PEOPLE'S BIBLE COMMENTARY

PROVERBS

ROLAND CAP EHLKE

CONCORDIA PUBLISHING HOUSE · SAINT LOUIS

Revised edition first printed in 2005.
Copyright © 1993 Concordia Publishing House
3558 S. Jefferson Ave., St. Louis, MO 63118-3968
1-800-325-3040 • www.cph.org

All rights reserved. No part of this publication may be reproduced, stored in a retrieval system, or transmitted, in any form or by any means, electronic, mechanical, photocopying, recording, or otherwise, without the prior written permission of Concordia Publishing House.

Commentary and pictures are reprinted from PROVERBS (The People's Bible Series), copyright © 1992 by Northwestern Publishing House. Used by permission.

Interior illustrations by Glenn Myers.

Unless otherwise stated, the Scripture quotations in this publication are taken from the HOLY BIBLE, NEW INTERNATIONAL VERSION®. NIV®. Copyright © 1973, 1978, 1984 by International Bible Society. Used by permission of Zondervan Publishing House. All rights reserved.

Manufactured in the United States of America

ISBN 0-7586-0458-0

1 2 3 4 5 6 7 8 9 10   14 13 12 11 10 09 08 07 06 05

CONTENTS

Editor's Preface	v
Introduction to Proverbs	1
Prologue: purpose and theme (1:1-7)	9
Exhortations to embrace wisdom (1:8–9:18)	17
First collection of Solomon's proverbs (10:1–22:16)	85
Appendixes to the first collection (22:17–24:34)	217
Second collection of Solomon's proverbs— Hezekiah's collection (25:1–29:27)	245
Appendixes to the second collection (30:1–31:31)	295
Endnotes	318
Topical index	319

ILLUSTRATIONS

Let the wise listen	10

Let your eyes look straight ahead	48
The house of the righteous stands firm	111
Better a patient man than a warrior	158
"It's no good, it's no good!" says the buyer	193
Honey from the comb is sweet	236
Like a roaring lion . . . is a wicked man ruling	281

EDITOR'S PREFACE

The *People's Bible Commentary* is just what the name implies—a Bible and commentary for the people. It includes the complete text of the Holy Scriptures in the popular New International Version. The commentary following the Scripture sections contains personal applications as well as historical background and explanations of the text.

The authors of the *People's Bible Commentary* are men of scholarship and practical insight gained from years of experience in the teaching and preaching ministries. They have tried to avoid the technical jargon which limits so many commentary series to professional Bible scholars.

The most important feature of these books is that they are Christ-centered. Speaking of the Old Testament Scriptures, Jesus himself declared, "These are the Scriptures that testify about me" (John 5:39). Each volume of the *People's Bible Commentary* directs our attention to Jesus Christ. He is the center of the entire Bible. He is our only Savior.

We dedicate these volumes to the glory of God and to the good of his people.

The Publishers

Introduction to Proverbs

Title

The first verse of Proverbs gives us the book's title: "The Proverbs of Solomon." The word *proverb* is a translation of the Hebrew word *mashal,* which means "parallel" or "similar." It refers to a method of describing and teaching by way of comparison. One truth is set in a parallel position to another. For example, 14:34 states, "Righteousness exalts a nation, but sin is a disgrace to any people." Here we see next to each other the results of both righteousness and sin upon a country.

A proverb may be a short two lines; it can also be a longer discourse. We find examples of both in the book of Proverbs. In many ways the biblical proverbs are not so different from wise sayings of more recent vintage. Our language is full of such expressions: A bird in the hand is worth two in the bush. A stitch in time saves nine. As we shall see later, biblical proverbs are also similar to some ancient literature from countries outside Israel. People everywhere and in every age have developed their own proverbs. What makes the biblical proverbs unique is that they are a part of God's inspired Word.

Although the book's title is "The Proverbs of Solomon," it includes other collections besides those of King Solomon. We'll discuss this when we get to the individual sections of the book.

The opening verse, however, refers to *Solomon's* proverbs, indicating that he is the main author. Solomon was king of Israel from 970 to 931 B.C. He was known for his extraordinary wisdom. First Kings 4:29-34 describes the breadth of Solomon's wisdom:

Introduction

> God gave Solomon wisdom and very great insight, and a breadth of understanding as measureless as the sand on the seashore. Solomon's wisdom was greater than the wisdom of all the men of the East, and greater than all the wisdom of Egypt. He was wiser than any other man, including Ethan the Ezrahite—wiser than Heman, Calcol and Darda, the sons of Mahol. And his fame spread to all the surrounding nations. He spoke three thousand proverbs and his songs numbered a thousand and five. He described plant life, from the cedar of Lebanon to the hyssop that grows out of walls. He also taught about animals and birds, reptiles and fish. Men of all nations came to listen to Solomon's wisdom, sent by all the kings of the world, who had heard of his wisdom.

According to an old tradition, Proverbs is the product of Solomon's middle age; the Song of Songs was written in his youth and Ecclesiastes in his old age. The content of these books lends credence to this tradition. Proverbs reflects the wisdom of a mature man, the Song of Songs depicts youthful love, and Ecclesiastes contains the reflections of an old man looking back over life. In addition to these writings, Solomon wrote Psalms 72 and 127.

Wisdom literature

Along with Job and Ecclesiastes, Proverbs is often classified as part of the Bible's wisdom literature. Sometimes the Song of Songs and Psalms are included in this category. Jeremiah 18:18 refers to this category of Scripture as "counsel from the wise" and places it side by side with "the teaching of the law by the priest" and "the word from the prophets."

Introduction

The wisdom of Proverbs discusses how to live a good life here on earth. As we've already indicated, this type of literature is not limited to the Bible. Other ancient people outside the chosen nation of Israel also had their wisdom books. One such book from Egypt, the *Wisdom of Amenemope,* resembles Proverbs 22:17–24:22. (We'll say more about that resemblance in our commentary on that passage.) The quote from 1 Kings chapter 4 compared Solomon's wisdom with that of "all the men of the East, and . . . the wisdom of Egypt."

Even without special revelation from God, people everywhere have been able to distill certain helpful truths about human behavior. While this is true, biblical wisdom literature rises above all the rest. Its source lies not in the observations of sinful human beings but in the Lord, who created life and knows best how it is to be lived.

The Bible's proverbs are rooted in "the fear of the LORD" (1:7). Consequently, they are entirely reliable and true. As one commentator observes, the Bible's proverbs shine with a "stronger and steadier light." James 3:17 sums up biblical wisdom's superiority over mere human wisdom: "The wisdom that comes from heaven is first of all pure; then peace-loving, considerate, submissive, full of mercy and good fruit, impartial and sincere."

In the Bible's wisdom literature, Job emphasizes *faith* amid life's trials, the Psalms are alive with *hope,* and Proverbs is the wisdom born of *love.* Proverbs has been called the Sermon on the Mount of the Old Testament. Just as in that sermon Christ directs us how to live lives of love, so does Proverbs.

In the Hebrew language in which it was originally written, Proverbs uses a number of different words to distinguish various aspects of wisdom. Because the distinction between words does not always come through in translation, we'll

3

Introduction

take a brief look at three key words. The most frequently used word is *hokmah;* this refers to practical wisdom. A second key word is *binah;* the emphasis in this word is on understanding and the ability to distinguish. A third important word is *tushiyyah,* referring to intellectual insight. While it is not important to remember these and other Hebrew terms for wisdom, it is good to keep in mind that Proverbs covers every phase of wisdom from theoretical insight to its practical application.

A striking feature of Proverbs is the frequent use of the word *heart* (almost one hundred times). Although the book deals with human behavior, it constantly points to the source of that behavior, namely, the condition of our hearts. The Old Testament Hebrew word for heart (*leb*) was rarely used for the physical organ. Rather, it referred to the entire inner life of emotions, will, intellect, and personality. If there is to be true change in outward behavior, it must start from within the heart.

Biblical wisdom finds its highest fulfillment in Jesus Christ, who is the very wisdom of God. Only the gospel of Christ can work a true change of heart and make us "wise for salvation" (2 Timothy 3:15).

Purpose

In our discussion of wisdom literature, we've already touched on the book's purpose—namely, that it directs believers to live godly lives. In his introduction to Proverbs, Martin Luther remarked, "It may properly be called a book of good works, for in it he [Solomon] teaches how to lead a good life before God and the world." Luther also notes that Solomon "pays special attention to young people."[1]

Another author has noted that Proverbs "is like medicine." While you can't live on it alone (since it does not focus on

Introduction

God's plan of salvation in Jesus Christ), "you should indulge in it often, but not in large doses. The 'stuff' of Proverbs has been distilled so that its advice comes in highly concentrated form."[2]

Proverbs points out the superiority of the godly life over the ungodly life. At times ungodly people prosper (Ecclesiastes points this out); often the godly suffer (see Job). Yet in the end, the righteous life is best.

Proverbs not only directs us to a godly life, but it also shows the folly of ungodly living, which ends in sorrow and ruin. In this respect Proverbs gives us training in the hard facts of life.

If we are to live as God wants, we need *knowledge*. How can we do the right thing if we don't know what that is? We also need *trust*. We need to trust that what God tells us is the right way, even when it goes against our own instincts. Proverbs 3:5,7 says: "Trust in the LORD with all your heart and lean not on your own understanding. Do not be wise in your own eyes."

We might sum up the purpose of Proverbs in this way: Proverbs leads us to know and to trust God's wisdom for living a good life.

Unlike most other Old Testament books, Proverbs does not focus on the Hebrew nation, the people of Israel. As a matter of fact, the term *Israel* occurs nowhere in the book. The book's tone is general throughout. Its observations relate to family situations, both agricultural and city life, business, politics, and the military. These observations apply to people of all times and places.

Poetry

As well as being a part of Scripture's wisdom literature, Proverbs is listed among the poetical books of the Bible. The

Introduction

other poetical books are Job, Psalms, Ecclesiastes, and the Song of Songs.

The main feature of Hebrew poetry is not rhyme or rhythm but *parallelism*. This means that one line of a verse is followed by a thought parallel to it. There are three basic types of parallelism: synonymous, antithetic, and synthetic.

In *synonymous* parallelism the poetical lines repeat the same thought in different words. Here are two examples:

> Evil men will bow down in the presence of the good,
>> and the wicked at the gates of the righteous (14:19).

> A fool's mouth is his undoing,
>> and his lips are a snare to his soul (18:7).

In *antithetic* parallelism opposite or contrasting thoughts are presented:

> The righteous eat to their hearts' content,
>> but the stomach of the wicked goes hungry (13:25).

> A cheerful heart is good medicine,
>> but a crushed spirit dries up the bones (17:22).

In *synthetic* parallelism the thought of the first line is expanded upon in the next line:

> A man's wisdom gives him patience;
>> it is to his glory to overlook an offense (19:11).

> "It's no good, it's no good!" says the buyer;
>> then off he goes and boasts about his purchase (20:14).

At times Hebrew parallelism includes more than two lines, but the same basic principles apply. A number of verses in Proverbs teach important truths by means of comparisons or similarities. For instance, Proverbs 25:11 says,

> A word aptly spoken
>> is like apples of gold in settings of silver.

Introduction

Place in the Bible

Over 20 quotations from Proverbs appear in the New Testament. This shows that the inspired writers of the New Testament recognized Proverbs as a part of the Scriptures. James 4:6 puts it very clearly: "That is why *Scripture* says: 'God opposes the proud but gives grace to the humble.'" This is a quote of Proverbs 3:34, and James refers to it as Scripture.

For a time, some of the later Jewish scholars questioned whether Proverbs belonged in the Bible. They thought there was a contradiction between Proverbs 26:4 and 5 (which we'll treat in our commentary on those verses), and they were bothered by the explicitness of some of the book's antiadultery passages (such as 7:7-27). Yet these objections are so minor and the New Testament endorsement so strong that the book's place in Scripture is secure.

Outline

Proverbs does not fit our modern ideas of how a book should be neatly outlined and flow in a smooth progression of thought. This does not detract from the usefulness and value of Proverbs. One scholar has described it this way: "Proverbs is truly a collection of sayings with no arrangement, outline, order, or progression. When you think about it, however, life is like that."[3]

Although it follows no definite pattern, the book does break down into several units, or sections. It's helpful to think of Proverbs not so much as a single unit but as a collection of wise sayings that were composed at various times and eventually gathered into what is now the book of Proverbs. The book breaks into six major sections, with a number of subsections:

Introduction

I. Prologue: purpose and theme (1:1-7)

II. Exhortations to embrace wisdom (1:8–9:18)
   A. Ten discourses for the young (1:8–7:27)
   B. Wisdom's sevenfold appeal (8:1–9:18)

III. First collection of Solomon's proverbs (10:1–22:16)

IV. Appendixes to the first collection (22:17–24:34)
   A. Sayings of wise men (22:17–24:22)
   B. Further sayings of wise men (24:23-34)

V. Second collection of Solomon's proverbs—
   Hezekiah's collection (25:1–29:27)

VI. Appendixes to the second collection (30:1–31:31)
   A. Sayings of Agur (30:1-33)
   B. Sayings of King Lemuel (31:1-9)
   C. Epilogue: the wife of noble character (31:10-31)

From this outline, we can see that the core of the book consists of collections of Solomon's proverbs, with other collections added in, in what are referred to as appendixes. As we read Proverbs, we'll note a number of repetitions within the book. We will also note a difference between the two collections of Solomon's proverbs. While the first is directed toward youth, the second is geared for older people, especially for those in positions of responsibility.

Now it is time to get into Proverbs itself. Notice the different types of poetry. But, more important, savor each precious truth. Apply it to your own circumstances, and ask God to help you put it into practice. God will enrich your life beyond measure as you live in the wisdom of Proverbs!

PART ONE

Prologue: Purpose and Theme
(1:1-7)

1 **The proverbs of Solomon son of David, king of Israel:**

We have already discussed this verse in the Introduction. It serves as a title for the entire book.

A few more comments regarding the term *proverbs* are in order here. Throughout the Old Testament, the original Hebrew word (*mashal*) is used in a number of ways and has a wider range of meaning than our English word *proverb*. The New International Version (NIV) translates it in numerous ways. For example, it may signify a "saying" (1 Samuel 10:12), a "parable" (Ezekiel 17:2), a "taunt" (Isaiah 14:4), a "mournful song" (Micah 2:4), an "oracle" (Numbers 23:7), and a "discourse" (Job 29:1). The Hebrew term clearly carries a wide variety of uses. In each instance, however, the use has to do with knowledge and the communication of knowledge.

As stated in the Introduction, not all of Proverbs was written by Solomon. But since he was the main author, we feel safe in assuming that unless the biblical text itself indicates otherwise, Solomon is the author of the various sections of Proverbs. This includes the verses of the Prologue:

> [2] **for attaining wisdom and discipline;**
> **for understanding words of insight;**
> [3] **for acquiring a disciplined and prudent life,**
> **doing what is right and just and fair;**

Let the wise listen

Proverbs 1:2,3

In verses 2 to 6 of the Prologue, Solomon sets forth the purpose of the book. He directs the child of God to wisdom, discipline, and understanding. A number of words for wisdom occur here, piled one on top of the other. Together they show that Proverbs intends to cover a wide range of knowledge and wisdom.

Verse 2 sets the pace. Our first duty is to attain wisdom. Once we become wise in God's ways, we need to allow them to rule over our lives. In both steps we are dependent on God. Our knowledge of him and his will comes through his Word, the Bible; the desire and ability to apply that knowledge come through the Holy Spirit, who is at work in the Word. Philippians 2:13 reminds us, "It is God who works in you to will and to act according to his good purpose."

In the Introduction we discussed the word *wisdom* (Hebrew *hokmah,* see page 4). Elsewhere in the Old Testament, this word is used when describing the skills of an artisan. It occurs over 40 times in Proverbs, where it focuses on the skill of living a God-pleasing life in a godless world. One commentator remarks, "Not sagacity, abstract learning, or philosophical speculation is intended, but an understanding of the principles which control and direct human living at its highest and best."[4] Practical wisdom is the chief emphasis of Proverbs.

Discipline is another key concept in Proverbs. It is that quality of being able to follow through and apply our God-given wisdom. We might call it self-discipline. The ancient Jewish rabbis had a saying, "The wicked are under the control of their impulses, but the righteous have their impulses under their control."

Self-discipline is especially important for us to keep in mind, since our society encourages just the opposite. In a thousand different ways we are told, "If it feels good, do it!" We are urged to follow our impulses rather than control

11

Proverbs 1:2,3

them. As a result, we have a society caught in the throes of massive drug problems; illicit sex; lack of responsibility in school, work, and home life; and a general tendency for people to do whatever pleases them—the me-first ethic.

Proverbs does not deny emotions their due. Joy and self-satisfaction have their place. But they are fully realized only when kept within the limits of God's Word. God sets up rules for living, not to make us unhappy but to bring us real, lasting happiness.

Verse 2 presents another of Proverbs' key words in the term *understanding* (*binah,* see Introduction page 4). This word is related to the spatial concept of between and refers to the ability to make distinctions. Young King Solomon prayed for this type of wisdom early in his reign: "Give your servant a discerning heart to govern your people and to *distinguish between* right and wrong" (1 Kings 3:9).

Life constantly calls on us to distinguish between what is good and bad or between what is a wise choice and what is an even better choice. How we make such choices does much to determine the course of our lives. When we face important decisions in life, how do we distinguish between the options? Do we merely act on impulse? Do we follow the advice of friends? Do we read books to gain insight? All these are important factors in life's choices. But it is even more important that we consult God's Word (including the scriptural advice of wise Christian friends, counselors, and pastors) and that we ask God's guidance in prayer.

Verse 3 parallels verse 2. It again speaks of discipline and goes on to apply what is right: "doing [literally, taking hold of] what is right and just and fair." The Christian life can never stop with worship or with Bible study. It always goes further and expresses itself in deeds. The Bible often presents this truth. One entire book, James, deals with this subject:

Proverbs 1:4-6

"What good is it, my brothers, if a man claims to have faith but has no deeds? . . . Faith by itself, if it is not accompanied by action, is dead" (James 2:14,17).

The supreme example of doing what is right and just and fair is Jesus Christ. His love toward us is active. He, the eternal Son of God, left his heavenly throne and came into this world, took on our flesh and blood, lived a perfect life of doing good to others, and then died a sacrificial death to pay for our sins. Jesus says to us, "My command is this: Love each other as I have loved you" (John 15:12). Proverbs is directed toward this same end—love in action.

Notice that verses 2 and 3 apply to the student of Proverbs. He is to attain and acquire wisdom, discipline, and understanding. In the verses coming up, Solomon turns from the student to the instructor, who is to dispense knowledge as well as add to his own storehouse of learning.

Whether we are being taught or are helping to teach others, Proverbs is for us.

> **⁴ for giving prudence to the simple,
>   knowledge and discretion to the young—
> ⁵ let the wise listen and add to their learning,
>   and let the discerning get guidance—
> ⁶ for understanding proverbs and parables,
>   the sayings and riddles of the wise.**

The word translated "simple" has the root meaning "to be open." It refers to a person of undecided views, who is wide open and susceptible to bad as well as good influences. The word translated "young" signifies an immature person without experience.

Left to themselves, the young and the simple are not likely to find true wisdom. The notion that by themselves such people will choose the best course of action is without scriptural basis. Sinful by nature, we are all likely to follow the easiest

Proverbs 1:4-6

path—namely, that which satisfies our personal inclination to act out of selfishness, lust, and whatever seems best for our personal interests, with little thought of what God wants or what may be good for others. It is especially foolish to assume that somehow young people, if left on their own, will do what is best. Some parents neglect the spiritual training of their children with the idea that the children can decide for themselves when they are older. This too is contrary to God's Word, which teaches us to "bring them up in the training and instruction of the Lord" (Ephesians 6:4).

Throughout Proverbs we find many different words for wisdom. Likewise, we will find many words for its opposite, foolishness. In speaking of the "simple" and the "young," verse 4 directs us to people caught in two types of foolishness. The young are in need of instruction. The simple may have had some instruction but are gullible and easily swayed toward evil. Both lack wisdom because they lack practical experience, and both need to be taught. Their foolishness is not as serious as that of people who know better and still defy God's Word.

Verse 5 is directed toward those who already are among the "wise" and "discerning." They still need to add to their learning; they still need guidance. The wiser we become in godly living, the more we realize how far we still must go. As Saint Paul wrote: "Now we see but a poor reflection as in a mirror; then we shall see face to face. Now I know in part; then I shall know fully, even as I am fully known" (1 Corinthians 13:12). We struggle to know ourselves and others and God. Life is also a constant struggle to live with ourselves and others and God as God wants us to. Proverbs guides us in that struggle.

Verse 6 speaks of understanding "proverbs," "parables," "sayings," and "riddles." In our study of Proverbs 1:1, we saw the wide range of meanings connected with the word *proverb.*

Proverbs 1:7

In addition to *proverb,* Solomon uses several other words to depict different types of wise sayings. One of them is the word *parable,* which signifies a figure of speech. For instance, Proverbs 9:17 states, "Stolen water is sweet; food eaten in secret is delicious!" To understand this parable is to realize the meaning behind the figure of speech: it refers to the attractiveness of the forbidden.

Some translations, such as the King James Version (KJV), translate the term "riddles" as "dark sayings." It is the same word used in 1 Kings 10:1: "When the queen of Sheba heard about the fame of Solomon and his relation to the name of the LORD, she came to test him with hard questions." Growth in godly wisdom will help us find answers to life's riddles, its hard questions.

**⁷ The fear of the LORD is the beginning of knowledge,
but fools despise wisdom and discipline.**

The Prologue's final verse is the theme for Proverbs. This is the motto of the Bible's wisdom writings in general. It reappears in somewhat altered form later in Proverbs (9:10; 15:33) and in Job 28:28 and Psalm 111:10.

"The fear of the LORD" is godly reverence. It is not terror. In fact, the fear of the Lord delivers us from fear! Solomon's father, David, described it in Psalm 34:4,7,9:

I sought the LORD, and he answered me;
    he delivered me from all my fears.
The angel of the LORD encamps around
        those who fear him,
    and he delivers them.
Fear the Lord, you his saints,
    for those who fear him lack nothing.

"The beginning" is the starting point, the foundation, upon which true knowledge rests. It is not something we leave

Proverbs 1:7

behind as we move on, any more than an accomplished athlete, artist, or musician leaves behind the basics of his or her trade. Everything rests on the foundation.

Solomon is saying that to live life as it should be lived, we need to have a proper relationship with the Lord, the God of free and faithful grace. In reverence submit to him. Follow his Word. Then you are on the right footing. All of life should be lived this way, not just certain parts.

In striking contrast to this, "fools despise wisdom and discipline." The fool in Proverbs is a person who is morally and spiritually foolish. He might be highly intelligent, and by worldly standards he may be very shrewd. But in God's sight he is a fool. Jesus spoke of such a man in his parable of the rich fool. The man was a successful farmer and businessman. In order to provide room for all his harvest, he determined to build bigger barns. Then he decided he would "take life easy; eat, drink and be merry." God had other plans. "God said to him, 'You fool! This very night your life will be demanded from you. Then who will get what you have prepared for yourself?'" (Luke 12:16-21). Though worldly wise, the man did not give any thought to God and, consequently, was a fool. So it is with all who do not make the fear of the Lord the beginning of knowledge.

To ignore God or put him in the background is to "despise wisdom and discipline." It is to play the fool. In the end the fool will have good reason to fear God—not to stand in reverence before his amazing grace but to cringe before his wrath.

Throughout the rest of Proverbs, we will see this contrast between wisdom and foolishness. May God guide us in the former and preserve us from the latter!

The triune God is the fountainhead of knowledge. He is our Creator, our Savior, and our Sanctifier. With this beginning, we move into the wisdom of Proverbs.

PART TWO

Exhortations to Embrace Wisdom
(1:8–9:18)

Ten discourses for the young

This section makes up one of the book's six major divisions, second in length only to the First Collection of Solomon's Proverbs (10:1–22:16). Although the Exhortations do not specifically say they come from Solomon, there is good reason to think they are his. The heading for the entire book of Proverbs is "The proverbs of Solomon." Moreover, portions not written by Solomon name specific authors (see 30:1; 31:1).

The Exhortations break into two subsections. The first consists of Ten Discourses for the Young (1:8–7:27), each directed to "my son" or "my sons." This portion focuses on guiding the young toward godly maturity. The second subsection is Wisdom's Sevenfold Appeal (8:1–9:18).

Warning against enticement
First discourse

In Proverbs 1:7 Solomon had contrasted the fear of the Lord with the way of fools. In the warning he is about to issue, he contrasts these two ways of life. First, he talks about the godly:

> **⁸ Listen, my son, to your father's instruction**
> **and do not forsake your mother's teaching.**
> **⁹ They will be a garland to grace your head**
> **and a chain to adorn your neck.**

Ancient wisdom literature often used the term *son* to refer to a student. It shows the closeness between an instruc-

17

Proverbs 1:8,9

tor and a pupil. This is the first of more than 20 such occurrences in Proverbs. Much of what follows applies to "my daughter" as well. Yet in Solomon's day, men were more in need of the instruction, because the responsibilities described fell chiefly to them. It's interesting that Solomon mentions both father and mother as participating in the instruction of their children. The responsibility—and the privilege!—rests with both parents.

In our day lack of respect for parents is common, even in Christian homes. As Saint Paul foretold: "There will be terrible times in the last days. People will be lovers of themselves, lovers of money, boastful, proud, abusive, disobedient to their parents, ungrateful . . ." (2 Timothy 3:1-9). God's command to honor one's parents still stands.

Young people concerned about living as God's children will recognize their parents as the Lord's gifts. Children might be tempted to think: "My parents don't understand. They've forgotten what it's like to be young." To the contrary, godly parents give advice because they do understand and have not forgotten. Of course, no parents are perfect, and obedience to God takes precedence over any earthly relationship. Yet, when all is said and done, God calls on children to honor their parents.

Children who honor their parents' instruction will discover God's blessings. Solomon describes parental teaching as a garland for the head and a chain for the neck. The garland symbolizes beauty and the chain honor. Joseph and Daniel wore chains around their necks (Genesis 41:42; Daniel 5:29). Young persons who follow their parents' good guidance possess a dignity and beauty that go deeper than outward appearance.

Solomon proceeds to contrast this with the way of the ungodly:

18

Proverbs 1:10-19

¹⁰ My son, if sinners entice you,
  do not give in to them.
¹¹ If they say, "Come along with us;
  let's lie in wait for someone's blood,
  let's waylay some harmless soul;
¹² let's swallow them alive, like the grave,
  and whole, like those who go down to the pit;
¹³ we will get all sorts of valuable things
  and fill our houses with plunder;
¹⁴ throw in your lot with us,
  and we will share a common purse"—
¹⁵ my son, do not go along with them,
  do not set foot on their paths;
¹⁶ for their feet rush into sin,
  they are swift to shed blood.
¹⁷ How useless to spread a net
  in full view of all the birds!
¹⁸ These men lie in wait for their own blood;
  they waylay only themselves!
¹⁹ Such is the end of all who go after ill-gotten gain;
  it takes away the lives of those who get it.

In contrast to the godly father and mother who have their children's welfare in mind, we now are introduced to sinners who entice young people to their ruin. Proverbs focuses especially on two enticements: (1) toward sexual sins and (2) toward wrongful material gain.

The inspired writer here deals with the second. To people who are blind to the spiritual side of life, material gain becomes all-important. Wealth becomes a god. The quest for the almighty dollar is especially alluring when it is an "easy buck." No work is involved, just robbery. We don't have to look far to see the reality of this in our day. And when wealth has become a god, people will do anything—even commit murder—in pursuit of that idol.

Proverbs 1:20,21

Yet for all that people are willing to do for riches, they get little in return. At the end of their rainbows, there are no long-awaited pots of gold. Instead, there are nothing but tubs of trouble.

Very often the wicked get caught in their own scheming. Solomon uses a picture to show the folly of this wrongful pursuit of wealth: it's as ridiculous as trying to catch birds by spreading a net out in the open (verse 17). You won't catch any birds that way, but you may get entangled in the net yourself.

In the end it will cost the wicked their own lives. Even if they should escape judgment in this life, they will not escape God's judgment. To continue impenitent on this path leads to damnation. The Bible lists "thieves" and "the greedy" among those who "will not inherit the kingdom of God" (1 Corinthians 6:9,10).

Warning against rejecting wisdom

[20] Wisdom calls aloud in the street,
she raises her voice in the public squares;
[21] at the head of the noisy streets she cries out,
in the gateways of the city she makes her speech:

Here, for the first time in Proverbs, we see wisdom personified. The fact that wisdom is depicted as calling out in the streets indicates that wisdom is practical for a man in the street. Moreover, wisdom is also for leaders, since wisdom calls aloud also in the sheltered gateways of ancient cities at which the city elders would meet to discuss important matters of business.

God's saving Word goes out to all. It calls out to people to turn to Christ, the wisdom of God, and be saved. Sadly, God's wisdom is "foolishness" to many (1 Corinthians 1:18), who prefer the wisdom of this unbelieving world. In the parable of

Proverbs 1:22-27

the wedding banquet (Matthew 22:1-14), Jesus describes a king sending his servants into the streets to invite people to the wedding of his son. Christ concludes the parable with the words "For many are invited, but few are chosen."

Proverbs goes on to speak of what happens when people don't heed the call:

> **22 "How long will you simple ones love your simple ways?**
>   **How long will mockers delight in mockery**
>   **and fools hate knowledge?**
> **23 If you had responded to my rebuke,**
>   **I would have poured out my heart to you**
>   **and made my thoughts known to you.**
> **24 But since you rejected me when I called**
>   **and no one gave heed when I stretched out my hand,**
> **25 since you ignored all my advice**
>   **and would not accept my rebuke,**
> **26 I in turn will laugh at your disaster;**
>   **I will mock when calamity overtakes you—**
> **27 when calamity overtakes you like a storm,**
>   **when disaster sweeps over you like a whirlwind,**
>   **when distress and trouble overwhelm you.**

In teaching the way of wisdom, the Lord through his inspired writers often does so by using contrast. As a skilled artist who sets his subject matter against a contrasting background, the Lord sets the bright gem of wisdom against the dismal backdrop of foolishness. Here we see some of that backdrop.

It's important to remember that when the Bible in general—and Proverbs in particular—speaks of foolishness, it points to a moral and *spiritual* condition. We should not confuse this with lack of academic prowess or a low IQ. Thus, some people who are brilliant may, in God's eyes, be fools. For example, Psalms 14:1 and 53:1 state, "The fool says in his heart, 'There is no God.'"

21

Proverbs 1:22-27

In Proverbs the fool is one who does not have a proper fear of the Lord. Consequently, he is apt to be led astray from what God says. Or else he simply ignores it in the first place.

Solomon uses several Hebrew words to describe the foolish person. One of them describes a person who is "gullible," or, as the NIV translates the word, "simple." We might also describe him as naive and inexperienced. He drifts along aimlessly until he falls easy prey to temptation. Of the various types of fool, this one is the least hardened, compared, for example, with the fool who says there is no God.

If this "simple" person doesn't learn, he may well move to the next level of foolishness and become a full-fledged "fool." While the various Hebrew terms for fool have different shades of meaning, they all point to the person who believes and lives contrary to what God's Word teaches.

In addition to the fool, we encounter other undesirable characters in the pages of Proverbs. Like the fool, they stand in bold contrast to the child of God. One is "the person who ridicules" (NIV translates "mocker"). Unlike the wise person, this individual would much rather make fun of others than be at the receiving end of constructive criticism: "Do not rebuke a mocker or he will hate you; rebuke a wise man and he will love you" (9:8).

Another acquaintance we have yet to make in our gallery of the ungodly is the "lazy" person.

Whether observing the fool, the mocker, or the one who is lazy, the believer realizes, "There but for the grace of God go I." King Saul began his reign wisely, only to fall into sin and have to admit, "I have acted like a fool" (1 Samuel 26:21). Even the author of Proverbs, wise King Solomon himself, became such a fool that he later fell into idolatry (1 Kings 11:4-11).

Proverbs 1:28-33

Those who continue in godlessness will in the end meet God's rejection. Although God in his wisdom would pour out his heart (verse 23, literally, pour out his "spirit"), yet when he receives nothing but rejection, wisdom will stop calling. This can happen to individuals, to entire nations (see Isaiah 1:4), and to church bodies. Jesus himself had to proclaim this harsh reality to some of his followers: "The words I have spoken to you are spirit and they are life. Yet there are some of you who do not believe" (John 6:63,64).

When the Lord speaks of laughing "at your disaster," it is not that he is heartless. Rather, it is a reference to the absurdity of unbelief. The Hebrew term for "storm" in verse 27 signifies a storm that causes devastation. Such is the end of those who foolishly reject God's wisdom.

> [28] **"Then they will call to me but I will not answer;**
>   **they will look for me but will not find me.**
> [29] **Since they hated knowledge**
>   **and did not choose to fear the LORD,**
> [30] **since they would not accept my advice**
>   **and spurned my rebuke,**
> [31] **they will eat the fruit of their ways**
>   **and be filled with the fruit of their schemes.**
> [32] **For the waywardness of the simple will kill them,**
>   **and the complacency of fools will destroy them;**
> [33] **but whoever listens to me will live in safety**
>   **and be at ease, without fear of harm."**

Again, the Savior's words come to mind. This time he was speaking to the Pharisees: "I am going away, and you will look for me, and you will die in your sin. Where I go, you cannot come" (John 8:21).

Many people put off God's Word as if it's something they'll get around to later in life. "I'll worry about that when I'm old and retired and have nothing else to do" is their atti-

Proverbs 2:1-8

tude. The tragic fact is that most people who reject the Word in their youth won't be able to grasp it in their old age either. Their hearts and minds will be too hardened. Procrastination is not a virtue, especially not in spiritual matters. "Now is the time of God's favor, now is the day of salvation" (2 Corinthians 6:2).

Happily, this section of warning concludes on a positive note. Whoever listens to the Lord enjoys safety and freedom from fear. The Lord watches over us and physically protects us. Even if he should allow bodily harm to come our way, we know that spiritually and eternally we still rest in his almighty arms.

Only by the grace of God and through his Word do we become wise and continue to grow in wisdom. The remedy against foolishness is to make God's words our daily companion and take them to heart.

Moral benefits of wisdom

Second discourse

2 My son, if you accept my words
　　and store up my commands within you,
² turning your ear to wisdom
　　and applying your heart to understanding,
³ and if you call out for insight
　　and cry aloud for understanding,
⁴ and if you look for it as for silver
　　and search for it as for hidden treasure,
⁵ then you will understand the fear of the LORD
　　and find the knowledge of God.
⁶ For the LORD gives wisdom,
　　and from his mouth come knowledge
　　　　and understanding.
⁷ He holds victory in store for the upright,
　　he is a shield to those whose walk is blameless,

Proverbs 2:1-8

**⁸ for he guards the course of the just
and protects the way of his faithful ones.**

We are now in the second of the ten discourses to "my son" (2:1-22). In contrast to a life of wickedness, Solomon presents the moral benefits of wisdom. When Solomon speaks of accepting "my words," he is writing by inspiration and equating them with God's words. Similarly, the words of the prophets, sacred historians, evangelists, and apostles were God's words. They come "from his mouth."

With the ears (or eyes, if reading) we take these words in. Then, in the heart we store them. Notice how the acquisition of godly wisdom seems to grow in intensity. First it is a matter of accepting and storing up. Later it becomes a crying aloud for and a searching for as "for hidden treasure." Job also spoke of divine wisdom as a rare, hidden treasure. "Neither gold nor crystal can compare with it, nor can it be had for jewels of gold" (28:17).

The word "commands" in verse 1 is not merely a reference to the Ten Commandments but to all of God's words. How important it is for Christian parents to teach their children "the holy Scriptures, which are able to make you wise for salvation through faith in Christ Jesus" (2 Timothy 3:15).

The first four verses of this discourse set up a condition, "If you accept my words," etc. From this condition a fivefold conclusion follows:

- "You will understand the fear of the LORD . . ." (verses 5-8).
- "You will understand what is right and just . . ." (verses 9-11).
- "Wisdom will save you from the ways of wicked men . . ." (verses 12-15).
- "It will save you also from the adulteress . . ." (verses 16-19).

Proverbs 2:9-11

- "Thus you will walk in the ways of good men . . ." (verses 20-22).

Many blessings, both earthly and spiritual, will follow if we seek godly wisdom. This is similar to Jesus' remark, "Seek first [God's] kingdom and his righteousness, and all these things will be given to you as well" (Matthew 6:33).

The fact remains that many people simply do not search out such wisdom. Some do not believe it is important. Some are not interested in God and the things of God. Some are concerned only with the delights of this short life. Some feel wisdom is only for the highly educated. And some think they know enough. Whatever the reason, it is tragic. In our materialistic and shallow age, we will want to look past the tinseled appeal of possessions and passing pleasures to the lasting treasures of God's Word.

The search for wisdom finds its reward in "the *fear* of the LORD" and in "the *knowledge* of God." One commentator describes these as "the two classic Old Testament terms for true religion—the poles of awe and intimacy."[5] Martin Luther defines what fearing God means for the believer: "To fear God is simply to serve God with the heart inwardly and with our doing outwardly, and this consists in holding him in honor and reverencing him."[6]

As we grow to know God better, we stand in awe of his greatness and of his love in Jesus Christ, "in whom are hidden all the treasures of wisdom and knowledge" (Colossians 2:3).

Such godly wisdom involves much more than head knowledge; it means to walk in God's ways:

> [9] **Then you will understand what is right and just**
> **and fair—every good path.**
> [10] **For wisdom will enter your heart,**
> **and knowledge will be pleasant to your soul.**

Proverbs 2:12-15

**¹¹ Discretion will protect you,
and understanding will guard you.**

Traveling through life is a pilgrimage. As we make our way, we can say with Solomon's father, David, "The Lord is my shepherd. . . . He leads me beside quiet waters. . . . He guides me in paths of righteousness. . . . Even though I walk through the valley of the shadow of death, I will fear no evil, for you are with me (Psalm 23:1-4).

What David described in the most famous of all psalms as "paths of righteousness," Solomon speaks of as "every good path." It's not that we take a road map and plan our whole lives. That's impossible. No, we simply live each new day with the Lord—paying attention to what he says in the Bible and speaking to him in prayer. This is the way of wisdom.

Contrary to the popular slogan, ignorance is *not* bliss. Rather, the knowledge of God is. It brings a peace of mind, heart, and soul that can't be bought. As another slogan puts it, No Jesus, no peace. Know Jesus, know peace.

God does not promise that we will never face physical pains and dangers in this life. Wisdom does, however, keep us from those of our own making. Finally, it keeps us spiritually safe forever.

**¹² Wisdom will save you from the ways of wicked men,
from men whose words are perverse,
¹³ who leave the straight paths
to walk in dark ways,
¹⁴ who delight in doing wrong
and rejoice in the perverseness of evil,
¹⁵ whose paths are crooked
and who are devious in their ways.**

An honest man is hard to find. In our sin-infested world, "perverse" (literally, "upside down") words, little white lies, half-truths, and misleading innuendoes are part of everyday

27

Proverbs 2:16-19

life. Whether or not we care to admit it, none of us is completely honest with others or even with ourself.

Yet some people make dishonesty a way of life. It might be cheating on income taxes or on their wives. They have little time for honest, truthful dealings. Pilate's question, "What is truth?" (John 18:38) is not their concern.

Not only do dishonest words and actions play a major role in this world's affairs, so does outright wickedness. Often brazenly wicked people become rich and famous. We see this, and the devil whispers in our ears, "If you can't beat 'em, join 'em!"

Verse 13 speaks of "straight paths" as opposed to "dark ways." The Bible associates straight with what is right, just as it uses light to symbolize goodness and darkness to represent evil.

People who leave the straight paths to walk in dark ways may actually come to "delight" and "rejoice" in this lifestyle. At first we may find evil repulsive; then we dabble in it, and it doesn't seem so bad; finally we join "those who call evil good and good evil" (Isaiah 5:20). That's why it's crucial not to get involved with wicked men in the first place.

Wisdom saves us from such people. It was godly wisdom that saved a discouraged Asaph, who sighed, "I envied the arrogant when I saw the prosperity of the wicked" (Psalm 73:3). God led him to understand "their final destiny. . . . How suddenly are they destroyed, completely swept away by terrors!" (Psalm 73:17,19).

In addition to saving us from wicked men, wisdom also saves from the wicked woman:

> **¹⁶ It will save you also from the adulteress,**
> **from the wayward wife with her seductive words,**
> **¹⁷ who has left the partner of her youth**
> **and ignored the covenant she made before God.**

Proverbs 2:16-19

**¹⁸ For her house leads down to death
and her paths to the spirits of the dead.
¹⁹ None who go to her return
or attain the paths of life.**

The Hebrew word translated "adulteress" literally is "stranger" or "foreigner." Anyone except one's own spouse is to be off limits, that is, to be regarded as a foreigner or stranger in matters of sexual intimacy.

In the idolatrous nations bordering ancient Israel, prostitution was customary. God's chosen people were to keep themselves pure from the false worship of those nations and from their immoral lifestyles. But the temptation was always there. Hence, Proverbs has several strong warnings against sexual immorality. Sad to say, God's people didn't always heed his warnings. The prophet Jeremiah, for example, lamented, "The land is full of adulterers" (23:10).

We do not know exactly what an Old Testament marriage ceremony entailed. Verse 17 indicates that a vow or covenant was a part of it. Elsewhere Solomon stresses that vows made before the Lord are not to be taken lightly: "Do not protest . . . 'My vow was a mistake'" (Ecclesiastes 5:6). This is as true today as it was three thousand years ago. Marriage is meant to last "so long as you both shall live."

It is of interest that the "partner of her youth" is, literally, "the lord of her youth." In Israel women married at an early age, and the man was the head of the house. In Christian marriages women are to "submit to your husbands, as to the Lord. For the husband is the head of the wife as Christ is the head of the church" (Ephesians 5:22,23). On the other hand, husbands are told, "Love your wives, just as Christ loved the church and gave himself up for her" (Ephesians 5:25).

Sadly, our age falls far short of the ideal. "The land is full of adulterers" . . . and broken marriages and unhappy marriages. We need the Lord's forgiveness and strength.

29

Proverbs 2:20-22

In Old Testament times, adultery called for the death penalty (Leviticus 20:10). While that isn't the case today, our newspapers recount many a case in which an angry spouse takes matters into his or her own hands and commits murder. Even if that doesn't happen, there are always the pangs of conscience adulterers must live with.

Adultery leads to more than unhappy consequences in this life. It leads to spiritual death. Those who do not repent of their immorality will go to hell. "Neither the sexually immoral nor idolaters nor adulterers . . . will inherit the kingdom of God" (1 Corinthians 6:9,10).

> **20 Thus you will walk in the ways of good men**
> **and keep to the paths of the righteous.**
> **21 For the upright will live in the land,**
> **and the blameless will remain in it;**
> **22 but the wicked will be cut off from the land,**
> **and the unfaithful will be torn from it.**

The closing verses of the first discourse to "my son" depict the happy state of the godly and the miserable end of the wicked. These verses again refer back to the original condition of the discourse: "*If* you accept my words and store up my commands . . . *if* you call out for insight and cry aloud for understanding . . . *if* you look for it as for silver . . ."

Then blessings will follow. One blessing is walking the same way with others who are headed in the right direction. Another is living in the land of the "upright" and "blameless."

God had promised the land of Canaan to his Old Testament people. With that promise went a warning. Before they entered the land, the Lord had told them through his servant Moses: "If you do not carefully follow all the words of this law [of God] . . . you will be uprooted from the land you are entering to possess" (Deuteronomy 28:58,63).

30

Proverbs 3:1,2

Some five centuries after Moses and following the death of King Solomon, the people's disregard for that warning bore dreadful fruit. The nation fell from God's ways, was torn in two, and eventually saw both the Northern and Southern Kingdoms carried into exile—the Northern never to return.

In his Sermon on the Mount, Jesus made a similar promise: "Blessed are the meek, for they will inherit the earth" (Matthew 5:5). Those who humbly entrust their lives to God enjoy his blessings in whatever land they live. Indeed, whole nations prosper and grow strong where the gospel flourishes. Alas, the reverse is also true. Arrogant, self-reliant unbelief sooner or later leads to a loss of God's blessings.

Of course the most priceless land of promise is heaven. It is God's gift through Jesus Christ. Lord, keep us from ever losing that land through wickedness and unbelief! Guide us day by day on the path to that dear land of rest!

Further benefits of wisdom

Third discourse

3 **My son, do not forget my teaching,**
but keep my commands in your heart,
² for they will prolong your life many years
and bring you prosperity.

The third discourse to "my son" (3:1-35) speaks of the devout life. As we look at this life, we see three distinct aspects to it: (1) its *inner quality,* submission to God (verses 1-12); (2) its *foundation,* the eternal wisdom of God (verses 13-20); and (3) its *external expression,* relationship with oneself (verses 21-26) and with others (verses 27-35).

Solomon speaks of keeping "my commands in your heart." The heart to the Hebrews was not merely the place of emotions, as we tend to think of it today. It included a per-

31

Proverbs 3:3,4

son's inner life of thoughts, will, emotions, and personality. In other words, divine wisdom is to be a part of our entire inner lives. We take it in, think about it, absorb it, and let it permeate us.

The promise of long life is similar to that given in connection with the Fourth Commandment: "Honor your father and mother, so that you may live long in the land" (Exodus 20:12) and to the promise tied to loving God: "Now choose life, so that you and your children may live and that you may love the LORD your God. . . . For the LORD is your life, and he will give you many years in the land (Deuteronomy 30:19,20).

In addition to long life, God promises "prosperity." This is the common Hebrew word *shalom*. It includes a wide range of concepts: peace, harmony, wholeness, prosperity— everything that makes existence complete and worthwhile.

Staying close to God and his Word often brings earthly blessings, such as a long and peaceful life. In Jesus Christ we realize the supreme fruition of this promise. Through the Savior we enjoy peace with God and eternal life.

> **³ Let love and faithfulness never leave you;**
> **bind them around your neck,**
> **write them on the tablet of your heart.**
> **⁴ Then you will win favor and a good name**
> **in the sight of God and man.**

Love and faithfulness are two key Old Testament concepts. Both find their source in God, the giver of all good gifts.

God's love, as expressed in Jesus, is to find reflection in our lives as well. "My command is this," says the Savior, "Love each other as I have loved you" (John 15:12).

Our word *amen* comes from the Hebrew word for faithfulness. Tied to it are the ideas of truthfulness and honesty.

Proverbs 3:5,6

This is another trait that is reflected in the lives of God's people.

We are to wear such virtues as ornaments; that is, as a way to glorify God and serve others. In Deuteronomy 6:8 Moses told the Israelites: "Tie them [God's words] as symbols on your hands and bind them on your foreheads." The Jews copied portions of the Scriptures, put them into little boxes called phylacteries, and then wore them on their foreheads and the backs of their hands. Yet many of them missed the point. Jesus spoke against the attitude of the religious leaders of his day: "Everything they do is done for men to see: They make their phylacteries wide" (Matthew 23:5). This was showy hypocrisy.

Wearing God's Word means far more than wearing a phylactery (or a cross on a necklace or lapel). It means living a life that is both pleasing to God and beneficial to others. Reflective of the words of Proverbs, we are told that as a 12-year-old child, Jesus "grew in wisdom and stature, and in favor with God and men" (Luke 2:52).

This is the model for God's children today . . . no matter how old we might be.

> ⁵ **Trust in the LORD with all your heart**
> **and lean not on your own understanding;**
> ⁶ **in all your ways acknowledge him,**
> **and he will make your paths straight.**

True wisdom consists of listening to God, even when his Word goes against what we might think is best. This is a difficult proverb, since we have a tendency to lean on our own understanding. For example, human wisdom may tell us to resort to lying, slandering, adultery, unscriptural divorce, theft, abortion, cowardice, or other sinful options to escape some of life's unpleasant situations. Ultimately, such "solu-

Proverbs 3:7,8

tions" are no solutions at all. Moreover, by itself human wisdom simply is not capable of understanding life's great tragedies and dealing with death.

Instead, we are to trust in, lean on, and acknowledge the Lord. To *trust* in him is to commit our lives entirely to him. To *lean* on him means just what it says. Of course to do this, we have to be confident that God isn't going to pull away and let us fall flat on our faces. To *acknowledge* him literally is to "know" him. We need to become well acquainted with God through his self-revelation, the Bible. Everything else depends on this. We're not going to trust in him and lean on him until we really know what he's like.

When the Israelites sent 12 men to scout the land they were to enter, only two—Joshua and Caleb—felt confident that the Lord would give them the land. The other ten were afraid: "The people who live there are powerful, and the cities are fortified and very large. . . . We can't attack those people; they are stronger than we are" (Numbers 13:28,31). But Caleb said, "We should go up and take possession of the land, for we can certainly do it" (Numbers 13:30).

The Lord commended Caleb: "My servant Caleb has a different spirit and follows me wholeheartedly" (Numbers 14:24). God allowed only Joshua and Caleb to enter the Promised Land. They had leaned on God and not on their own understanding.

The Lord is just as loving and powerful today. He still makes "paths straight," removing obstacles and helping us walk the way we should go. Trust him.

> [7] **Do not be wise in your own eyes;**
>   **fear the LORD and shun evil.**
> [8] **This will bring health to your body**
>   **and nourishment to your bones.**

Proverbs 3:9,10

"Do not be wise in your own eyes" is another way of telling us not to lean on our own understanding. One commentator paraphrases, "Don't take yourself too seriously." We can be serious about life and relaxed at the same time, when we put everything in God's hands.

We can't be that way if we indulge ourselves in evil. Then we'll know nothing but nagging consciences and the displeasure of God.

Indeed, physical health is often related to our mental and spiritual conditions. The Hebrew in verse 8 literally speaks of "healed navels" and "moist bones."

> ⁹ **Honor the LORD with your wealth,**
> **with the firstfruits of all your crops;**
> ¹⁰ **then your barns will be filled to overflowing,**
> **and your vats will brim over with new wine.**

Just as a godly life can be related to physical well-being, it can also bring material blessings. The Old Testament Israelites were required to bring the firstfruits of their crops and animals to God's representative, the priest. (See Leviticus 23:10; Numbers 18:12,13.)

They were to offer to God the first and the best of what they had. In regard to giving as he told them to, the Lord laid out this challenge: "Test me in this . . . and see if I will not throw open the floodgates of heaven and pour out so much blessing that you will not have room enough for it" (Malachi 3:10). Since Hebrew society was largely agricultural, they thought of wealth in terms of overflowing barns and brimming vats of wine. Unfortunately, the people often didn't take up the Lord's challenge. They gave God the leftovers and the worst of what they had.

While New Testament believers don't have regulations as to how much to give, we still have God's challenges and

Proverbs 3:11,12

promises. For example, Jesus says: "Give, and it will be given to you. A good measure, pressed down, shaken together and running over, will be poured into your lap. For with the measure you use, it will be measured to you" (Luke 6:38).

Sometimes that "good measure" comes in material ways. Other times God pours out gifts such as friendships and happiness. How do we respond to the Lord's challenges? Secure in the love of Christ, we can boldly, generously honor the Lord with our gifts for his work, the work of his church.

As we know, life is far from an uninterrupted holiday of physical health and material wealth. Lest we get that wrong impression, Solomon now moves to another aspect of life:

> **11 My son, do not despise the LORD's discipline**
> **and do not resent his rebuke,**
> **12 because the LORD disciplines those he loves,**
> **as a father the son he delights in.**

Side by side with life's pleasures come trials. They too are blessings from God. The New Testament writer to the Hebrews quotes these two verses from Proverbs as he encourages Christians: "Endure hardship as discipline. . . . God disciplines us for our good" (see Hebrews 12:4-11).

In many ways and in numerous places, the Bible deals with human suffering, focusing especially on the trials that believers are called upon to endure. The entire book of Job, for instance, deals with this subject.

Although we don't always see it at the time, our sufferings in this life are for our good. Rather than resenting such troubles, the believer learns to recognize them for what they are. Through life's sicknesses, pains, and heartaches, our heavenly Father tempers us, teaches us patience, and summons us to rely more completely on his strength.

Proverbs 3:13-18

One of the psalms puts it this way: "It was good for me to be afflicted so that I might learn your decrees, [O LORD]" (Psalm 119:71). What is probably the best-known passage on the subject has this to say: "We know that in all things God works for the good of those who love him, who have been called according to his purpose" (Romans 8:28).

Believers, then, love God and his Word not simply out of hope for earthly rewards, but they love him because they know that in all circumstances he is loving them! Job was the ideal example of this. When he lost all his children and worldly possessions, he exclaimed, "The LORD gave and the LORD has taken away; may the name of the LORD be praised" (Job 1:21).

This kind of wisdom brings real, lasting happiness.

> **13 Blessed is the man who finds wisdom,**
> **the man who gains understanding,**
> **14 for she is more profitable than silver**
> **and yields better returns than gold.**
> **15 She is more precious than rubies;**
> **nothing you desire can compare with her.**
> **16 Long life is in her right hand;**
> **in her left hand are riches and honor.**
> **17 Her ways are pleasant ways,**
> **and all her paths are peace.**
> **18 She is a tree of life to those who embrace her;**
> **those who lay hold of her will be blessed.**

In this chapter of Proverbs, we've already seen how the person with wisdom enjoys long life, health, and prosperity . . . along with the Lord's discipline. Now we get a look at more of the riches of godly wisdom. The phrase "blessed is the man" may also be translated as "happy is the man." This happiness comes from knowing God's care.

Except for "riches," the blessings spoken of here are beyond what money can buy: long life, honor, pleasant ways, peace.

37

Proverbs 3:19,20

But, we ask, aren't there many faithful Christians who don't enjoy such blessings? God always keeps his promises. A person might be poor in material wealth but rich with contentment. A believer might suffer unpleasant trials or persecutions yet find great pleasure in knowing he walks with God. Another child of God might suffer an early death, only to enter more quickly into heaven's eternity.

We need not look for earthly fulfillment of these promises. Nor do we need to rule out the possibility. In his wisdom God deals with us as he sees fit. At any time during life, we can be confident that through difficult and easy circumstances the Lord is taking care of us in the best possible way.

Verse 18 contains the first of four references in Proverbs to "a tree of life." (The others are 11:30; 13:12; 15:4.) It directs our thoughts back to the Garden of Eden with its tree of life (Genesis 2:9). Through true wisdom we have access into the second Eden, heaven itself.

Jesus Christ is the wisdom of God, and the cross of Christ is "a tree of life to those who embrace her."

> ¹⁹ **By wisdom the Lᴏʀᴅ laid the earth's foundations,**
> **by understanding he set the heavens in place;**
> ²⁰ **by his knowledge the deeps were divided,**
> **and the clouds let drop the dew.**

Not only does wisdom direct our thoughts back to the Garden of Eden, it goes beyond that—to creation itself.

As modern science discovers more of the wonders of the universe, we capture a glimpse of God's infinite wisdom in creation. For example, our planet earth is really a 6.5 trillion ton ball hurtling through space at the rate of 66,000 miles an hour.

But the earth is tiny compared to the sun and to our Milky Way galaxy, which is one hundred thousand light-

Proverbs 3:21-26

years wide. (One light-year is six trillion miles!) This galaxy, in turn, is but one of billions of other galaxies. All of this God watches over, controls, and keeps running with precision.

Solomon turns from the earth and the vast realms of the heavens to the water in the mighty seas and in the clouds. His mention of the dividing of the waters may be a reference to the second day of creation: "And God said, 'Let there be an expanse between the waters to separate water from water.' So God made the expanse and separated the water under the expanse from the water above it. . . . God called the expanse 'sky'" (Genesis 1:6-8).

Water is essential. During the long dry seasons in the Middle East, the soil depends on dew for moisture. Without water, there can be no life.

The massive foundations of the earth, the expanses of the heavens, a tiny drop of dew—God's entire creation reflects his awesome wisdom.

> ²¹ **My son, preserve sound judgment and discernment,**
> **do not let them out of your sight;**
> ²² **they will be life for you,**
> **an ornament to grace your neck.**
> ²³ **Then you will go on your way in safety,**
> **and your foot will not stumble;**
> ²⁴ **when you lie down, you will not be afraid;**
> **when you lie down, your sleep will be sweet.**
> ²⁵ **Have no fear of sudden disaster**
> **or of the ruin that overtakes the wicked,**
> ²⁶ **for the LORD will be your confidence**
> **and will keep your foot from being snared.**

In his wisdom God has provided for our physical lives on earth. To possess spiritual wisdom is to hold the source of other blessings as well. "Sound judgment and discernment . . . will be life for you" (literally, "for your soul").

Proverbs 3:27,28

In a picturesque way, Solomon shows how wisdom enriches every aspect of life. It is "an ornament" for the neck. That is, it brings favor from others. They admire this quality in people who possess it, just as they might see and admire a piece of jewelry.

Wisdom brings safety. An awareness of God's love gives us the assurance spoken of in the psalm: "[The angels] will lift you up in their hands, so that you will not strike your foot against a stone" (Psalm 91:12).

Godly wisdom brings the blessing of sweet, undisturbed sleep. It keeps us from fear of sudden disaster, because we know our lives are in the hands of our loving Savior-God.

Having known these truths from infancy on, many believers might take them for granted. Maybe we don't even think of this knowledge as *wisdom* but assume it's something everybody knows. However, most people do not possess such insights. People who don't know the true God simply cannot have the confidence that believers possess.

Without the Lord, people don't have this priceless wisdom, no matter how knowledgeable they might be in every other area of life. That's why it's vital for Christians to share the gospel of Christ, the wisdom of God.

> [27] **Do not withhold good from those who deserve it,**
>   **when it is in your power to act.**
> [28] **Do not say to your neighbor,**
>   **"Come back later; I'll give it tomorrow"—**
>   **when you now have it with you.**

We sometimes speak of two types of sins—those of commission and those of omission. We easily fall into thinking that if we avoid *committing* sins, we're doing pretty well. Meanwhile, we overlook all the things we are *omitting,* which God wants us to do. Solomon reminds us that to withhold good is wrong.

Proverbs 3:31,32

With all the people in need of help today, we don't have to look far to see where we Christians can do good. There are victims of famines and floods. There are also those who are spiritually starving without the gospel. With our contributions for relief and for missions, with our prayers, and with our personal efforts, we can reach out to help. And the time to do it is now, not tomorrow.

> **²⁹ Do not plot harm against your neighbor,**
> **who lives trustfully near you.**
> **³⁰ Do not accuse a man for no reason—**
> **when he has done you no harm.**

God warns against the mind-set that would take advantage of a trusting neighbor (or anyone, for that matter). Out of a personal sense of insecurity, some might suspiciously plot against others or accuse them of wrongs they haven't done. Do not do that.

Christians, especially, have no reason to be so calculating and suspicious. We are secure in our Savior's love. Martin Luther's explanation to the Eighth Commandment puts it this way: "We should fear and love God that we do not tell lies about our neighbor, betray him, or give him a bad name, but defend him, speak well of him, and take his words and actions in the kindest possible way."

Instead of tearing others down, we can build them up.

> **³¹ Do not envy a violent man**
> **or choose any of his ways,**
> **³² for the LORD detests a perverse man**
> **but takes the upright into his confidence.**

Violent men often seem to get what they want in life: power, riches, position, women, respect from others. They simply and boldly seize whatever they can get. Don't envy them, says Solomon, and don't try to be like them.

41

Proverbs 3:33-35

The Almighty is not impressed with them. They are perverse, headed away from God and toward destruction. Their moment in the sun will soon be gone.

While God detests the wicked, he takes the upright "into his confidence." That is, those who trust in him are his friends and are privy to the intimate advice of his Word.

> ³³ **The Lord's curse is on the house of the wicked,**
> **but he blesses the home of the righteous.**
> ³⁴ **He mocks proud mockers**
> **but gives grace to the humble.**
> ³⁵ **The wise inherit honor,**
> **but fools he holds up to shame.**

These final three verses of chapter 3 consist of three comparisons between the righteous and the wicked.

Verse 33 contrasts God's curse upon the wicked's house with his blessing on the home of the righteous. The house in which ungodliness prevails is filled with strife and sorrow. Although the righteous still struggle with sin, they also know God's love and promises of help.

Verse 34 is quoted twice in the New Testament (James 4:6; 1 Peter 5:5). In the *Magnificat,* Mary the mother of Jesus expresses a similar thought: "He has brought down rulers from their thrones but has lifted up the humble" (Luke 1:52). This often-emphasized Bible truth is ironic— the very people who exalt themselves are put down, while those who lower themselves before God are lifted up. God laughs at feeble human attempts at self-glorification: "The One enthroned in heaven laughs; the Lord scoffs at them" (Psalm 2:4). But those who humbly recognize their unworthiness before him, God, in his grace, forgives and uplifts.

Verse 35 contrasts the honor of the wise with the shame of fools. Sometimes already in this life, the wise are recognized

Proverbs 4:1-6

by their fellowmen, while ungodly fools are held in contempt. Even if it must wait until the life to come, this Word of God holds true.

Wisdom is supreme

Fourth discourse

4 **Listen, my sons, to a father's instruction;**
    pay attention and gain understanding.
² **I give you sound learning,**
    so do not forsake my teaching.
³ **When I was a boy in my father's house, still tender,**
    and an only child of my mother,
⁴ **he taught me and said,**
    "Lay hold of my words with all your heart;
    keep my commands and you will live.
⁵ **Get wisdom, get understanding;**
    do not forget my words or swerve from them.
⁶ **Do not forsake wisdom, and she will protect you;**
    love her, and she will watch over you.

We are now in the fourth (4:1-9) of ten discourses. It is different in that it addresses "my sons," plural, instead of simply "my son." As we'll see, this discourse depicts wisdom as a bride to be sought and won.

Solomon here speaks more as a father than as a teacher. He recalls his own childhood (verse 3). His reference to himself as "a boy . . . still tender" recalls his father David's words: "My son Solomon is young and inexperienced" (1 Chronicles 22:5; 29:1).

What Solomon is passing down to the next generation, then, is godly wisdom from his own father (verse 4). Through the centuries it has always been this way among God's people. More than four hundred years before Solomon, Moses declared to the Israelites: "These commandments that I give you today are to be upon your hearts.

43

Proverbs 4:7-9

Impress them on your children. Talk about them when you sit at home and when you walk along the road, when you lie down and when you get up" (Deuteronomy 6:6,7). Christian fathers of today continue to pass the priceless heritage of God's Word on to their children. There is no greater gift that we can give to the next generation.

The word for "teaching" in verse 2 is also the word for the first five books of the Bible—the writings of Moses, the Pentateuch—namely, the Hebrew word *Torah*. The "teaching" we are concerned with handing down is nothing less than the Bible itself.

Verse 5 brings out the metaphor of wisdom being a bride to be sought. "*Get* wisdom, *get* understanding" is, literally, "buy," or "purchase." In Old Testament times, the bridegroom would purchase the bride from her father (see, for example, Genesis 29:14-30).

The believer's relationship with wisdom is not cold and merely academic. It is one of love (verse 6). We love and treasure God's Word, and through that Word, God himself protects us.

> [7] **Wisdom is supreme; therefore get wisdom.**
>   **Though it cost all you have, get understanding.**
> [8] **Esteem her, and she will exalt you;**
>   **embrace her, and she will honor you.**
> [9] **She will set a garland of grace on your head**
>   **and present you with a crown of splendor."**

Wisdom is our priority; we are to be willing to give anything for it. Jesus spoke of the kingdom of God as such a treasure: "The kingdom of heaven is like a merchant looking for fine pearls. When he found one of great value, he went away and sold everything he had and bought it" (Matthew 13:45,46). To have God's wisdom is to possess the kingdom, namely, God's gracious ruling in our hearts. For

Proverbs 4:10-17

what is the kingdom but knowing "the holy Scriptures, which are able to make you wise for salvation through faith in Christ Jesus" (2 Timothy 3:15)?

In verses 8 and 9, we see more of the intimate, even passionate, relationship between wisdom and its possessor. Wisdom places a garland and crown on one's head. Such adornment was customary at ancient weddings (see Song of Songs 3:11; Ezekiel 16:12). God himself has in store for believers "the crown of righteousness," which we will receive on the day Christ returns (2 Timothy 4:8).

Fifth discourse

> [10] Listen, my son, accept what I say,
>   and the years of your life will be many.
> [11] I guide you in the way of wisdom
>   and lead you along straight paths.
> [12] When you walk, your steps will not be hampered;
>   when you run, you will not stumble.
> [13] Hold on to instruction, do not let it go;
>   guard it well, for it is your life.
> [14] Do not set foot on the path of the wicked
>   or walk in the way of evil men.
> [15] Avoid it, do not travel on it;
>   turn from it and go on your way.
> [16] For they cannot sleep till they do evil;
>   they are robbed of slumber till they make someone fall.
> [17] They eat the bread of wickedness
>   and drink the wine of violence.

In the fifth discourse to youth (4:10-19), the way of righteousness is sharply distinguished from the way of the wicked.

When a child learns to walk, at first he is hesitant and stumbles and falls. Later in life, that same child might become a track star. When we learn to ride a bike, at first it

Proverbs 4:18,19

seems to be an impossible balancing act. Later, it becomes second nature.

That's the way it is with many activities in life, including growing in God's wisdom. As we travel God's way, we become more confident and stronger, provided we continue to be nourished from God's Word.

The promise of long life (verse 10) is often connected with wisdom (see 3:16). This can refer to a longer, fuller life here on earth and certainly points believers to the life to come.

To walk wisdom's path is to tread on smooth paths (verse 12). Palestine is a hilly and rocky country. Leaving the beaten path invites turning one's ankle and stumbling. Spiritually, to leave God's way is to invite a fall (verses 14,15).

The wicked like nothing more than to see the godly fall (verse 16). They can't get to sleep until they've dreamed up some evil. It's their bread and drink (verse 17). One commentator calls these two verses a "picture of upside-down morality." God's people will avoid doing anything that causes a "brother to fall" (Romans 14:21); and their "food"—as was Christ's—is to do our heavenly Father's will (John 4:34).

Those who feed their minds on wickedness and evil (including through books and television) come to see this as a legitimate way of life. Avoid it, says Solomon. The two ways lead to opposite destinations:

> **¹⁸ The path of the righteous is like the first gleam of dawn,**
> **shining ever brighter till the full light of day.**
> **¹⁹ But the way of the wicked is like deep darkness;**
> **they do not know what makes them stumble.**

Verse 18 is a beautiful picture of our heavenward walk. At daybreak the light is dim. By noon the sun is overhead and beaming brightly. When we enter heaven, we will be in the

Proverbs 4:20-27

resplendent presence of him who is Light itself. What a glorious future lies ahead!

Since the wicked are walking in darkness, they are bound to stumble. The darkness is so deep that they can't even see what they're falling over! They spend this life stumbling about in the dark, only to be hurled into an eternity of more darkness.

The contrasting picture of light and darkness occurs throughout Scripture. God uses it to compare righteousness and sin, wisdom and folly, belief and unbelief, heaven and hell.

Sixth discourse

> [20] **My son, pay attention to what I say;**
> **listen closely to my words.**
> [21] **Do not let them out of your sight,**
> **keep them within your heart;**
> [22] **for they are life to those who find them**
> **and health to a man's whole body.**
> [23] **Above all else, guard your heart,**
> **for it is the wellspring of life.**
> [24] **Put away perversity from your mouth;**
> **keep corrupt talk far from your lips.**
> [25] **Let your eyes look straight ahead,**
> **fix your gaze directly before you.**
> [26] **Make level paths for your feet**
> **and take only ways that are firm.**
> [27] **Do not swerve to the right or the left;**
> **keep your foot from evil.**

The sixth of ten discourses (4:20-27) is structured around parts of the body—the heart, mouth, lips, eyes, feet, and entire body. Each is to be used in the service of God. We are reminded of Saint Paul's words: "Therefore, I urge you, brothers, in view of God's mercy, to offer your bodies as living sacrifices, holy and pleasing to God—this is your spiritual act of

Let your eyes look straight ahead

Proverbs 5:1-6

worship" (Romans 12:1). We also think of the well-known hymn "Take My Life and Let It Be," in which the hymn writer Frances Havergal offers herself entirely to God— hands, voice, feet, lips (*Christian Worship* [CW] 469).

Notice especially verse 23, in which the heart is called the "wellspring of life." It is the very source of life. In the Bible the heart represents the entire inner life of human beings. This means that not only the emotions but also the intellect and will spring from the heart. That's why God is constantly looking past outward appearances and directly into the heart.

If the heart is evil, then evil, including evil speech, will flow from it. Jesus says: "The good man brings good things out of the good stored up in his heart, and the evil man brings evil things out of the evil stored up in his heart. For out of the overflow of his heart his mouth speaks" (Luke 6:45).

Sinful speech, in turn, can have the effect of hardening our hearts. Complaining, cynicism, innuendoes, and off-color joking can become habitual. Hence, "put away perversity from your mouth" (verse 24).

Looking straight ahead (verse 25) stands in contrast to having shifty eyes, behind which lurks a deceitful heart. A godly person will keep focused on what is right and true.

The level paths and straight walk of the last two verses represent the righteous, godly way through life. Like road signs, God's Word shows the way.

Warning against adultery
Seventh discourse

5 **My son, pay attention to my wisdom,**
   listen well to my words of insight,
 ² that you may maintain discretion
   and your lips may preserve knowledge.
 ³ For the lips of an adulteress drip honey,
   and her speech is smoother than oil;

Proverbs 5:1-6

> ⁴ **but in the end she is bitter as gall,**
>   **sharp as a double-edged sword.**
> ⁵ **Her feet go down to death;**
>   **her steps lead straight to the grave.**
> ⁶ **She gives no thought to the way of life;**
>   **her paths are crooked, but she knows it not.**

The seventh discourse (5:1-23) warns against involvement with an adulterous woman. Three of the ten discourses to youth (also numbers nine and ten) call for sexual purity. Obviously, God considers it a very important subject. Like the prophets and New Testament writers, Proverbs sees our sexual morality as a reflection of our faithfulness or unfaithfulness to God, who is our heavenly Bridegroom.

The intimate connection between sexual chastity and devotion to the Lord led the Bible writers to speak of idolatry as prostitution. Ezekiel chapters 16 and 23 offer powerful examples of how God's people left him and became, as he called them, "you prostitute." Moreover, in times of widespread unbelief, one of the first areas to break down is the family. Marital infidelity follows close upon spiritual indifference. We see this everywhere today.

In the first six verses of this section, we learn the basic facts about the adulteress. Her speech is inviting. ("Honey" and "oil" represent what is sweet and smooth.) She promises every kind of delight, always with the lie that you'll get away with it.

In the end, of course, there is nothing but misery. ("Gall," sometimes translated as "wormwood," is a bitter herb.) A person might be filled with self-recrimination and despair. Physical death may come at the hands of a jealous spouse or by venereal disease. Spiritual and eternal death can result from hardening one's conscience.

Perhaps the most striking line in these verses is the last: "Her paths are crooked, but she knows it not." She is so hard-

Proverbs 5:7-14

ened in sin and so used to excusing her ways, that she no longer even sees how far astray she has gone. Sin can do that to people.

> ⁷ Now then, my sons, listen to me;
>   do not turn aside from what I say.
> ⁸ Keep to a path far from her,
>   do not go near the door of her house,
> ⁹ lest you give your best strength to others
>   and your years to one who is cruel,
> ¹⁰ lest strangers feast on your wealth
>   and your toil enrich another man's house.
> ¹¹ At the end of your life you will groan,
>   when your flesh and body are spent.
> ¹² You will say, "How I hated discipline!
>   How my heart spurned correction!
> ¹³ I would not obey my teachers
>   or listen to my instructors.
> ¹⁴ I have come to the brink of utter ruin
>   in the midst of the whole assembly."

These verses offer preventative medicine for avoiding the adulteress. Don't play with fire. Stay away from this woman. Paul urges, "Flee the evil desires of youth" (2 Timothy 2:22). Lest we forget, this advice can work the other way too. Women should avoid the adulterous man.

The cost of lustful indulgence is high. The story of the person caught in an adulterous web is often a tragedy of wasted years, cover-ups, lost wealth, drained energy, and ruined health. The sweet-sounding adulteress turns out to be cruel. She takes the money she has gotten and spends it with her friends.

Whether verse 11 refers to an actual physical disease or to one's drained strength is immaterial. Either way, the piti-ful soul is left groaning.

Proverbs 5:15-20

These verses do not end with the usual contrast between the two ways. Instead they describe only one side, the regrets of the man who doesn't take the sage's advice. Verses 12 to 14 list those regrets: he hated discipline, spurned correction, didn't obey his teachers, and didn't listen to his instructors.

Now he has come to the brink of ruin. Only by God's grace can one escape complete destruction. His near ruin includes public embarrassment in the "assembly," the local group that made pronouncements of censure.

Deuteronomy 22:22 describes the Mosaic punishment for adultery: "If a man is found sleeping with another man's wife, both the man who slept with her and the woman must die. You must purge the evil from Israel." The Christian church is not under the civil laws of ancient Israel. And the harshness of God's Old Testament law may at times stun us. Yet it shows the utter seriousness of sin.

One of the sad realities of our time is that too many Christian churches treat adultery lightly. Church members carry on affairs, live together outside of marriage, get unscriptural divorces, and remarry unscripturally (all of which are variations of adultery). Meanwhile, churches look the other way, offering no censure and even condoning what goes on. But God sees and will judge.

> ¹⁵ **Drink water from your own cistern,**
> **running water from your own well.**
> ¹⁶ **Should your springs overflow in the streets,**
> **your streams of water in the public squares?**
> ¹⁷ **Let them be yours alone,**
> **never to be shared with strangers.**
> ¹⁸ **May your fountain be blessed,**
> **and may you rejoice in the wife of your youth.**
> ¹⁹ **A loving doe, a graceful deer—**
> **may her breasts satisfy you always,**
> **may you ever be captivated by her love.**

Proverbs 5:15-20

[20] **Why be captivated, my son, by an adulteress?**
Why embrace the bosom of another man's wife?

Using a delightful picture of clear, pure, running water, God declares that sexual fulfillment is to be with one's own wife. In Song of Songs, the lover says to his bride: "You are a spring enclosed, a sealed fountain. . . . You are a garden fountain, a well of flowing water" (4:12,15). Like a privately owned well or cistern from which one draws refreshing, uncontaminated water, she is kept just for him. The Bible looks at sex in marriage as a beautiful gift from the Creator.

Solomon points to the other side of the picture when he says, Don't contaminate this wonderful blessing by sharing her with strangers (verses 16,17). Some see these two verses not as a question and exhortation but as statements. The overflow is a reference to the children coming from the marriage. They play in the streets but belong to you. Although this is a possibility, the former interpretation seems better.

The message is that we should be content with our spouses. "The wife of your youth" is a significant phrase. As couples grow older together, they are to work at keeping their love alive. Some men grow tired of the wives they married when they were young. So they seek other women, often younger ones, as if in doing so they can return to their own youth. In the days of the prophet Malachi, God condemned those Israelites who were divorcing "the wife of your youth, . . . though she is your partner, the wife of your marriage covenant. . . . 'I hate divorce,' says the LORD God of Israel" (Malachi 2:14,16).

Verse 19 is reminiscent of Song of Songs. There too the wife is pictured as a lovely, graceful animal: "Your two breasts are like two fawns, like twin fawns of a gazelle" (Song of Songs 4:5). Clearly, God approves of the delights of sensual love—within marriage.

Proverbs 5:21-23

Which brings Solomon to the closing question: Why throw it all away and go chasing after another man's wife? Given the blessings of marriage and the misery of adultery, only a fool would opt for the latter.

> ²¹ **For a man's ways are in full view of the LORD,**
>   **and he examines all his paths.**
> ²² **The evil deeds of a wicked man ensnare him;**
>   **the cords of his sin hold him fast.**
> ²³ **He will die for lack of discipline,**
>   **led astray by his own great folly.**

Even if one gets away with adultery before human eyes, God sees. Nothing escapes his judgment.

The wicked are ensnared by their own evil in one of two ways. For one thing, a particular sin can become an unbreakable habit. What began as flirtation with the sin of adultery, for example, can turn into a life-consuming nightmare. We hear of a growing number of people "addicted" to sexual immorality, whether it be adultery or some other form. Evil can also ensnare in that one sin leads to another. For instance, a person is unfaithful; then he or she turns to lying to cover up; this is followed by stealing to pay for the sin; and so on. Eventually the web of sin has become so strong that it completely entangles the sinner. At the last, what started as a foolish lack of discipline culminates in death.

Is there no way out? Thanks be to the triune God, there is! The chain can be broken. After including adulterers among the wicked who will not "inherit the kingdom of God," the apostle Paul declares: "And that is what some of you were. But you were washed, you were sanctified, you were justified in the name of the Lord Jesus Christ and by the Spirit of our God" (1 Corinthians 6:9,11). Through Christ there is forgiveness and power against the viselike grip of sin.

Proverbs 6:1-5

Warning against folly

Eighth discourse

6 **My son, if you have put up security for your neighbor,**
   if you have struck hands in pledge for another,
² if you have been trapped by what you said,
   ensnared by the words of your mouth,
³ then do this, my son, to free yourself,
   since you have fallen into your neighbor's hands:
   Go and humble yourself;
   press your plea with your neighbor!
⁴ Allow no sleep to your eyes,
   no slumber to your eyelids.
⁵ Free yourself, like a gazelle from the hand of the hunter,
   like a bird from the snare of the fowler.

The eighth discourse to youth (6:1-19) furnishes a digression from the subject of sexual morality, before returning to it for the final two discourses. In this discourse Solomon discusses situations into which the naive commonly fall.

The first situation is that of making oneself responsible for another's debt. A related example from the book of Genesis is Judah's offering himself as surety for his brother Benjamin's safety. Judah said to his father: "I myself will guarantee his safety; you can hold me personally responsible for him. If I do not bring him back to you and set him here before you, I will bear the blame before you all my life" (43:9).

While Judah's was a noble act, Solomon refers to a reprehensible attitude. He strongly warns against pledging for our neighbor or "another," literally, a stranger. Although it can happen at any age, the young are less experienced and more likely to make foolish financial commitments, such as offering to support a friend or stranger in some business transaction. The striking of hands was the equivalent of our modern handshake to confirm the deal.

Proverbs 6:9-11

So strongly does Solomon warn against such deals that he urges, "Go and humble yourself" to get out of it. "Humble yourself" in the Hebrew is "trample upon yourself." In other words, forget about your dignity; be prepared to humiliate yourself to be free from your pledge.

He adds, "Press your plea." Keep pestering your neighbor until he lets you off the hook! Don't let another day go by until you have gotten out of this snare.

Our material resources are gifts of God. As is the case with everything we have, we will want to use them wisely.

> **⁶ Go to the ant, you sluggard;**
> **consider its ways and be wise!**
> **⁷ It has no commander,**
> **no overseer or ruler,**
> **⁸ yet it stores its provisions in summer**
> **and gathers its food at harvest.**

A second common error into which the young often fall is that of laziness. Solomon points to the tiny ant for this lesson. The Bible tells us that wise King Solomon was well acquainted with the world of plants and animals: "He described plant life, from the cedar of Lebanon to the hyssop that grows out of walls. He also taught about animals and birds, reptiles and fish" (1 Kings 4:33).

Ants receive mention only twice in the entire Bible. The other reference is in Proverbs 30:25. In both cases they are representatives of industriousness.

The sluggard can learn from these tiny creatures. They have initiative; they don't need a leader standing over them. They do not procrastinate. They plan ahead and store up for the winter.

> **⁹ How long will you lie there, you sluggard?**
> **When will you get up from your sleep?**

Proverbs 6:12-15

> **¹⁰ A little sleep, a little slumber,**
> **a little folding of the hands to rest—**
> **¹¹ and poverty will come on you like a bandit**
> **and scarcity like an armed man.**

One translation renders "you sluggard" as "you lazy bum." You can almost see the sluggard hearing about the ant and then rolling over on his side for a bit more sleep. Or else, he folds his hands over his stomach—the common position when taking a nap—and mumbles: "I'll be with you in a minute. Give me just a little more sleep." We get the picture.

Solomon turns from the positive example of the ant to a warning of what will happen if the sluggard doesn't get moving. Poverty lies ahead.

The Bible doesn't advocate workaholism. Jesus himself took time for rest and relaxation. But God does not want us wasting away our time in laziness. When it comes to doing the Lord's work, we have only *now* to act, before the night of death comes and work must cease.

Verses 10 and 11 are repeated in Proverbs 24:33,34, another passage warning against laziness.

> **¹² A scoundrel and villain,**
> **who goes about with a corrupt mouth,**
> **¹³ who winks with his eye, signals with his feet**
> **and motions with his fingers,**
> **¹⁴ who plots evil with deceit in his heart—**
> **he always stirs up dissension.**
> **¹⁵ Therefore disaster will overtake him in an instant;**
> **he will suddenly be destroyed—without remedy.**

Just as Solomon observed the little ant, he also watched human behavior in detail. Long before modern psychology took up the study of body language, the wise king of Israel had observed how even the slightest motions can tell volumes about a person.

57

Proverbs 6:16-19

Here he focuses his powers of observation on the "scoundrel and villain." The scoundrel is, literally, the man of Belial. The term *Belial* means "worthlessness" and "wickedness" and later came to be applied to the devil himself (2 Corinthians 6:15), who is the epitome of wickedness.

Solomon describes several telltale signs of a wicked man. First, his mouth is corrupt. Lies, filthy talk, slander, and a general disregard for God characterize his speech.

The other signs consist of that body language mentioned earlier. His eyes wink. This is the knowing wink that one liar gives to another; it is also the wink of mockery directed against one who tries to stand for what is right. Even his feet give signals. This might indicate a scraping with one's foot to give a sign to a wicked accomplice. Finally, he uses his fingers. Perhaps in obscene gestures or as a come-on to evil.

Whether openly or more subtly, the scoundrel stirs up dissension. Friendships and marriages are broken. Business, trade, politics, and international affairs all suffer from his handiwork.

Sooner or later his evil catches up with him. When disaster comes, it is sudden, complete, and irreversible. Over and over in Proverbs, we see this truth repeated. Evildoers do not get away with it. God watches. There is judgment.

To underscore God's attitude against wickedness, Solomon calls to our attention seven things that the Lord hates and detests:

> [16] **There are six things the LORD hates,**
> **seven that are detestable to him:**
> [17]   **haughty eyes, a lying tongue,**
> **hands that shed innocent blood,**
> [18]   **a heart that devises wicked schemes,**
> **feet that are quick to rush into evil,**
> [19]   **a false witness who pours out lies**
> **and a man who stirs up dissension among brothers.**

Proverbs 6:16-19

This is one of the so-called numerical proverbs, in which the sage presents a listing. (We'll see several of them in Proverbs 30.) The "six . . . seven" form is a poetic way of expression. Solomon is not saying that God hates six things, and then there are seven he detests. He detests and hates all seven.

In most numerical proverbs, the second line increases by one the number given in the first line. (Proverbs 30:7-9 and 24-28 are exceptions.) We also find this form in the books of Job (5:19) and Amos (1:3–2:6).

Returning to the proverb at hand, Solomon enumerates seven evils. Seven suggests completeness, and this list might be a summary listing of sin in general. This list is not to be confused with the "seven deadly sins," which, later in church history, some came to see as especially harmful (pride, covetousness, lust, anger, gluttony, envy, sloth).

Each of the seven sins in Solomon's list is important enough to come up several times throughout Proverbs. To emphasize their seriousness as well as God's anger against them, we list this catalog of sins, along with at least one cross-reference for each (although they occur more often):

- haughty eyes—reflecting a proud heart (11:2)
- lying tongue—reflecting a deceitful heart (12:19; 17:7)
- hands that shed innocent blood—murder, not capital punishment (1:11)
- a heart devising wicked schemes—the heart, at the center of human activity for good or ill (1:31; 24:2)
- feet rushing into evil—yet slow to do what God wills (1:16)
- a false witness—the cause of great harm (12:17)
- a man stirring up dissension (6:14)

This list strikes us in how closely it resembles the description of the scoundrel we just studied (6:12-15). No

Proverbs 6:20-29

doubt it follows immediately upon that passage as a summary. It also serves as a warning that God looks at every sin as an abomination—whether it be a sin of thought (in the heart), word, or deed.

Most striking of all, we are able to see ourselves in this list. How often haven't we fallen in one way or another into all sorts of sins! And rather than calling some sins deadlier than others, the Bible informs us that any breaking of God's law is deadly: "Whoever keeps the whole law and yet stumbles at just one point is guilty of breaking all of it" (James 2:10).

We can be thankful that God, who hates sin, has taken out his wrath on his own Son. "God made him who had no sin to be sin for us, so that in him we might become the righteousness of God" (2 Corinthians 5:21). On the cross Jesus suffered the "disaster" (verse 15) that should have overtaken us because of our sins.

Ninth discourse

²⁰ **My son, keep your father's commands**
and do not forsake your mother's teaching.
²¹ **Bind them upon your heart forever;**
fasten them around your neck.
²² **When you walk, they will guide you;**
when you sleep, they will watch over you;
when you awake, they will speak to you.
²³ **For these commands are a lamp,**
this teaching is a light,
and the corrections of discipline
are the way to life,
²⁴ **keeping you from the immoral woman,**
from the smooth tongue of the wayward wife.
²⁵ **Do not lust in your heart after her beauty**
or let her captivate you with her eyes,

Proverbs 6:20-29

²⁶ **for the prostitute reduces you to a loaf of bread,**
   and the adulteress preys upon your very life.
²⁷ **Can a man scoop fire into his lap**
   without his clothes being burned?
²⁸ **Can a man walk on hot coals**
   without his feet being scorched?
²⁹ **So is he who sleeps with another man's wife;**
   no one who touches her will go unpunished.

In the ninth discourse to "my son" (6:20-35), Solomon returns to the topic of sexual morality. He spends several introductory verses (20-23) exhorting the young person to listen to his father and mother. With this introduction, he is saying something like this: I'm repeating a topic I spoke of before. But it's so important that you need to pay close attention once more.

Indeed, the lure of sins of the flesh is so powerful and widespread that it calls for added emphasis. Our modern society has accepted the "new morality" of sexual freedom, which of course is neither new nor moral. On a daily basis we witness its lure in magazines, advertising, TV shows, hit songs, and popular slogans ("If it feels good, do it"). We also witness its dire consequences: ruined careers and reputations, including those of highly visible politicians and church leaders; widespread venereal disease and abortion; broken homes; emotionally scarred children; crimes of revenge and violence.

Solomon guides young people through the maze. Cling to the Bible's teachings, which you learned from your parents (verse 20). Keep these teachings in your heart, and let them adorn your outward behavior (verse 21). They are a sure guide to light your way (verse 22). Psalm 119:105 uses this same imagery in speaking of God's Word: "Your word is a lamp to my feet and a light for my path."

Proverbs 6:20-29

In verse 24 we come to the point of this discourse. Godly teaching keeps one from the immoral woman. This woman stands in brazen distinction to the moral training the young man received from his father and mother. Again, Solomon mentions her smooth tongue (see 5:3).

He says, "Do not lust." Sin begins in the heart. Jesus spoke of the close connection between the desire and the deed when he said, "Anyone who looks at a woman lustfully has already committed adultery with her in his heart" (Matthew 5:28). And the Tenth Commandment declares, "You shall not covet your neighbor's wife" (Exodus 20:17).

Solomon seems to say that getting involved with an adulteress brings more serious consequences than involvement with a prostitute (verse 26). The prostitute can reduce you to poverty, so you end up living with the bare minimum, a loaf of bread. The adulteress can cost you your very life.

The following verses explain why, as Solomon describes adultery as playing with fire (verses 27-29). The answer to the two rhetorical questions is, No. You can't scoop fire into your lap and not burn your clothes. Nor can you walk on hot coals and not scorch your feet.

Since adultery involves taking another man's wife, the adulterer can expect the husband to seek revenge. Punishment is sure to come. If not from a vengeful husband, then in some other way.

The Old Testament called for the death penalty for adultery (Deuteronomy 22:22), the same as for murder. In a way adultery was, and is, a form of murder. It cuts at the heart of a marriage.

Not all sexual sins called for the death penalty. Although it was not honorable, prostitution did not ensure death (see, for example, Leviticus 21:7). This is not to say that going to prostitutes is all right, while adultery isn't. Both are sins. Yet

Proverbs 6:30-35

the fact is that the Old Testament dealt more severely with the latter, and Solomon warns against it in this discourse.

> **³⁰ Men do not despise a thief if he steals**
> **to satisfy his hunger when he is starving.**
> **³¹ Yet if he is caught, he must pay sevenfold,**
> **though it costs him all the wealth of his house.**
> **³² But a man who commits adultery lacks judgment;**
> **whoever does so destroys himself.**
> **³³ Blows and disgrace are his lot,**
> **and his shame will never be wiped away;**
> **³⁴ for jealousy arouses a husband's fury,**
> **and he will show no mercy when he takes revenge.**
> **³⁵ He will not accept any compensation;**
> **he will refuse the bribe, however great it is.**

Having just pictured adultery as playing with fire, Solomon now compares it to stealing. People can understand and sympathize with a thief who steals because he is starving. Yet, if caught, he has to pay in full. Mosaic Law required payment of between twofold and fivefold as penalty for stealing (Exodus 22:1-9). Without designating a specific amount, "sevenfold" represents full payment (seven being the number of completeness).

If people are understanding of a thief and he still has to pay the penalty, how will they be toward the adulterer? Not nearly so understanding. No one has to commit adultery to stay alive; it's merely a matter of satisfying one's lust. He can expect he's going to pay dearly for it.

Even in our society, which is accepting of sexual immorality, the stigma of adultery is still strong enough to cost politicians their offices and clergy their calling. If we ever reach complete indifference, there won't be much society left. There should always be a willingness to forgive but never an excusing of the sin.

Proverbs 7:1-5

While many today view the playboy and playgirl as sophisticates, Solomon says the adulterer "lacks judgment." God says, "Call them simpletons!"

Solomon closes this warning against adultery with a description of the wronged husband's anger and the adulterer's punishment. Since he doesn't mention death by stoning, we may conclude that this punishment was not always carried out in Solomon's day. Yet the guilt, shame, suffering, and hurt remained. That hasn't changed in our day either.

Warning against the adulteress

Tenth discourse

7 **My son, keep my words**
and store up my commands within you.
² Keep my commands and you will live;
guard my teachings as the apple of your eye.
³ Bind them on your fingers;
write them on the tablet of your heart.
⁴ Say to wisdom, "You are my sister,"
and call understanding your kinsman;
⁵ they will keep you from the adulteress,
from the wayward wife with her seductive words.

The tenth and last discourse for youth (7:1-27) takes up the subject of sexual morality once more. As in the previous discourse, Solomon begins with several verses of encouragement to follow wisdom.

He says we are to make wisdom both an inward and an outward part of life—written in the heart and tied to one's fingers (verse 3). As people tie a string around their fingers as a reminder, so wisdom is to be our constant reminder of what's right. Unless it becomes a way of life, even the best advice is useless in the face of powerful temptations.

64

Proverbs 7:6-9

The apple of the eye in verse 2 refers to the pupil of the eye. It is vital for vision and has to be carefully protected. Similarly, we are to guard and keep wisdom's teachings. And how do we do that? By carefully studying God's Word and, with his help, firmly holding to its teachings.

The reference to wisdom as "my sister" and "kinsman" prepares us for the next section of Proverbs, in which wisdom is personified. It also underscores the closeness we are to have with wisdom. "Sister" was a term of endearment sometimes applied to one's sweetheart or bride (see Song of Songs 4:9,10,12; 5:1,2).

Even as he guards wisdom's teachings and keeps them in his heart, they protect the young man . . . from the adulterous wife of another man:

> **⁶ At the window of my house**
> **I looked out through the lattice.**
> **⁷ I saw among the simple,**
> **I noticed among the young men,**
> **a youth who lacked judgment.**
> **⁸ He was going down the street near her corner,**
> **walking along in the direction of her house**
> **⁹ at twilight, as the day was fading,**
> **as the dark of night set in.**

This warning against the adulterous woman differs from the others in that Solomon presents it as an eyewitness story. Looking through the cross strips of wood that formed the lattice to his window, he observed what went on in the busy street beneath. There he saw a young man who "lacked judgment."

Several details are of note. For one thing, this particular youth was not the only "simple" one. There were other young men who were naive and inexperienced. But unlike the others, this one lacked the good judgment to avoid the

Proverbs 7:10-13

adulteress. The term translated "young men" in verse 7 is actually "sons." This ties it to the objects of Solomon's ten discourses, which are directed to "my son" and in the fourth discourse to "my sons" (see also verse 24). In other words, he's saying, this young man was one of you.

It should strike us modern readers in the same way. This kind of sin could seduce us just as well. We ought humbly take to heart the words of Paul, "So, if you think you are standing firm, be careful that you don't fall!" (1 Corinthians 10:12).

Perhaps the young man was simple enough not to be aware that he was headed into an area of ill-repute. Or he may have known and yet felt nothing would happen if he just walked by. But he was playing with fire.

Verse 9 paints the backdrop: darkness was setting in. The three expressions—"at twilight, as the day was fading, as the dark of night set in"—describe the succession from late afternoon until night. As the afternoon fades, the cool breeze sets in. (The twilight actually refers to the breeze that arises in the late afternoon.) And then comes darkness.

In dramatic fashion Solomon continues the scene as it unfolds:

> **¹⁰ Then out came a woman to meet him,**
> **dressed like a prostitute and with crafty intent.**
> **¹¹ (She is loud and defiant,**
> **her feet never stay at home;**
> **¹² now in the street, now in the squares,**
> **at every corner she lurks.)**
> **¹³ She took hold of him and kissed him**
> **and with a brazen face she said:**

There is nothing subtle about this woman's appearance. In Bible times this may have meant she was wearing a veil (see Genesis 38:14,15). Perhaps her dress was brightly colored.

Proverbs 7:14-20

At any rate, she is dressed in a way designed to seduce, or, as some might say, she is dressed to kill.

Behind this brazen exterior, she is crafty. Though she seems to offer love and pleasure to the youth, she is really concerned only about herself. Her interest is in her own enjoyment, not that of the young man.

The woman is "loud," the same way in which folly is later described (9:13). Although she "lurks" about, once she has found her prey, she goes right at him (verse 13). She takes hold of him, maybe taking his hand or embracing him, and she kisses him. Then she speaks:

> ¹⁴ "I have fellowship offerings at home;
>   today I fulfilled my vows.
> ¹⁵ So I came out to meet you;
>   I looked for you and have found you!
> ¹⁶ I have covered my bed
>   with colored linens from Egypt.
> ¹⁷ I have perfumed my bed
>   with myrrh, aloes and cinnamon.
> ¹⁸ Come, let's drink deep of love till morning;
>   let's enjoy ourselves with love!
> ¹⁹ My husband is not at home;
>   he has gone on a long journey.
> ²⁰ He took his purse filled with money
>   and will not be home till full moon."

Her first words are striking. She talks about fellowship offerings (also called peace offerings) and vows! (See Leviticus 7:11-21.) Perhaps she had vowed to offer a gift for some blessing, such as a safe trip.

In light of the immorality that follows, it seems strange that she should be concerned with vows and offerings. Upon reflection, however, it may not seem so strange at all. We think, for example, of our Christmas holidays. This woman

Proverbs 7:14-20

might mention to the naive young man at an office party, "I even made it to church this year." And then she proceeds to seduce him.

When people still maintain the outward trappings of religion, yet live immoral lives, God declares: "I hate, I despise your religious feasts; I cannot stand your assemblies. Even though you bring me burnt offerings and grain offerings, I will not accept them. Though you bring choice fellowship offerings, I will have no regard for them" (Amos 5:21,22). We're only fooling ourselves if we think we can disregard God's commandments and then buy him off by dropping money in the offering plate.

Apparently, the young man walked by regularly, since the woman looked for him (verse 15) and had everything ready. He had been flirting with danger, and now he would get it.

Her bed is ready, with linens from Egypt and perfumes. Fine Egyptian linen was valued (Ezekiel 27:7). The three fragrant spices—myrrh, aloes, cinnamon—are also mentioned in the wedding scene in the Song of Songs (4:14). What in one setting adds to the joy of "the marriage bed kept pure" (Hebrews 13:4), in another situation becomes a tool of the devil.

In the Song of Songs, the bride and groom are invited, "Eat, O friends, and drink; drink your fill, O lovers" (5:1). The adulteress invites the young man, "Come, let's drink deep of love till morning" (verse 18). But her next words set her worlds apart from the lovers in the Song: "My husband is not at home."

"My husband"—she literally refers to him in a derogatory way as "the man"—has enough money with him for an extended journey. In those days money in the form of silver pieces was carried in little sacks. Her reference to the full moon reminds us that the Jewish calendar was lunar.

68

Proverbs 7:21-23

The woman has appealed to all five senses. She dressed provocatively (sight), took hold of him (touch), prepared a meal (taste), and perfumed her bed (smell). With flattering words she continues her appeal to his sense of hearing:

> [21] **With persuasive words she led him astray;**
> **she seduced him with her smooth talk.**
> [22] **All at once he followed her**
> **like an ox going to the slaughter,**
> **like a deer stepping into a noose**
> [23] **till an arrow pierces his liver,**
> **like a bird darting into a snare,**
> **little knowing it will cost him his life.**

The words "all at once" (verse 22) point to the youth's sudden turn from indecision to action. He goes with her . . . to his slaughter. Like a dumb ox or deer or bird, he doesn't know what's happening to him. A decision made in a moment of passion will affect the rest of his life. We grieve for the many young people today who, seduced by popular lies about easy sex, make quick and foolish decisions, sometimes in the name of love (verse 18), only to spend a lifetime of regret.

The arrows that will pierce him are not Cupid's. Disease, remorse, financial loss, emotional upheaval, a vengeful husband, and perhaps an early death are some of the arrows in the quiver of the adulterous woman.

The young man's openness to temptation is markedly different from the behavior of another young man described in the Bible. When Joseph was tempted by his master's wife, "he refused to go to bed with her or even be with her." Although his refusal brought Joseph false accusations and imprisonment, God used the entire experience to strengthen and prepare him for a role of worldwide importance. (Read the account in Genesis chapter 39.)

Proverbs 7:24-27

²⁴ **Now then, my sons, listen to me;**
   pay attention to what I say.
²⁵ **Do not let your heart turn to her ways**
   or stray into her paths.
²⁶ **Many are the victims she has brought down;**
   her slain are a mighty throng.
²⁷ **Her house is a highway to the grave,**
   leading down to the chambers of death.

Solomon closes this discourse by addressing "my sons." Everyone should heed these warnings.

Although this extended warning against adultery dramatized a specific situation, it is a general warning for everyone. In spite of such warnings, many continue to find out the hard way that God's Word is right. The word translated "grave" in verse 27 can also be translated "hell" (Hebrew *sheol*). That is the final destination of unrepented sin.

One of the great tragedies of Bible history is that Solomon himself fell prey to sins of the flesh. Having gathered a large harem to himself, he let his wives lead him into idolatry. It's possible that he repented later in life. Yet the damage had been done. Strife haunted his senior years and, following his death, the next generation saw Solomon's mighty kingdom split into two divisions. He lived with the awareness that this would happen, because God himself had told Solomon. First Kings chapter 11 recounts these events from Solomon's last years.

It happened to Solomon; it could happen to any of us. If we have not fallen prey to such temptations, it is only by God's grace. If we have, that same grace brings us forgiveness in Christ.

The Ten Discourses for the Young are at an end. May they warn, encourage, and strengthen today's young men and women, even as they did the youth of King Solomon's day, almost three thousand years ago.

Proverbs 8:1-11

Wisdom's sevenfold appeal

Proverbs 1:8–7:27 consisted of ten discourses to "my son." The next two chapters (8:1–9:18) contain seven appeals from wisdom. We are urged to listen to wisdom. Among these appeals of wisdom, we find what has been called the major messianic text of the Bible's wisdom literature (8:22-31).

In the first of these seven subsections, we see wisdom personified; that is, described as a person.

Wisdom's "divine call"

① Wisdom personified

8 Does not wisdom call out?
     Does not understanding raise her voice?
² On the heights along the way,
     where the paths meet, she takes her stand;
³ beside the gates leading into the city,
     at the entrances, she cries aloud:
⁴ "To you, O men, I call out;
     I raise my voice to all mankind.
⁵ You who are simple, gain prudence;
     you who are foolish, gain understanding.
⁶ Listen, for I have worthy things to say;
     I open my lips to speak what is right.
⁷ My mouth speaks what is true,
     for my lips detest wickedness.
⁸ All the words of my mouth are just;
     none of them is crooked or perverse.
⁹ To the discerning all of them are right;
     they are faultless to those who have knowledge.
¹⁰ Choose my instruction instead of silver,
     knowledge rather than choice gold,
¹¹ for wisdom is more precious than rubies,
     and nothing you desire can compare with her.

The opening verse asks two rhetorical questions, emphasizing the fact that, yes, wisdom does call out. Wisdom is out

71

Proverbs 8:12-21

in public. Wisdom's approach is different from that of the harlot. Unlike the harlot who "lurks" at every street corner (7:12), wisdom loudly calls out. Wisdom's purpose is also different. It's not to deceive and destroy but to enlighten and give life.

Wisdom calls out as we travel along life's way. She also calls out "where the paths meet," at the crossroads of life, when we need to make important decisions. If we are not to lose our way, we need to listen to wisdom.

Wisdom makes an appeal for everyone. "All mankind" in verse 4 is, literally, "the sons of Adam." All the descendants of Adam need wisdom, for we are all part of a fallen race. We are lost unless God shares his wisdom with us. That wisdom calls to all shows that this wisdom is not merely for people with higher education. The wisdom God offers does not have to do with one's mental capacity. It is a spiritual matter. It involves what we believe and how we live, not simply how much information we can cram into our heads.

When Solomon became king of Israel, God appeared to him in a dream and said, "Ask for whatever you want me to give you" (1 Kings 3:5).

Solomon replied, "Give your servant a discerning heart to govern your people and to distinguish between right and wrong" (1 Kings 3:9).

The Lord was pleased with this request. He gave Solomon wisdom and added the blessings of riches and honor, things for which the king had not asked.

God wants us to choose his wisdom. Make the Bible your top priority and God will see to it that everything else is taken care of too.

Wisdom's self-description

> [12] **"I, wisdom, dwell together with prudence;**
> **I possess knowledge and discretion.**

Proverbs 8:12-21

¹³ To fear the LORD is to hate evil;
    I hate pride and arrogance,
      evil behavior and perverse speech.
¹⁴ Counsel and sound judgment are mine;
    I have understanding and power.
¹⁵ By me kings reign
    and rulers make laws that are just;
¹⁶ by me princes govern,
    and all nobles who rule on earth.
¹⁷ I love those who love me,
    and those who seek me find me.
¹⁸ With me are riches and honor,
    enduring wealth and prosperity.
¹⁹ My fruit is better than fine gold;
    what I yield surpasses choice silver.
²⁰ I walk in the way of righteousness,
    along the paths of justice,
²¹ bestowing wealth on those who love me
    and making their treasuries full.

Again, wisdom speaks. Since true wisdom comes from God, wisdom hates whatever God hates. In Proverbs 6:16-19, we saw seven things that are detestable to the Lord. Heading the list was "haughty eyes." Here the top item is "pride." The eyes are but a reflection of what is in the heart, and haughty eyes are evidence of a prideful heart. Throughout the Bible we see pride as something God does not tolerate. For example, Jesus saved his harshest words for the proud teachers of the law and Pharisees (see Matthew 23).

What is it about pride that makes it so hateful? The proud cut themselves off from God's grace in a way that other sinners don't. Proud people fail to see their need for God; they are self-sufficient. Jesus said to the proud leaders of the Jews, "I tell you the truth, the [lowly] tax collectors and the prostitutes are entering the kingdom of God ahead of you" (Matthew 21:31).

Proverbs 8:22-31

True wisdom, however, begins in humble fear of the Lord (verse 13). This includes the recognition of our sinfulness and of our complete dependence on God's grace. Whatever of value we are or have or hope to be comes from above.

Having described what she hates, wisdom turns to what she is and has and offers (verses 14-21). We've seen that when Solomon became king of Israel he prayed for wisdom to rule God's chosen nation. Along with wisdom, God promised Solomon other, unasked-for blessings, "so that in your lifetime you will have no equal among kings" (1 Kings 3:13).

When we pursue the wisdom of God, we find that God blesses us in unexpected ways. But we can't feign interest in God's Word with the ulterior motive of getting what we really want—namely, earthly riches and power. No, God sees into our hearts. Let's seek God's wisdom for the sheer joy and love of it (verse 17)! Then let God surprise us in whatever ways he chooses.

So far in chapter 8, we've seen wisdom personified. Following the NIV translation, we have referred to wisdom as "she." But that is not to say wisdom is a woman. At times we use feminine pronouns to personify what is not necessarily female. We might, for instance, point to a ship and say, "There she is!" This little aside is important at this point, as we now turn to what some interpreters consider the most profound section in the entire book, Proverbs 8:22-31:

Wisdom's eternal existence

²² **"The Lord brought me forth as the first of his works,**
　　before his deeds of old;
²³ **I was appointed from eternity,**
　　from the beginning, before the world began.
²⁴ **When there were no oceans, I was given birth,**
　　when there were no springs abounding with water;

Proverbs 8:22-31

²⁵ **before the mountains were settled in place,**
  before the hills, I was given birth,
²⁶ **before he made the earth or its fields**
  or any of the dust of the world.
²⁷ **I was there when he set the heavens in place,**
  when he marked out the horizon on the face of
    the deep,
²⁸ **when he established the clouds above**
  and fixed securely the fountains of the deep,
²⁹ **when he gave the sea its boundary**
  so the waters would not overstep his command,
 and when he marked out the foundations of the earth.
³⁰ **Then I was the craftsman at his side.**
 I was filled with delight day after day,
  rejoicing always in his presence,
³¹ **rejoicing in his whole world**
  and delighting in mankind.

Some commentators see here no more than a continued personification of wisdom, which belongs with God from eternity and is evident in his creation. This interpretation works well and is consistent with other personifications of abstract terms, such as folly in Proverbs 9:13-18.

Others, however, see wisdom moving beyond personification; we watch as wisdom does more than take on godly characteristics. Here wisdom takes on the nature of God himself and plays a role in the creation of the world. Therefore, those commentators and this author understand this portion of Proverbs chapter 8 as referring to Jesus Christ, the very Son of God.

Notice that wisdom says, "The Lord brought me forth . . . from eternity . . . before the world began" (verses 22,23). Wisdom was present already in eternity, before the creation of the world and, consequently, before there even was such a thing as time. Along the same lines, Jesus said, "And now, Father, glorify me in your presence with the glory I had with you before the world began" (John 17:5).

75

Proverbs 8:22-31

Although present from eternity, wisdom is "given birth" by God (verses 24-26). Likewise, Jesus is God's only begotten Son, "his one and only Son" (John 3:16).

Wisdom is described as present with God at creation (verses 27-29). John's gospel begins with a description of Jesus as "the Word." This connects him intimately with the wisdom of Proverbs, which calls out and makes its appeals. John declares: "In the beginning was the Word, and the Word was with God, and the Word was God. He was with God in the beginning" (John 1:1,2).

"I was the craftsman at his [God's] side," says wisdom (verse 30). John's gospel says of Jesus, "Through him all things were made; without him nothing was made that has been made" (John 1:3). Hebrews 1:2 asserts, "[God] has spoken to us by his Son . . . through whom he made the universe." And Colossians 1:15-17 declares: "He is the image of the invisible God, the firstborn over all creation. For by him all things were created: things in heaven and on earth, visible and invisible, whether thrones or powers or rulers or authorities; all things were created by him and for him. He is before all things, and in him all things hold together."

Already in Genesis chapter 1, the mystery of the Trinity is hinted at. "God created the heavens and the earth. . . . The Spirit of God was hovering. . . . And God said [repeated each day of creation, indicating the presence of the Word], . . . God said, 'Let us make man in our image.'"

Note too the parallel time sequence between Genesis chapter 1 and Proverbs. On day one God created the world (Genesis 1:1-5—Proverbs 8:23), on day two the waters (Genesis 1:6-8—Proverbs 8:24), on day three the dry land (Genesis 1:9-13—Proverbs 8:25,26).

God's delight in his creation (verses 30,31) is also seen in his assessment at the end of the sixth day: "God saw all that he had made, and it was very good" (Genesis 1:31).

Proverbs 8:32-36

In the fourth century after Christ, a controversy raged in the Christian churches. Focusing on this portion of Proverbs, the followers of Arius argued that Jesus was a created being and not eternal. There was a time when he was not, they contended. (In our day the Jehovah's Witnesses have taken up this ancient heresy.) Much of their argument rested on a faulty Greek translation of verse 22: "The LORD *created* me," instead of "The LORD brought me forth."

Orthodox Christians, led by the church father Athanasius, recognized that although begotten (or "brought forth"), Jesus is coeternal with God the Father. Out of this research into God's Word came the Nicene Creed, in which we still confess our faith in Jesus Christ, "the only Son of God, eternally begotten of the Father, God from God, Light from Light, true God from true God, begotten, not made, of one being with the Father. Through him all things were made."

When we come to the eternally begotten Son and other mysteries concerning the triune God, we are in realms beyond human comprehension. We can no more capture the eternal, omnipotent God within our minds than we could put the ocean into a bucket.

But the wonder of all wonders is that the great Creator has come to us to save us! Jesus is God. He is also our brother, who has suffered and died for us. Jesus is "the wisdom of God" (1 Corinthians 1:24), the one "in whom are hidden all the treasures of wisdom and knowledge" (Colossians 2:3).

Wisdom's warning

[32] "Now then, my sons, listen to me;
blessed are those who keep my ways.
[33] Listen to my instruction and be wise;
do not ignore it.

Proverbs 8:32-36

> ³⁴ **Blessed is the man who listens to me,**
> **watching daily at my doors,**
> **waiting at my doorway.**
> ³⁵ **For whoever finds me finds life**
> **and receives favor from the LORD.**
> ³⁶ **But whoever fails to find me harms himself;**
> **all who hate me love death."**

"Now then . . ." having stood in awe at the glory of wisdom, we are invited, "Listen to me." Who wouldn't want to listen to wisdom? Only the fool!

We are invited to receive gifts from wisdom's treasuries. Wisdom promises blessings, life, and favor from the Lord.

The word *blessed* means "happy." To enjoy God's blessing is to possess more than the passing pleasures of the moment. It's having the happiness that comes from knowing that no matter what the circumstances of life, we are in the loving hands of the eternal, almighty God. Jesus says, "Blessed rather are those who hear the word of God and obey it" (Luke 11:28). We enjoy God's blessings as we listen to his Word and take it to heart.

Earlier "my son" was urged to stay away from the door of the adulteress' house (5:8). Now wisdom urges us to sit and wait "at my doorway." Here, not at the other place, is where true blessings await us.

So many human beings are concerned about winning the favor of other people. Jesus warns about that kind of person: "Everything they do is done for men to see" (Matthew 23:5). Wisdom says it is far more important to have God's favor. We can learn from the example of the apostle Paul who said: "I care very little if I am judged by you or by any human court. . . . It is the Lord who judges me" (1 Corinthians 4:3,4).

Finally, to turn away from wisdom is really to hate life and to love death (verse 36)! We think it's tragic when we see

Proverbs 9:1-6

someone drink himself to death or ruin his life in some other self-destructive way. Ultimately, anyone who turns from the wisdom of God in Christ and tries to go his or her own way is doing the same thing. All roads that lead away from God end up in eternal death, no matter how pleasant and appealing they might seem in this world.

To find wisdom, though, is to find life! Following the Bible is the only way to live life to the fullest now and into eternity.

Invitations of wisdom and of folly

Wisdom's invitation

9 **Wisdom has built her house;**
    she has hewn out its seven pillars.
  2 She has prepared her meat and mixed her wine;
    she has also set her table.
  3 She has sent out her maids, and she calls
    from the highest point of the city.
  4 "Let all who are simple come in here!"
    she says to those who lack judgment.
  5 "Come, eat my food
    and drink the wine I have mixed.
  6 Leave your simple ways
    and you will live; walk in the way of understanding.

Here wisdom is personified as a woman. She is preparing her house for company. At the close of this chapter (verses 13-18), we'll see wisdom's counterpart, folly, inviting passersby into her house.

One of life's more enjoyable experiences is getting together with friends and relatives for a dinner. The Bible reminds us that there is a more important feast than earthly, physical food: "Man does not live on bread alone but on every word that comes from the mouth of the LORD" (Deuteronomy 8:3).

79

Proverbs 9:7-9

Wisdom invites us to feast on God's Word—by going to church, attending Bible classes, reading and sharing the Word at home and with friends.

Wisdom's house has seven pillars. Seven is the biblical number symbolizing completeness. Perhaps the use of this number is a way of saying that her house is ready.

She calls out from the highest point in the city. That is, wisdom does not try to hide her invitation. She also sends out her maids. We are reminded of Jesus' parable of the king's invitation to the wedding banquet for his son (Matthew 22:1-14). He sent out servants to invite people in. Both the maids and the servants might represent God's messengers who go out with the glorious gospel invitation.

To accept wisdom's invitation, we must first admit that we need it, that we are among the "simple" and "those who lack judgment" (verse 4). Then we also need to follow through and taste of the banquet—"eat my food and drink the wine" (verse 5). "Do not merely listen to the word, and so deceive yourselves," writes James. "Do what it says" (James 1:22). All this begins to take place in our lives when the Holy Spirit brings us to faith in Jesus.

Wisdom's feast in this life is but a foretaste of heaven, where we will join in "the wedding supper of the Lamb" (Revelation 19:9).

Wisdom's effect

> [7] **"Whoever corrects a mocker invites insult;**
> **whoever rebukes a wicked man incurs abuse.**
> [8] **Do not rebuke a mocker or he will hate you;**
> **rebuke a wise man and he will love you.**
> [9] **Instruct a wise man and he will be wiser still;**
> **teach a righteous man and he will add to his learning.**

Wisdom has called out and made appeals, prepared her house, and shown to all who come in what she has to offer.

Proverbs 9:10-12

Now we see the two possible responses to that appeal—wisdom is either accepted or ignored.

The mocker rejects God's wisdom. He belittles it and insults it. He calls it a crutch for the weak or foolishness or a waste of time. Jesus used a striking picture to illustrate this: "Do not give dogs what is sacred; do not throw your pearls to pigs. If you do, they may trample them under their feet, and then turn and tear you to pieces" (Matthew 7:6). In ancient Israel the unclean street dogs were nothing but scavengers. Pigs were unclean animals. Some wicked people simply will not listen to God's Word. They despise it, mock it, trample all over it.

Moreover, a mocker will hate you for offering him constructive criticism. Don't even bother trying, says Solomon.

Of course, we can't prejudge anyone to be a mocker. Let's not excuse ourselves from witnessing to others simply because some will reject it.

Sad to say, most people do reject wisdom's invitation. Returning to Jesus' parable of the wedding feast, the Lord ended the parable on this note: "For many are invited, but few are chosen" (Matthew 22:14).

A wise man isn't like that. He gladly receives the invitation. And he is open to the correction of God's Word. May we, by God's grace, never become proud and "above" rebuke! Rather, may we always be open to correction and instruction, especially in spiritual truths.

Solomon places the "wise man" and the "righteous man" in parallel lines. The two are synonymous. Biblical wisdom is not mere head knowledge. It has to do with being righteous. And our righteousness comes through Jesus Christ.

> [10] **"The fear of the LORD is the beginning of wisdom,**
> **and knowledge of the Holy One is understanding.**
> [11] **For through me your days will be many,**
> **and years will be added to your life.**

Proverbs 9:13-18

> ¹² **If you are wise, your wisdom will reward you;**
> **if you are a mocker, you alone will suffer."**

Again we have the key refrain of Proverbs: "The fear of the LORD is the beginning of wisdom." The book keeps coming back to this because it is central. We cannot and are not going to find wisdom, understanding, and lasting happiness aside from the Lord. These final words of wisdom summarize the first nine chapters of Proverbs.

Following biblical wisdom means living a healthier lifestyle, which, in a way, prolongs our lives. But it's really God who decides. The ultimate prolonging of life is the eternal life that is ours through Christ.

Verse 12 has been called "perhaps the strongest expression of individualism in the Bible."[7] While we are influenced by others and, in turn, influence them, each person stands alone before God. Finally, we live and die as individuals. "Each one should test his own actions. Then he can take pride in himself, without comparing himself to somebody else, for each one should carry his own load" (Galatians 6:4,5).

Wisdom's opponent

> ¹³ **The woman Folly is loud; she is undisciplined**
> **and without knowledge.**
> ¹⁴ **She sits at the door of her house,**
> **on a seat at the highest point of the city,**
> ¹⁵ **calling out to those who pass by,**
> **who go straight on their way.**
> ¹⁶ **"Let all who are simple come in here!"**
> **she says to those who lack judgment.**
> ¹⁷ **"Stolen water is sweet;**
> **food eaten in secret is delicious!"**
> ¹⁸ **But little do they know that the dead are there,**
> **that her guests are in the depths of the grave.**

Proverbs 9:13-18

Exhortations to Embrace Wisdom (1:8–9:18), one of the lengthier sections of Proverbs, is coming to an end. Solomon concludes it with a personification of wisdom's opponent, folly.

It might be more to our modern taste to end a work—whether a story, sermon, or article—on an upbeat note. Yet many individual proverbs and some larger sections of the book end on a downbeat, talking about the wicked or the foolish. Several Old Testament books (Ecclesiastes, Isaiah, Lamentations, Malachi) end with sharp words of judgment, and a number of Jesus' parables end in strongly negative words (see the last several verses of Matthew chapter 22, the story of the wedding banquet).

Solomon closes wisdom's sevenfold call with the call of folly. Folly is like the adulteress of chapter 7, in that both are seductive. While that is the true nature of folly, she tries to imitate wisdom. As wisdom called from the city heights, so does folly. In our day we might argue that folly has seized the most prominent places for calling out. Think of how folly controls TV, the movies, and much of the publishing world.

Verse 16 is an exact repetition of verse 4. Folly uses the same words as wisdom: "Let all who are simple come in here!" The simple are open to either good or evil. How especially true this is of young people! What kind of exposure are our children getting? Is it a constant diet of spiritual junk food and trash from television? How much of God's Word are they being exposed to and hearing?

"Those who lack judgment" are going to have that vacuum filled. The question is—what's going to fill it?

Folly offers lies: "Stolen water is sweet." Sex with someone else's spouse might seem more exciting than with one's own. The shady business deal may hold out promises of things you've always wanted to have but have never been

83

Proverbs 9:13-18

able to afford. It's the old deception Satan used with Eve in the Garden of Eden. "When the woman saw that the fruit of the tree was good for food and pleasing to the eye, and also desirable for gaining wisdom, she took some and ate it. She also gave some to her husband, who was with her, and he ate it" (Genesis 3:6). The forbidden fruit was inviting.

Adam and Eve soon found out that they had been deceived. Many continue to find out, sometimes too late. Inside of folly's house are not the promised pleasures but the bones of dead men. "The depths of the grave" can also be translated "the depths of hell" (Hebrew *sheol*). That's where folly ends up.

Only by God's grace can we hope to escape the ensnarements of folly and enter the house that wisdom built.

PART THREE

First Collection of Solomon's Proverbs
(10:1–22:16)

10 The proverbs of Solomon:

The text itself indicates that here we have a division in Proverbs. Having finished his exhortations to embrace wisdom (chapters 1–9), Solomon now presents some of that wisdom we are to embrace.

This is the largest single section of the book, forming its core and consisting of 375 proverbs. All the verses in this collection consist of short two-line proverbs. Usually when we think of a proverb, this type comes to mind.

Most of these proverbs are antithetic in form. That is, the second part of the verse expresses a thought that contrasts with the first. In general, the first part of the verse presents the advantage of the good life; the contrasting thought, introduced by *but,* shows the harm brought about by evil.

There seems to be no comprehensive plan to the section. Each proverb stands by itself, without a connection with the preceding or following proverb. As one commentator notes, "each is in itself a small perfected and finished whole."[8]

A wise son

A wise son brings joy to his father,
but a foolish son grief to his mother.

Unlike the books of Job and Ecclesiastes, these proverbs do not deal extensively with the question of why righteous people often suffer while the wicked prosper. Rather, they

Proverbs 10:2,3

show the earthly advantages of a godly life. Yet here we see that already in this life evil has consequences that can tragically affect even those not directly involved in the wrong.

Certainly this proverb will spur parents to make the most of their parenting responsibilities. The time and effort expended in training children according to God's Word will bring joy as the child grows into a God-fearing adult. Conversely, children who are neglected or not nourished on the Bible can bring much grief later in life.

The triumph of righteousness

> ² **Ill-gotten treasures are of no value,**
> **but righteousness delivers from death.**
>
> ³ **The Lord does not let the righteous go hungry**
> **but he thwarts the craving of the wicked.**

Ill-gotten treasures may bring temporary happiness, but they cannot bring lasting satisfaction (see 21:6). Many a person who has devoted his life to money has discovered this. Like becoming involved with an adulteress (2:18), the unprincipled pursuit of wealth can lead to an untimely death. On the other hand, a clear conscience lets one sleep at night and "delivers from death."

Even when the wicked get ahead in the world, they still don't really satisfy their cravings. Why not? Because they are looking for fulfillment in the wrong places. The person who craves wealth will never have enough. Likewise, the person who lives for satisfying the desires of the flesh will never find lasting satisfaction.

The Bible teaches us to place our confidence in the Lord, seek his kingdom first, and be satisfied with his blessings. He will never let us down.

Proverbs 10:4,5

Work habits

⁴ **Lazy hands make a man poor,
but diligent hands bring wealth.**

⁵ **He who gathers crops in summer is a wise son,
but he who sleeps during harvest is a disgraceful son.**

Entrusting our lives to God does not mean we sit back and do nothing. The Lord gives us various abilities, and we are to use those abilities. Christians who are lazy are inviting correction, as Saint Paul wrote to the Thessalonians: "We gave you this rule: 'If a man will not work, he shall not eat.' We hear that some among you are idle. They are not busy; they are busybodies. Such people we command and urge in the Lord Jesus Christ to settle down and earn the bread they eat. And as for you, brothers, never tire of doing what is right" (2 Thessalonians 3:10-13).

Martin Luther spoke of work as being the "mask" behind which God gives us his blessings:

> When riches come, the godless heart of man thinks: I have achieved this with my labors. It does not consider that these are purely blessings of God, blessings that at times come to us through our labors and at times without our labors, but never because of our labors; for God always gives them because of his undeserved mercy. For, as we have said above, he uses our labor as a sort of mask, under the cover of which he blesses us and grants what is his, so that there is room for faith and we do not imagine that by our own efforts and labors we have achieved what is ours.[9]

Verse 5 reminds us of the old English proverb to make hay while the sun shines. Solomon put it this way in the book of Ecclesiastes: "Whatever your hand finds to do, do it with all

Proverbs 10:6,7

your might, for in the grave, where you are going, there is neither working nor planning nor knowledge nor wisdom" (9:10). He isn't saying there is no life after death, but as far as doing anything in this world, *now* is the time. We can't come back and do what we didn't get done during our lives on earth.

Blessings of righteousness

**⁶ Blessings crown the head of the righteous,
but violence overwhelms the mouth of the wicked.**

**⁷ The memory of the righteous will be a blessing,
but the name of the wicked will rot.**

The first line of verse 6 is reminiscent of Jacob's words of blessings to the sons of Joseph: "Let all these [blessings] rest on the head of Joseph, on the brow of the prince among his brothers" (Genesis 49:26). To picture God's blessings as a sort of crown is a wonderful way to think of them. They bring honor and a dignified bearing to the godly.

The wicked, on the other hand, bring about their ultimate destruction. The trouble they have caused with their deceitful or evil talk will come back to them. David expressed a similar thought in one of the psalms: "Let the heads of those who surround me be covered with the trouble their lips have caused" (140:9).

Blessings come to the head of the righteous, and troubles come back upon the head of the wicked. Likewise, the righteous will eventually be honored, while the wicked will be disgraced. Certain people, such as Judas, have acquired such a rotten reputation that no parents name their children after them.

Even if no one else remembers the godly, the Lord does. He remembers them, as well as those who have afflicted his people. "For he who avenges blood remembers; he does not ignore the cry of the afflicted" (Psalm 9:12).

Proverbs 10:8-14

Pros and cons concerning the mouth

⁸ **The wise in heart accept commands,
but a chattering fool comes to ruin.**

⁹ **The man of integrity walks securely,
but he who takes crooked paths will be found out.**

¹⁰ **He who winks maliciously causes grief,
and a chattering fool comes to ruin.**

¹¹ **The mouth of the righteous is a fountain of life,
but violence overwhelms the mouth of the wicked.**

¹² **Hatred stirs up dissension,
but love covers over all wrongs.**

¹³ **Wisdom is found on the lips of the discerning,
but a rod is for the back of him who lacks judgment.**

¹⁴ **Wise men store up knowledge,
but the mouth of a fool invites ruin.**

Some people are so busy talking that they never have time to listen. The wise, on the other hand, are more thoughtful. They are ready to listen, and they do what God commands.

The Bible often portrays life as a journey. The "man of integrity" in verse 9 is the upright person, who walks by faith and tries to live by God's Word. What a wonderful assurance that, as we walk through life, the almighty God will keep us secure in his protection. "We know that in all things God works for the good of those who love him, who have been called according to his purpose" (Romans 8:28). The wicked, of course, have no such assurance. Sooner or later they "will be found out." Saint Paul put it this way: "The sins of some men are obvious, reaching the place of judgment ahead of them; the sins of others trail behind them. In the same way, good deeds are obvious, and even those that are not cannot be hidden" (1 Timothy 5:24,25).

To wink maliciously (verse 10) is to wink in a derisive way, with evil intent. It's the kind of facial expression that puts

89

Proverbs 10:8-14

people down and hurts feelings. The chattering fool speaks without considering what he or she is saying. This behavior also often hurts others. In the end, it too comes to ruin.

By contrast, the righteous weigh their words and use their mouths to build others up, sometimes by encouraging and other times by means of constructive criticism. Such good talk is a fountain, with its source deep within a person. The ancient Roman philosopher Seneca (first century A.D.) recognized the connection between what we say and what is inside of us: "Speech is the index of the mind." More important, Jesus says: "The good man brings good things out of the good stored up in his heart, and the evil man brings evil things out of the evil stored up in his heart. For out of the overflow of his heart his mouth speaks" (Luke 6:45). That's one reason it's so vital that the Holy Spirit dwell in our hearts! What's in our hearts affects the way we talk and everything else we do.

Notice that verse 11b is exactly the same as verse 6b. In each case Solomon contrasts this truth about the wicked with a different truth about the righteous. In the end, it is the difference between life and death.

Verse 12a is self-evident. The contrasting thought that follows it is quoted twice in the New Testament (James 5:20; 1 Peter 4:8). But just what is meant by love *covering* wrong? This covering is not of a deceitful nature, as when we might lie to cover up some wrong we've done. Rather, it is the willingness to overlook and forgive the sins of others.

In verse 13 we find the first of several passages that speak of physical punishment. (See 14:3; 19:29; 26:3 for some other examples.) At times, the Old Testament also called for capital punishment—death by stoning—for certain serious crimes. Yet it never told God's people to engage in the mutilation practiced by Israel's neighbors—such as

Proverbs 10:15-17

plucking out eyes, cutting off thumbs and toes, or displaying dead bodies. While Christian parents might spank their children, they will never abuse them. Sadly, the Bible's healthy teachings on discipline are often lost today, when many people oppose any form of corporal punishment and equate it with child abuse.

Verse 14 returns to a similar thought as we found in verse 8. While the wise are busy taking in wisdom and storing it up as the priceless treasure it is, the foolish are busy talking their way to disaster. In both verses the same Hebrew term is used for the foolish; it depicts someone who is stubborn in his foolishness and becoming persistent and more hardened.

It's interesting how often the Hebrew writers of the Old Testament use very concrete, physical illustrations to relate ethical and spiritual truths. The righteous and the wicked *walk* a *path;* the *mouth* is a *fountain;* love *covers* wrongs; the wicked get the *rod* on their *backs;* wisdom is *stored up.* The kind of vivid language we see in this small portion of Proverbs is typical. It helps the proverbs come alive.

Resources for living

> ¹⁵ **The wealth of the rich is their fortified city,**
> **but poverty is the ruin of the poor.**
>
> ¹⁶ **The wages of the righteous bring them life,**
> **but the income of the wicked brings them punishment.**
>
> ¹⁷ **He who heeds discipline shows the way to life,**
> **but whoever ignores correction leads others astray.**

Worldly wealth can bring a degree of security. Along with riches come power, influence, and connections. In this way wealth is like a "fortified city," protecting those within its walls.

Poverty can be ruinous. The poor don't have ready access to the best education or medical help; they sometimes want

Proverbs 10:18-21

for basic food and shelter; and their pleas for help can easily be overlooked.

In verse 16, however, Solomon moves beyond those social observations. Spiritually, the rich are those who trust in the Lord—no matter how materially rich or poor they might be. They inherit eternal life, something all the money in the world can't buy. The wicked end up bankrupt— whether they are materially wealthy or impoverished. They end up forever separated from the source of all good gifts, God himself. These truths are expressed in Romans 6:23: "The wages of sin is death, but the gift of God is eternal life in Christ Jesus our Lord."

As noted in our Introduction to Proverbs, the key word in Proverbs is *wisdom* (Hebrew *hokmah*). It occurs 42 times in the book and is the central theme of Proverbs. There is, however, a related term that occurs some 30 times; that is the word *discipline* (Hebrew *musar*). It is similar to our idea of athletes in training and has to do with instruction as given by a coach or leader. Discipline can come as positive reinforcement or negative warning. It involves the practice of self-discipline.

According to verse 17, the person who follows the way of discipline is on the way to life (and can help others too). Again, the most important application is spiritual. As we follow Christ, we are on the right way. After all, he is "the way and the truth and the life" (John 14:6). The ungodly are headed in the opposite direction and leading others down that path.

Verbal expression

**18 He who conceals his hatred has lying lips,
and whoever spreads slander is a fool.**

**19 When words are many, sin is not absent,
but he who holds his tongue is wise.**

Proverbs 10:18-21

²⁰ **The tongue of the righteous is choice silver,**
   but the heart of the wicked is of little value.

²¹ **The lips of the righteous nourish many,**
   but fools die for lack of judgment.

The proverbs in this short section of four verses deal with verbal expression. We might well ask ourselves: How am I using my mouth? What kind of person do my words make me?

Do we conceal hatred; that is, pretend friendliness when it's not really there? Psychologists tell us that it is better to express anger, get it out, and deal with it in a constructive way. This can be difficult in a society that avoids confrontation. But in the long run it's healthier for everyone involved. We also need to confess our sins of hatred before God, so there can be forgiveness and renewal.

Do we use our lips to spread slander? Gossip is easy to fall into. But we need to ask if what we say about others is for their good or merely to build ourselves up by putting other people down.

James chapter 3 warns against the unbridled tongue, from which flow many words and in which sin is not absent:

> When we put bits into the mouths of horses to make them obey us, we can turn the whole animal. Or take ships as an example. Although they are so large and are driven by strong winds, they are steered by a very small rudder wherever the pilot wants to go. Likewise the tongue is a small part of the body, but it makes great boasts. Consider what a great forest is set on fire by a small spark. The tongue also is a fire, a world of evil among the parts of the body. It corrupts the whole person, sets the whole course of his life on fire, and is itself set on fire by hell. (verses 3-6)

93

Proverbs 10:22,23

In contrast to the unbridled tongue is that of the righteous. It's a treasure, like "choice silver." Notice how Solomon again connects the tongue with the heart. What flows off the tongue—whether good or ill—is only a reflection of what resides in the heart.

May our lips offer nourishing words—words that are food for thought and that bring to others Jesus, who is the Bread of Life (John 6:35). Without him, there can only be spiritual starvation and death.

Blessings and riches versus human efforts and plans

²² **The blessing of the LORD brings wealth,**
   and he adds no trouble to it.

²³ **A fool finds pleasure in evil conduct,**
   but a man of understanding delights in wisdom.

Every spiritual treasure comes as a free gift from God's grace: forgiveness, peace with God, eternal life. As for earthly riches, they too come from our gracious God. "The earth is the LORD's, and everything in it" (Psalm 24:1). Since it all belongs to him, he freely dispenses it as he sees fit.

The second line of verse 22 could be translated, "and hard work adds nothing to it." That is, God's blessings, not our efforts, are the real source of whatever we have. If we follow the NIV translation, we can understand it in the sense that God's gift of wealth is quite different from the "ill-gotten treasures" (10:2) of the wicked. They bring with them all kinds of trouble, including the judgment of God.

Verse 23 sets the godly lifestyle in stark contrast to that of the ungodly. It's either one or the other. Either a person's heart is set on God and his wisdom or on the pursuit of the riches of this world. "Evil conduct" can be openly, crassly evil. Or it can be more subtle, as in the secret idolatry of worldly wealth. No matter how successful in worldly terms

Proverbs 10:24-32

an ungodly person might be, in God's sight he is still "a fool."

The righteous and the wicked

²⁴ **What the wicked dreads will overtake him;**
what the righteous desire will be granted.

²⁵ **When the storm has swept by, the wicked are gone,**
but the righteous stand firm forever.

²⁶ **As vinegar to the teeth and smoke to the eyes,**
so is a sluggard to those who send him.

²⁷ **The fear of the LORD adds length to life,**
but the years of the wicked are cut short.

²⁸ **The prospect of the righteous is joy,**
but the hopes of the wicked come to nothing.

²⁹ **The way of the LORD is a refuge for the righteous,**
but it is the ruin of those who do evil.

³⁰ **The righteous will never be uprooted,**
but the wicked will not remain in the land.

³¹ **The mouth of the righteous brings forth wisdom,**
but a perverse tongue will be cut out.

³² **The lips of the righteous know what is fitting,**
but the mouth of the wicked only what is perverse.

The wicked person gets exactly what he fears—namely, calamity, disaster, and distress (1:27). There is something ironic in verse 24. Many people live their lives without God, vainly hoping somehow to find security and peace of mind. Yet they must constantly be looking back over their shoulders, for their consciences will give them no peace. In the end, they get not what they desperately seek but what they most fear—the judgment of the Almighty.

But the righteous get just what they desire. And what is that? Jesus explained it this way in his Sermon on the Mount: "Blessed are those who hunger and thirst for righteousness,

Proverbs 10:24-32

for they will be filled" (Matthew 5:6). This righteousness, moreover, is a free gift from God.

So, while the wicked strive with all their might, they end up empty-handed. But the righteous simply take, by faith, God's good gifts. Along with that, God also supplies our earthly needs. As Jesus continued his sermon, "Seek first [God's] kingdom and his righteousness, and all these things will be given to you as well" (Matthew 6:33).

Continuing his comparison of the righteous and the wicked, Solomon contrasts the one's stability with the other's being swept away (verse 25). The Bible uses different pictures to show this contrast. Psalm 1, for example, speaks of the godly as a firmly planted tree and the ungodly as "chaff that the wind blows away." In the Sermon on the Mount, Jesus said the godly person "is like a wise man who built his house on the rock," while the ungodly person "is like a foolish man who built his house on sand" (Matthew 7:24-27).

Vinegar irritates the teeth as smoke does the eyes. Similarly a lazy person irritates those who send him on an errand. The errand doesn't get done or it's late or something goes wrong.

Long life lies ahead for those who fear the Lord (verse 27). While that life may be short here on earth, it lasts forever in heaven. Eternal joy also lies ahead (verse 28). Solomon's father, David, spoke of that joy: "You [LORD] have made known to me the path of life; you will fill me with joy in your presence, with eternal pleasures at your right hand" (Psalm 16:11). The wicked have nothing to look forward to after this brief life on earth. Their future is bleak, hopeless.

Incidentally, verse 27 is one of over a dozen "fear of the LORD" passages. Spread as they are throughout the book, from the first to the last chapter, these passages show the

Proverbs 10:24-32

importance of this concept. "The fear of the LORD is the beginning of knowledge" (see 1:7 and the comments there). It is also the middle and the end of true, godly knowledge and wisdom.

Verses 29 and 30 take up the happy, sure state of God's people, as opposed to the ruin awaiting unbelievers. We speak of having "roots." We feel a strong emotional attachment to our roots—the place where we grew up, the land our parents or grandparents came from, and so on. To be torn away from those roots brings terrible suffering. Because of their apostasy after the days of Solomon, God's Old Testament people were uprooted and taken into captivity in Babylon for 70 years. One of the psalms recounts that sadness: "By the rivers of Babylon we sat and wept when we remembered Zion" (137:1). In a sense, then, verse 30 was prophetic.

But it also speaks to people of all times. The believer's real roots are with the Lord. We are merely pilgrims traveling through this world on our way to heaven. Nothing can ever tear us away from our true home. The unbeliever, however, has set his heart on this world and the things of this world. He will be uprooted and torn away from all he loves.

In verses 31 and 32, Solomon returns once more to the subject of the tongue. Today many people think that what we say is not all that important. Vows are taken lightly; filthy talk and cursing are common; gossip is rampant. But God's Word declares that what we say does matter. Hence the Bible has many exhortations to speak in a God-pleasing manner and to avoid wrongful speech. When the proverb says that "a perverse tongue will be cut out," it is not referring to some Old Testament practice of cutting out people's tongues. It is more in the pattern of David's words in Psalm 12:3: "May the LORD cut off all flattering lips and every boastful

Proverbs 11:1-3

tongue." God is the one who finally puts an end to all ungodly speech.

Integrity

11 **The Lord abhors dishonest scales,**
   but accurate weights are his delight.
   ² When pride comes, then comes disgrace,
   but with humility comes wisdom.
   ³ The integrity of the upright guides them,
   but the unfaithful are destroyed by their duplicity.

"Use honest scales and honest weights," God had commanded in the Mosaic Law (Leviticus 19:35,36; also Deuteronomy 25:15). Obviously, not all Israelites paid attention to those laws. Hence, five centuries after Moses' time, Solomon had to remind the Jews of God's will. Later in Proverbs, Solomon returns to the topic (16:11; 20:10,23). Some two centuries after Solomon, the prophet Amos warned against "skimping the measure, boosting the price and cheating with dishonest scales" (8:5). And the prophet Micah took up the same refrain (6:11).

There is nothing new under the sun. The Lord still abhors dishonest scales but delights in honesty. While some might appear to get away with dishonesty, God sees everything. There will come a day of reckoning.

Just as false scales are wrong, so is a false, inflated sense of oneself. Whatever talents we have and whatever success we meet with—it's all a gift from God. An old rabbinic dictum says, "As water leaves a high level and goes to a lower level, so Torah [the Law] abandons him whose mind is haughty and cleaves to him whose mind is humble."

True humility recognizes our total dependence on God. He is our Creator; without him we would not exist. He is our Redeemer; without him we are lost and condemned. He

Proverbs 11:4-9

is our Sanctifier; without him we can do nothing good and have no hope of salvation. That's humility . . . and wisdom.

With this kind of honesty toward God, self, and other people, the upright can keep their bearings. Meanwhile, lacking guidance, the unfaithful resort to dishonesty, false pride, and duplicity—all of which lead to their destruction.

The value of righteousness

⁴ **Wealth is worthless in the day of wrath,**
but righteousness delivers from death.

⁵ **The righteousness of the blameless makes a straight way**
for them,
but the wicked are brought down by their
own wickedness.

⁶ **The righteousness of the upright delivers them,**
but the unfaithful are trapped by evil desires.

⁷ **When a wicked man dies, his hope perishes;**
all he expected from his power comes to nothing.

⁸ **The righteous man is rescued from trouble,**
and it comes on the wicked instead.

⁹ **With his mouth the godless destroys his neighbor,**
but through knowledge the righteous escape.

Wealth is a blessing from God, unless, of course, it is ill-gotten wealth. Yet earthly riches have severe limitations. All the wealth of the world is of no value in the hour of death and judgment. But righteousness is a priceless commodity. It delivers one.

Unfortunately, because of sin no one is righteous before the holy God. Solomon says in Ecclesiastes, probably written toward the end of his life: "There is not a righteous man on earth who does what is right and never sins" (7:20). What, then, does Solomon mean when he speaks of the righteousness that holds up in the day of wrath and that delivers from

Proverbs 11:4-9

death? He can be referring only to a righteousness that comes from God himself. Abraham, the father of the Jewish nation and also known as the father of believers, had that righteousness. "[He] believed the LORD, and he credited it to him as righteousness" (Genesis 15:6).

Living in the New Testament age, we see in Jesus Christ the full righteousness of God. His perfect life and sacrificial death become our righteousness as we are brought to faith in him (Romans 1:16,17). It is his righteousness that makes us righteous, that delivers from God's wrathful judgment and from eternal death in hell.

Although these doctrines are not full-blown in the Old Testament, we must not think that Solomon and other believers before Christ had a different kind of righteousness or were saved in some other way. Faith in the coming Savior was their righteousness, just as faith in the Savior who has come is ours.

The Bible also speaks of another kind of righteousness. This is the good that enables people to get along in this world; sometimes it's referred to as civic righteousness. While it's not sufficient to stand up in the day of God's wrath, judgment day, it does lead to harmony in society and personal relationships. Much of Proverbs speaks of these earthbound, temporal situations.

In verses 4 to 9, however, it seems Solomon is grappling with the eternal issues—the day of wrath, death, the way (through life), perishing, hope, destruction, rescue, escape.

In the end, the wicked have no hope. Notice especially verse 7: "When a wicked man dies, his hope perishes; all he expected from his power comes to nothing." What a gloomy future awaits those who live and die without God! Like a puff of smoke, everything they put their trust in comes to nothing in the hour of their deaths.

Proverbs 11:10,11

The righteous—that is, those righteous in Christ—know that their future is bright, no matter how miserable life on earth can be at times. Passages such as Psalm 73:27,28 show that ultimately the only safe place to be is near to God: "Those who are far from you will perish; you destroy all who are unfaithful to you. But as for me, it is good to be near God."

Verse 9 discusses the evil that the wicked can do with their mouths. They can destroy others emotionally and spiritually by deceit, enticement, lying, slander, and other evil uses of the tongue. But the righteous know God's Word, follow that Word, and escape.

Righteousness and a city's people

**10 When the righteous prosper, the city rejoices;
when the wicked perish, there are shouts of joy.**

**11 Through the blessing of the upright a city is exalted,
but by the mouth of the wicked it is destroyed.**

A city contains both righteous and unrighteous people. All of them rejoice when the righteous prosper. At first this might seem strange. But when we think about it, it makes sense. Even the ungodly would rather have good people in positions of influence, because even the wicked can't trust their own kind of people in power.

Similarly, even the wicked are happy to see their own kind perish. In mob wars, for example, the gangsters fight against one another.

It is the Christian's prayer that God will bless our cities and countries with good, upright leaders. One prayer that was frequently used in church services says: "Endue them [those in authority] with grace to rule after Thy good pleasure, to the maintenance of righteousness and to the hindrance and punishment of wickedness, that we may lead a quiet and peaceable life in all godliness and honesty."

Proverbs 11:12-19

On the other hand, it is a terrible tragedy when deceitful, dishonest people hold power. Cities and lands are left in ruin by their lying leadership. How necessary it is for us to pray that God will preserve us from such government and bless us with the upright.

Besides praying, we can also live as God's children. God calls us to be his righteous, upright people. Through us too, when we live by faith in Christ, God will bless our cities, states, and countries.

The right way to act

> ¹² A man who lacks judgment derides his neighbor,
> but a man of understanding holds his tongue.

> ¹³ A gossip betrays a confidence,
> but a trustworthy man keeps a secret.

> ¹⁴ For lack of guidance a nation falls,
> but many advisers make victory sure.

> ¹⁵ He who puts up security for another will surely suffer,
> but whoever refuses to strike hands in pledge is safe.

> ¹⁶ A kindhearted woman gains respect,
> but ruthless men gain only wealth.

> ¹⁷ A kind man benefits himself,
> but a cruel man brings trouble on himself.

> ¹⁸ The wicked man earns deceptive wages,
> but he who sows righteousness reaps a sure reward.

> ¹⁹ The truly righteous man attains life,
> but he who pursues evil goes to his death.

"If you can't say anything nice, don't say anything at all" is a modern paraphrase of verses 12 and 13. Sometimes we need to bite our lips when tempted to destroy someone's reputation. And when we've been told something in confidence, it should remain that way.

Proverbs 11:12-19

Old Testament law forbade slander: "Do not go about spreading slander among your people" (Leviticus 19:16). In the New Testament, it is placed along with other sins we are to rid ourselves of: "Rid yourselves of all malice and all deceit, hypocrisy, envy, and slander of every kind" (1 Peter 2:1).

Holding one's tongue when proper and keeping a secret do not rule out giving good advice when called for. At the governmental and military levels, guidance and advice are musts (verse 14). We could apply that to many other levels as well. In our homes, churches, and at work, we should seek out the advice of good people. It's the wise thing to do.

Verse 15 cautions against taking on financial responsibility for another (literally, for a "stranger"). The practice of striking hands was equivalent to our handshake, a demonstration that a deal was sealed.

Verse 16 contrasts a gentle, kindhearted woman with ruthless men. While these men's ruthless business techniques might gain them some financial success, the kindhearted woman is the one who gains people's respect. This truth from God's Word should give men pause who think they have to act tough, "macho," in order to win respect. True toughness, as verse 17 shows, can lie in being kind, in being willing to show love to those in need and those close to us. The kind (Hebrew "merciful") man will benefit himself by winning the love and respect of his family and other people. "Blessed are the merciful," says Jesus, "for they will be shown mercy" (Matthew 5:7). In our day of abusive fathers, boyfriends, and husbands, these verses are especially timely.

The wicked man's earnings are deceptive, both because they were earned dishonestly and because they bring him only a false security. As for reaping a reward from sowing righteousness, Saint Paul has this to say: "Do not be deceived:

Proverbs 11:20-23

God cannot be mocked. A man reaps what he sows. The one who sows to please his sinful nature, from that nature will reap destruction; the one who sows to please the Spirit, from the Spirit will reap eternal life. Let us not become weary in doing good, for at the proper time we will reap a harvest if we do not give up" (Galatians 6:7-9). Those who live by faith will receive the benefits of their faith.

Verse 19 contrasts the end of the righteous with that of the evil—life versus death. This judgment often comes to fruition here on earth and always in the world to come.

The inner nature

²⁰ **The Lord detests men of perverse heart**
but he delights in those whose ways are blameless.

²¹ **Be sure of this: The wicked will not go unpunished,**
but those who are righteous will go free.

²² **Like a gold ring in a pig's snout**
is a beautiful woman who shows no discretion.

²³ **The desire of the righteous ends only in good,**
but the hope of the wicked only in wrath.

Anyone who thinks that God is indifferent to sin and to sinners should read verse 20. The word that the NIV translates "detests" is in the KJV "abomination." The New Evangelical Translation has "disgusting."

What should terrify the ungodly all the more is that the all-knowing God looks into everyone's heart. No one can fool God. And no one can be blameless before him, except through the Savior Jesus Christ.

Although in this world the wicked often appear to prosper, we can be sure that God's justice will have its day. While the righteous often suffer, it is equally sure that their day will also come. The righteous (literally, "the seed of the

Proverbs 11:20-23

righteous") and their children who follow them will enjoy complete and eternal deliverance from the sorrows of this life.

At first verse 22 might seem unrelated to the previous verse. Yet both have a common theme, namely, the frequent contradiction between outward appearance and inner reality. In Old Testament times, women often wore nose rings. For example, we read that the beautiful Rebekah was given such a gold ring (Genesis 24:22,47). Solomon compares a beautiful woman without good judgment to a pig, an unclean animal, with a gold ring in its snout. The most valuable beauty is not outward but comes from within. Saint Peter reminds Christian wives:

> Your beauty should not come from outward adornment, such as braided hair and the wearing of gold jewelry and fine clothes. Instead, it should be that of your inner self, the unfading beauty of a gentle and quiet spirit, which is of great worth in God's sight. For this is the way the holy women of the past who put their hope in God used to make themselves beautiful. They were submissive to their own husbands. (1 Peter 3:3-5)

This is not to say that it's wrong for women to wear jewelry. But the greatest beauty is an inner quality.

Verse 23 reminds us that our inner hopes and dreams will eventually come to fruition. The wicked place their hopes in everything but in God. For them, disappointment—the wrath of God—lies ahead. Jesus tells us:

> Do not store up for yourselves treasures on earth, where moth and rust destroy, and where thieves break in and steal. But store up for yourselves treasures in heaven, where moth and rust do not destroy, and where thieves do not break in and

Proverbs 11:24-26

> steal. For where your treasure is, there your
> heart will be also. (Matthew 6:19-21)

When our hearts desire God and the things of God, there is nothing but good ahead!

Generosity compared with selfishness

> ²⁴ **One man gives freely, yet gains even more;**
> **another withholds unduly, but comes to poverty.**
>
> ²⁵ **A generous man will prosper;**
> **he who refreshes others will himself be refreshed.**
>
> ²⁶ **People curse the man who hoards grain,**
> **but blessing crowns him who is willing to sell.**

We often get the idea that the way to become wealthier is to hoard what we have. That may be the way of logic and common sense. The Bible presents another way: We become richer by being generous. Others appreciate our generosity, and we in turn are blessed. Those blessings may or may not be returned in kind, but they will be there. For instance, we may be blessed with love and many friendships. Not all riches are financial.

Speaking of giving generously to the needy—in particular, needy believers—the apostle Paul says: "Whoever sows sparingly will also reap sparingly, and whoever sows generously will also reap generously. . . . For God loves a cheerful giver" (2 Corinthians 9:6,7).

Verse 26 seems to have special application to times of scarcity. Some might be tempted to hoard their grain to drive the price up. This was not the case with a devout man like Joseph. During the famine in his day, Joseph opened Egypt's storehouses and sold the grain (Genesis 41:53-57). Nor should it happen that any Christian hoards and keeps from others what they need.

Proverbs 11:27-31

It certainly is not God's way of dealing with us. He freely gives us all we have, including his Son, who gave his life for our salvation. Knowing God's love and continuing generosity, can we ourselves be anything other than generous?

Inheriting rewards

²⁷ **He who seeks good finds goodwill,**
    but evil comes to him who searches for it.

²⁸ **Whoever trusts in his riches will fall,**
    but the righteous will thrive like a green leaf.

²⁹ **He who brings trouble on his family will inherit**
        only wind,
    and the fool will be servant to the wise.

³⁰ **The fruit of the righteous is a tree of life,**
    and he who wins souls is wise.

³¹ **If the righteous receive their due on earth,**
    how much more the ungodly and the sinner!

Instead of spending our lives in the pursuit of money, we are wise to spend our time seeking good. When we seek good—that is, the good of others—we'll find it for ourselves. The goodwill of others will come back to us. Those who seek evil—that is, evil for others—will find it for themselves. Their own evil will recoil back on them.

Jesus says that the treasures of this world can be destroyed by moths and rust and stolen by thieves (Matthew 6:19). Such riches, like leaves in autumn, dry up and wither. To trust in earthly riches, then, is self-destructive. But to trust in God is to prosper, to be constantly renewed, to "thrive like a green leaf."

How terrible to neglect one's own family (verse 29). That person will get nothing back. This is a warning to all parents. Never pursue money, power, or pleasure at the expense of the very families God has entrusted to you. We hear of many a present-day father, the head of the family, who has brought

Proverbs 12:1-4

sorrow and trouble to his family by selfishly following his own lusts. In the end, his family turns against him, and he is left with nothing but regret and sorrow. That's inheriting the wind!

He ends up with the wind—that is, with nothing of substance. So he must turn to the wise for advice, help, and, quite often, for work. In this way, he becomes "servant to the wise."

Again returning to the picture of a thriving plant, Solomon speaks of "a tree of life" (verse 30). The last chapter of the Bible speaks of the tree of life in paradise (Revelation 22:2,14,19). This is the final inheritance of the righteous. Until then, God's people will wisely do what they can to win other souls to God and to salvation (see 1 Corinthians 9:19-23).

Already in this life, both the righteous and the ungodly receive rewards. The righteous receive the rewards of grace—God's blessings of faith, hope, and love. The ungodly must live with burdened consciences and dread of future judgment.

Character determines direction

12 Whoever loves discipline loves knowledge,
but he who hates correction is stupid.

² **A good man obtains favor from the LORD,**
but the LORD condemns a crafty man.

³ **A man cannot be established through wickedness,**
but the righteous cannot be uprooted.

⁴ **A wife of noble character is her husband's crown,**
but a disgraceful wife is like decay in his bones.

It's been said that one's love of knowledge is no greater than one's love of correction. Although correction goes against the grain of our sinful pride, it is necessary if we are to grow in wisdom. To hate correction is "stupid," a word that actually means animallike, like a dumb beast.

Proverbs 12:1-4

Solomon has already talked about the wise man having God's favor (3:4; 8:35). When the angel announced to Mary that she would be the mother of Jesus, the angel said, "You have found favor with God" (Luke 1:30). Whatever favor we enjoy comes as a gift from our gracious God. On the other hand, the Lord condemns the crafty. Those who would scheme and seek wisdom apart from God are not going to get the genuine product. They may have a worldly form of wisdom but not the real thing. God says, "I will destroy the wisdom of the wise; the intelligence of the intelligent I will frustrate" (1 Corinthians 1:19).

Human theories and systems of philosophy are constantly being overturned and replaced with newer ones. That is a judgment of God upon those who seek to be wise without him. It is also part of the truth expressed in verse 3, that aside from God's blessings no one has a firm foundation. In the 20th century, the Nazis and Communists tried to build systems of government on evil foundations, involving atheism and the methodical destruction of masses of people. Those systems could not stand. What holds true for governments applies also to individuals.

The righteous, however, cannot be uprooted. They are "like a tree planted by streams of water" (Psalm 1:3). Their roots go deep into God's Word. They will live forever.

Moving from great general truths of life to a particular application, Solomon speaks of how a wife's character can affect her husband. The man with a noble wife is truly blessed. She is his crown, his honor. The closing verses of Proverbs are devoted to the rare and treasured wife of noble character (31:10-31). In contrast, a disgraceful wife is like bone cancer. Whether as an unfaithful wife (see chapter 7) or a nag (19:13), eventually she'll be the ruin of her husband.

Proverbs 12:5-7

Righteous and wicked profiles

⁵ **The plans of the righteous are just,**
  but the advice of the wicked is deceitful.

⁶ **The words of the wicked lie in wait for blood,**
  but the speech of the upright rescues them.

⁷ **Wicked men are overthrown and are no more,**
  but the house of the righteous stands firm.

Honesty, justice, and forthrightness are characteristics of God's people. Their plans are aboveboard. Not so with the wicked. Self-serving, ulterior motives characterize them. Their advice is not to be trusted, because they are probably manipulating you for some gain for themselves.

Wicked people use words as traps. With words they try to put down, embarrass, discredit, and, if necessary, do away with the upright. In the four gospels, we see many examples of how Jesus' enemies tried to trap him with words. One example comes from Matthew 22:15-22, where we read, "Then the Pharisees went out and laid plans to trap him in his words." They asked him whether or not it was right to pay taxes. The real purpose behind their question was to get Jesus to say something wrong. He saw through their scheming and said, "You hypocrites, why are you trying to trap me?"

Frustrated by their inability to catch him with words, "they left him and went away." Once again, Jesus' speech had rescued him from their attempts to entrap him. Eventually, they put all pretense of sincerity aside, brought in false witnesses to lie about Jesus, and had him crucified.

That's the pattern that often holds between the wicked and the righteous. As we align our speech with God's truth, we are rescued from the verbal traps of the wicked.

Although in this life the wicked might still seem to overcome the righteous, even as they crucified our Lord, eventu-

The house of the righteous stands firm

Proverbs 12:8-14

ally they are overthrown (verse 7). They "are no more" alludes to their descendants being cut off with them. Among the Jews, one's house included the entire family. For one's house to stand forever, then, meant that the family would live on generation after generation.

Obvious outcomes

[8] A man is praised according to his wisdom,
but men with warped minds are despised.

[9] Better to be a nobody and yet have a servant
than pretend to be somebody and have no food.

[10] A righteous man cares for the needs of his animal,
but the kindest acts of the wicked are cruel.

[11] He who works his land will have abundant food,
but he who chases fantasies lacks judgment.

[12] The wicked desire the plunder of evil men,
but the root of the righteous flourishes.

[13] An evil man is trapped by his sinful talk,
but a righteous man escapes trouble.

[14] From the fruit of his lips a man is filled with good things
as surely as the work of his hands rewards him.

The unbelieving world always seems to have a mixed attitude toward godly people. On the one hand, it doesn't like them; yet, on the other hand, it must acknowledge their valuable contributions. Those with warped minds, who bring destruction and dissension, are despised by everyone.

Some people are so enthralled with being "somebody" that they'll put on a false front of wealth simply for the sake of appearances (verse 9). Others don't put on any pretense. They appear to be "nobody," and yet have a servant to help them with their work. In our culture, with its stress on material possessions, many men and women will go heavily into

Proverbs 12:8-14

debt merely to maintain the image of being wealthy. This is not good.

The Mosaic Law called for kindness to animals: "Do not muzzle an ox while it is treading out the grain" (Deuteronomy 25:4). This injunction allowed for an ox to eat some grain while it was working. A godly man takes better care of his animals than an evil man does of his family. Child abuse and wife abuse bear evidence of that.

Stick to the task at hand, verse 11 is telling us. Working your land will make you sweat, but reaping the harvest will make it worthwhile. This is unlike the get-rich-quick approach. Winning the lottery or hooking up on some super business deal appeals to the fantasies of some.

In pursuit of easy money, the wicked will plunder their own kind. The mob wars of our times bear witness to this. Meanwhile, the righteous go about their honest work and, under God's hand, flourish.

We've seen how the wicked try to use words to trap others (verse 6). Often they get caught in their own trap, like the religious leaders who tried to trick Jesus. Perhaps we've experienced some of that self-entrapment ourselves. It may have come as we told a little white lie to cover ourselves, and then someone exposed the lie and embarrassed us. "But a righteous man escapes trouble." There's a saying that honest people don't need to have good memories.

Our words do matter. Jesus says: "I tell you that men will have to give account on the day of judgment for every careless word they have spoken. For by your words you will be acquitted, and by your words you will be condemned" (Matthew 12:36,37). A righteous person will try to fill his lips "with good things," with words that are uplifting, yet truthful.

113

Proverbs 12:17-20

What we do is to match what we say. Our words and actions are to work together and not be at odds with each other. God graciously rewards those efforts.

Notice that verses 13 and 14 make a pair. In this lengthy section of Solomon's proverbs (10:1–22:16), it's unusual to have two verses in a row that are tied together like that.

The stubbornness of a fool

¹⁵ The way of a fool seems right to him,
but a wise man listens to advice.

¹⁶ A fool shows his annoyance at once,
but a prudent man overlooks an insult.

Have you ever had this happen: you are sure you are driving in the right direction or you remember just where you put something or you have some "fact" straight, but as it turns out, you were mistaken? The fool lives his life like that. He simply knows he's headed on the right course.

The difference between the fool and the wise man is that the fool won't listen to anyone. When it's too late, he'll find out he was wrong. But the wise person listens to advice.

Perhaps because he is so set on his way, the fool is easily annoyed. He doesn't have time for the advice of others or for their problems. Whatever or whoever gets in his way annoys him.

The prudent, sensible person does more than listen to advice. He listens even to insults without letting them get the better of him. In this, we will try to follow the Savior's example: "When they hurled their insults at him, he did not retaliate; when he suffered, he made no threats. Instead, he entrusted himself to him who judges justly" (1 Peter 2:23).

The way of deceit

¹⁷ A truthful witness gives honest testimony,
but a false witness tells lies.

Proverbs 12:17-20

¹⁸ **Reckless words pierce like a sword,**
   but the tongue of the wise brings healing.

¹⁹ **Truthful lips endure forever,**
   but a lying tongue lasts only a moment.

²⁰ **There is deceit in the hearts of those who plot evil,**
   but joy for those who promote peace.

"You shall not give false testimony against your neighbor," declares the Eighth Commandment (Exodus 20:16). We can't have it both ways, says Solomon in verse 17; either we tell the truth, or we tell lies.

In the face of that truism, many still think they can be reckless with their speech. Their thoughtless words and lies about others wound. Sometimes we express it this way: "Those words cut into my heart!" The wise use the gift of speech differently. "Speaking the truth in love" (Ephesians 4:15), they try to heal with their words.

The truth endures. God's Word, the Bible, is forever true. As Isaiah said, "The grass withers and the flowers fall, but the word of our God stands forever" (Isaiah 40:8).

Think about it. Through the centuries, God's Word has been assailed by scoffers, "proven false" by scientists, misused and twisted by heretics and false prophets and cult leaders, disobeyed by people who claim to believe it, ignored by those who want to go their own way, considered weak and insignificant by the haughty, and contradicted by other "holy" books. Yet its prophecies have been fulfilled precisely in Jesus Christ; its assessment of human nature continually proves accurate, while psychologists go on changing their opinions; its historical record stands fast, while historians dig through desert sands for more evidence; its observations about nature remain correct, while scientific theories shift with each new generation; its good news of grace in Jesus continues to save, while other "holy" books offer the same

Proverbs 12:21-28

old tired message that never works, namely, you've got to save yourself.

Those who hold to the Bible and whose lips recite its truths are standing on an everlasting foundation. Those who spin their own notions of truth have their moment, and that's all (verse 19).

Because they are outside the Word, the wicked can plan nothing that's really good. The natural condition of the human heart is deceitful and evil. Those whose hearts God has changed can come up with something better than the self-serving plans of the wicked. Jesus describes them when he says, "Blessed are the peacemakers" (Matthew 5:9).

General advice and observations

> ²¹ **No harm befalls the righteous,**
> **but the wicked have their fill of trouble.**
>
> ²² **The LORD detests lying lips,**
> **but he delights in men who are truthful.**
>
> ²³ **A prudent man keeps his knowledge to himself,**
> **but the heart of fools blurts out folly.**
>
> ²⁴ **Diligent hands will rule,**
> **but laziness ends in slave labor.**
>
> ²⁵ **An anxious heart weighs a man down,**
> **but a kind word cheers him up.**
>
> ²⁶ **A righteous man is cautious in friendship,**
> **but the way of the wicked leads them astray.**
>
> ²⁷ **The lazy man does not roast his game,**
> **but the diligent man prizes his possessions.**
>
> ²⁸ **In the way of righteousness there is life;**
> **along that path is immortality.**

Reading verse 21, someone might argue, "But the righteous often do suffer harm!" Certainly Solomon knew enough about life in this sinful world to realize that the righteous suf-

Proverbs 12:21-28

fer. He speaks of this at length in the book of Ecclesiastes. His point here seems to be that no *lasting* harm befalls the righteous. While the righteous may suffer for a lifetime, even long-term trouble on earth resolves into eternal joy with God. And while the wicked may prosper for a time, their troubles far outweigh their passing pleasures, and they face an eternity without God.

As far as God is concerned, honesty isn't merely the best policy. It's the only policy (verse 22).

Being honest, however, does not mean that we blurt out whatever we know to anyone who will listen. There is a time for everything. The fool doesn't see this and is always speaking his mind, which is filled with foolishness (verse 23). Addicted to the widespread venting of foolishness, our age continues to pump out an endless array of television and radio talk shows, in which the famous and not-so-famous express themselves on every subject under the sun.

The "diligent hands" in verse 24 represent the whole person. The thought here is similar to Proverbs 10:4. Solomon wrote elsewhere: "Whatever your hand finds to do, do it with all your might" (Ecclesiastes 9:10).

Hard work does not mean we should be anxious. We are to do our best and then entrust the results to God. When we place our work in God's hands, there's really no room for anxiety.

As verse 25 points out, anxiety puts tremendous stress on the heart and wears people down. A thoughtful word of kindness can do wonders toward alleviating that stress. We might direct the anxious person to Scripture's promises, such as, "Cast all your anxiety on [God] because he cares for you" (1 Peter 5:7).

One cause of anxiety might be a person's circle of friends (verse 26). Getting into the wrong crowd can be disastrous.

117

Proverbs 13:1

"Bad company corrupts good character" (1 Corinthians 15:33). Therefore, the righteous are cautious before forming deep friendships. The wicked have no compunctions. They find their own kind and go astray together.

The word translated "roast" in verse 27 occurs only here in the entire Old Testament. Some conjecture that it should be translated "hunt" or "catch." One might wonder how the lazy man would have enough energy to hunt and catch his prey, much less roast it. However one renders that particular word, the idea is clear. A person can be so lazy that he doesn't even take care of life's basic necessities. Luther quoted with irony a proverb of his day: "Wait until a fried chicken flies into your mouth." The godly prize their possessions as gifts from the Lord. We will want to be faithful stewards of what God gives into our care during our earthly lives.

The way of righteousness that leads to life is God's way (verse 28). Christ's righteousness becomes ours by faith. Jesus tells us in the most famous verse in Scripture, "God so loved the world that he gave his one and only Son, that whoever believes in him shall not perish but have eternal life" (John 3:16).

A wise son

13 A wise son heeds his father's instruction,
but a mocker does not listen to rebuke.

The early chapters of Proverbs consisted of discourses to "my son." Proverbs 1:8 stated, "Listen, my son, to your father's instruction." Interspersed throughout the First Collection of Solomon's Proverbs (10:1–22:16) are reminders of those opening chapters. It's as if Solomon is saying, "Are you paying attention, son?"

The reverse side depicts the mocker. He does not listen. He scoffs. He goes his own way.

Proverbs 13:4

Using one's mouth to advantage

² **From the fruit of his lips a man enjoys good things,**
  but the unfaithful have a craving for violence.

³ **He who guards his lips guards his life,**
  but he who speaks rashly will come to ruin.

Because they have listened and learned, the wise can speak wisely. With words of correction, they help the erring. With words of kindness, they uplift the needy. The love and gratefulness they receive in return are "good things" they enjoy.

Meanwhile, the ungodly continue on their own way. Not having listened to rebuke, they pursue their own way, a way that treats others with disregard and violence.

The ability to control the tongue is a sign of wisdom. Later Solomon says, "The tongue has the power of life and death, and those who love it will eat its fruit" (18:21).

As the wicked are unable to control their passion for violence, they can't control their tongues either. Their end is ruin.

The lazy and the hardworking

⁴ **The sluggard craves and gets nothing,**
  but the desires of the diligent are fully satisfied.

This is one of many warnings against laziness and its consequences. Simply because one craves something doesn't mean he'll get it. The lazy have no reason to expect they'll get anything.

The proverb is also another recommendation for hard work and God's blessings upon it. "Fully satisfied," in line two, is rendered as "abundantly gratified" or simply "satisfied" in other translations. Solomon is not saying that hardworking people have their every last whim satisfied. Doing the work God has placed before them and trusting God's providence,

Proverbs 13:7,8

they find full satisfaction in knowing he will give them what is best.

Righteousness versus wickedness

5 The righteous hate what is false,
but the wicked bring shame and disgrace.

6 Righteousness guards the man of integrity,
but wickedness overthrows the sinner.

Righteous people reflect their Lord's attitude toward evil. It is not an attitude of mere indifference and ignoring what is wrong. No, the righteous *hate* what is false. In our day many Christians seem oblivious to the spiritual and moral rot all around. Whatever happened to the fiery hatred the prophets, the apostles, and Jesus himself had against everything evil?

The wicked bring shame upon themselves. Some become so hardened in immorality that "their glory is in their shame" (Philippians 3:19). That is, they boast about their sins.

Their sinful way of life will bring about the final ruin of sinners. "Their destiny is destruction" (Philippians 3:19). Protected by God's power, the righteous are kept safe, in time and for eternity.

The vanity of riches

7 One man pretends to be rich, yet has nothing;
another pretends to be poor, yet has great wealth.

8 A man's riches may ransom his life,
but a poor man hears no threat.

Truth is often stranger than fiction. By borrowing and putting purchases on credit, some people are able to give a pretense of wealth, when in reality they have nothing. Others, who live very humbly, are very wealthy. We ought not be too impressed by the appearance of wealth. Nor should we draw hard-and-fast conclusions from first impressions.

Proverbs 13:9-11

Verse 8 also deals with the topic of riches. The issue here is not whether or not one possesses earthly wealth but what value it has. On the one hand, riches can ransom a person's life. On the other hand, if you and your family are poor, no one will hold you up for ransom in the first place. Poverty does have its compensations.

Wealth often brings more anxiety, rather than the hoped-for security. In Ecclesiastes, Solomon remarked, "The sleep of a laborer is sweet, whether he eats little or much, but the abundance of a rich man permits him no sleep" (5:12).

Righteous and evil living

⁹ **The light of the righteous shines brightly,**
   but the lamp of the wicked is snuffed out.

¹⁰ **Pride only breeds quarrels,**
   but wisdom is found in those who take advice.

¹¹ **Dishonest money dwindles away,**
   but he who gathers money little by little makes it grow.

Light and the lamp symbolize life. Job put the two together in poetic parallelism: "Why is light given to those in misery, and life to the bitter of soul?" (3:20). For one's light to shine brightly meant long life, and one's lamp being snuffed out meant death. Verse 9, then, is a picturesque way of saying that the righteous will live long and the wicked won't. Jesus' parable of the ten virgins (Matthew 25:1-13) used the imagery of lamps to portray spiritual readiness (lamps with oil in them), over and against spiritual death (lamps with no oil).

Our sinful human pride doesn't like to take advice. It would rather quarrel than admit to being wrong. Wisdom admits when we need to be corrected and willingly takes advice.

Proverbs 13:12-14

Wealth gained by threats or by theft won't last. The prophet Jeremiah used this illustration: "Like a partridge that hatches eggs it did not lay is the man who gains riches by unjust means. When his life is half gone, they will desert him, and in the end he will prove to be a fool" (17:11).

The essence of life

¹² **Hope deferred makes the heart sick,
    but a longing fulfilled is a tree of life.**

¹³ **He who scorns instruction will pay for it,
    but he who respects a command is rewarded.**

¹⁴ **The teaching of the wise is a fountain of life,
    turning a man from the snares of death.**

Waiting for a long time drains one of life and energy. When Rachel waited and waited to have a child, she became discouraged and said to her husband Jacob, "Give me children, or I'll die!" (Genesis 30:1). When one's hope is finally realized, it's like having a new lease on life. In his wisdom God may keep us waiting for years before we receive an answer to a prayer. Sometimes his answer is that our hopes will not be realized until we're in heaven. Once we're there, all life's heartaches and longings will be past.

Verse 13 is appropriate today, when there is so much disrespect for authority in government, schools, and the church. Those who snub their noses at the instruction and commands of teachers and officials will pay. They'll find out the hard way that they should have paid attention and that they can't be a law unto themselves. Respect and obedience bring the rewards of friendship, contentment, and peace of mind.

Like the tree of life in verse 12, the fountain of life in verse 14 brings to mind pictures of paradise. The last chapter of the Bible speaks of "the river of the water of life" and "the tree of life" in heaven (Revelation 22:1,2). The end of

Proverbs 13:15-18

God's wisdom is eternal life and deliverance from eternal death in hell.

Wise and unwise behavior

**¹⁵ Good understanding wins favor,
but the way of the unfaithful is hard.**

**¹⁶ Every prudent man acts out of knowledge,
but a fool exposes his folly.**

**¹⁷ A wicked messenger falls into trouble,
but a trustworthy envoy brings healing.**

**¹⁸ He who ignores discipline comes to poverty and shame,
but whoever heeds correction is honored.**

Jesus is not only our Savior, but also our perfect example. As a boy he "grew in wisdom and stature, and in favor with God and men" (Luke 2:52). This kind of growing is the ideal for us and our children. Eventually, Jesus' goodness led to the hatred of sinful men who nailed him to the cross. Yet the generalization remains true that the godly are respected, while those who are faithless to the discipline of wisdom make life unnecessarily hard for themselves.

The fool goes through life with no higher guide than his own passions. It's evident that he is stumbling along. The prudent man—the man of understanding—"acts out of knowledge." That knowledge is based on the Scriptures.

The wicked messenger (verse 17) might be getting into trouble because he misrepresents those who sent him. The trustworthy envoy is dependable. The "healing" he brings probably means that everyone involved in his activities reaps the benefits of his reliability. What applies to messengers and envoys, we can apply to employees in general. God wants us to be reliable and trustworthy workers.

Solomon certainly knows how to drive home a point. You can't ignore discipline and not expect trouble—in verse 18

Proverbs 13:19,20

he mentions poverty and shame. To heed correction results in honor. Many times in Proverbs, he emphasizes that the way of the wicked ends in misery and the godly way leads to blessings. This is a truth that God Almighty has established. No human being can alter it.

Associate with wise people

> **¹⁹ A longing fulfilled is sweet to the soul,
> but fools detest turning from evil.**

> **²⁰ He who walks with the wise grows wise,
> but a companion of fools suffers harm.**

Although each is clear by itself, the two lines of verse 19 are somewhat difficult to tie together. The first line describes the sweet satisfaction of having a goal and reaching it. The second says that fools don't want to turn from their course of action.

The best explanation seems to be that goals are such strong motivations that people will do anything to reach them. If that's the case, the conjunction *but* in line two should be translated "so" (which is a possibility). The fool sets his heart on wealth (or fame or pleasure), and nothing can turn him from his evil drive to get it.

The same would hold true on the positive side. Jesus' goal was the salvation of the world, and so "for the joy set before him [he] endured the cross, scorning its shame" (Hebrews 12:2).

We have a saying, Birds of a feather flock together. Verse 20 says that—and more. If we weren't like them before, we tend to become like those with whom we associate. Do you want to become wiser? Then seek out the wise. Do you want to spend your time on nonsense? Then seek out the company of fools. But know that in doing so, you'll end up getting hurt.

Choose your friends carefully.

Proverbs 13:21,22

The reward of the righteous

²¹ **Misfortune pursues the sinner,**
 but prosperity is the reward of the righteous.
²² **A good man leaves an inheritance for his children's**
  children,
 but a sinner's wealth is stored up for the righteous.

Proverbs deals with general truths. One of those truths is that sin doesn't pay, in this world or the next. While the wicked may attain a degree of prosperity, and even become rich and famous, the fact remains that "misfortune pursues the sinner." That misfortune may come in the form of family troubles, envy and hatred from those he has mistreated, pangs of conscience and remorse, anxiety over the ever-present possibility of losing one's wealth.

While the righteous may not become fabulously wealthy, God blesses them sufficiently with food, clothing, and contentment to enjoy what they have. That is real prosperity.

The good man also has something to pass on to his children. Often through hard work he has saved up some material goods or money. More important, he passes down the spiritual heritage of God's Word.

The sinner's wealth is much less secure. Especially if he amassed it dishonestly, eventually he will lose it. In one way or another, it will end up in the hands of those who faithfully plod along at their daily tasks. Solomon expresses this thought also in Ecclesiastes 2:26. In a sense, because the ungodly live in fear of losing their wealth, they never fully possess what they have. But the godly possess the entire world, since God gives them contentment to enjoy all things. The thought is similar to Jesus' words in the Beatitudes: "Blessed are the meek, for they will inherit the earth" (Matthew 5:5).

Proverbs 13:23-25

Concerning society, family, and self

²³ **A poor man's field may produce abundant food,**
   but injustice sweeps it away.

²⁴ **He who spares the rod hates his son,**
   but he who loves him is careful to discipline him.

²⁵ **The righteous eat to their hearts' content,**
   but the stomach of the wicked goes hungry.

One of life's tragedies is the oppression of the poor. Just when they start to get ahead, "injustice sweeps it away." The injustice spoken of in verse 23 probably refers to the powerful grabbing food from the poor. Solomon's frequent mention of the poor bears a twofold lesson. We should never treat the poor unjustly. We should help them in any way we can.

Verse 24 is one of the best known passages in all of Proverbs. It is one of a number of proverbs dealing with the discipline of children (see also 19:18; 22:15; 23:13,14; 29:15,17).

Although a father might be inclined to indulge and spoil a child, that is very unloving. As the child grows older, his or her pampered background will be a hindrance rather than a help. Not having been disciplined, the child will not have internalized that discipline and become self-disciplined. It will be harder to stick with difficult tasks and relate to other people. The "rod" here and elsewhere in Proverbs quite clearly refers to physical correction, spanking.

The rod is not to be confused with child abuse, in which a child is harmed. Nor should parents be so strict as to "exasperate" their children (Ephesians 6:4). Christian parents will exhibit "the fruit of the Spirit," which is "love, joy, peace, patience, kindness, goodness, faithfulness, gentleness and self-control" (Galatians 5:22,23).

Verse 25 extols the earthly blessings of a godly lifestyle. While there might be exceptions to the rule, the general truth

Proverbs 14:1-3

stands. David wrote, "I was young and now I am old, yet I have never seen the righteous forsaken or their children begging bread" (Psalm 37:25).

The way of the wise

14 **The wise woman builds her house,**
but with her own hands the foolish one tears hers down.

² He whose walk is upright fears the LORD,
but he whose ways are devious despises him.

³ A fool's talk brings a rod to his back,
but the lips of the wise protect them.

The previous chapter began with a proverb about a wise son. This chapter opens with one about a wise woman. She builds her house, that is, she nurtures and encourages her family or household. (The Hebrew language does not have separate words for house and home.) In the ancient Jewish home—as in the modern Christian home—the woman had a great deal of responsibility (see 31:10-31).

But she doesn't build her home alone. The rest of the family takes part and, more important, the Lord takes part. In Psalm 127:1, Solomon wrote, "Unless the LORD builds the house, its builders labor in vain."

While a woman can't build her home alone, she can tear it down single-handedly. The foolish woman destroys her family life by unfaithfulness, laziness, or quarreling.

According to verse 2, the person who walks uprightly fears the Lord. One's outward behavior matches with his inner attitude toward the Lord. Those who despise God walk a different path. They make no genuine attempt to live uprightly. What righteousness they display comes not from fear of the Lord but from worldly motives.

The fool expresses his unbelief in what he says. If punishment does not come in this life, it'll come later. The wise

Proverbs 14:4-6

speak truthfully, in keeping with God's Word. They have God's own assurance of protection (verse 3).

Summarizing verses 2 and 3, we see that the godly and wicked differ in three key ways:

- their attitudes—fear of the Lord versus despising the Lord
- their behaviors—upright versus devious walk
- their ends—God's protection versus punishment

Strength of character

**⁴ Where there are no oxen, the manger is empty,
but from the strength of an ox comes an
abundant harvest.**

**⁵ A truthful witness does not deceive,
but a false witness pours out lies.**

**⁶ The mocker seeks wisdom and finds none,
but knowledge comes easily to the discerning.**

The Israelites used the ox for plowing and for threshing grain. The idea of verse 4 seems to be that if you want to enjoy the benefits of owning an ox, you have to be prepared to take care of the animal. The farmer with no oxen didn't have to put food in the manger. But he couldn't have as good a harvest without the help of this animal. In present-day terms, we might liken this to a teenager who wants to have a car, but doesn't want to keep it up. To enjoy certain benefits in life, we must be willing to pay certain costs.

Sprinkled throughout Proverbs are reminders of the differences between a truthful witness and a deceiver. In addition to verse 5, we find another one later in this chapter (verse 25). It may be that these verses have a double purpose. They keep the importance of being truthful ever before us. They also serve as little markers, saying, "These proverbs you are studying are the truth."

Proverbs 14:7-9

The mocker can't find wisdom, because he has started from the wrong premise. Instead of fearing the Lord—which is the "beginning of knowledge" (1:7)—he scoffs. Because the discerning person has started with the right foundation, he keeps building and increasing his knowledge through study of the Scriptures.

Fools compared with sensible people

**⁷ Stay away from a foolish man,
      for you will not find knowledge on his lips.**

**⁸ The wisdom of the prudent is to give thought to
      their ways,
      but the folly of fools is deception.**

**⁹ Fools mock at making amends for sin,
      but goodwill is found among the upright.**

In order to find true knowledge, we need to keep going back to God's Word. We certainly won't find it in the talk of a foolish person. If we stay around the fool and listen long enough, we run the risk of becoming foolish ourselves.

The point of verse 8 is that wisdom guides us through life. The foolish may have a form of wisdom, their theories about the meaning and purpose of life. But in the end it proves to be a delusion. "Where is the wise man [of this world]?" asks the apostle Paul. "Where is the scholar? Where is the philosopher of this age? Has not God made foolish the wisdom of the world?" (1 Corinthians 1:20).

The people of this world—namely, fools—consider the Bible's talk about sin and the need for forgiveness nonsense (verse 9). To them, the message of Christ crucified is "foolishness" (1 Corinthians 1:23). Consequently, they remain in their sinful condition and under the wrath of God. Those who believe—namely, the upright—experience God's goodwill.

Proverbs 14:10-13

So this world is divided into two camps: those who mock the things of God and those who find God's wisdom where the world sees nothing but foolishness. The one camp has the world's wisdom on its side. The other has God.

The essence of joy

> ¹⁰ **Each heart knows its own bitterness,**
> **and no one else can share its joy.**
>
> ¹¹ **The house of the wicked will be destroyed,**
> **but the tent of the upright will flourish.**
>
> ¹² **There is a way that seems right to a man,**
> **but in the end it leads to death.**
>
> ¹³ **Even in laughter the heart may ache,**
> **and joy may end in grief.**

In a sense, this cluster of proverbs is the most melancholic in the entire book. Solomon expresses the human condition of isolation in verse 10. We can know one another and share our joys and sorrows. But at the deepest level, no human is able to communicate to another exactly how he feels.

When an athlete trains for years and finally wins an Olympic gold medal, does anyone else truly feel the same exhilaration as he or she stands on the winner's podium? Even among fellow athletes, the experience is slightly different for each one. Who truly experiences the grief, entwined with countless memories, of the widow who stands beside the grave of her husband of more than 50 years?

Only one person completely understands and feels our hearts' deepest disappointments and greatest joys. That one, of course, is God. He knows us better than we know ourselves. He loves us and has promised, "Never will I leave you; never will I forsake you" (Hebrews 13:5). We need never be alone.

Proverbs 14:10-13

The wicked build their permanent houses in this world. But since this world is perishing, their houses will too (verse 11). The righteous live in tents. We are merely pilgrims, "looking for the city that is to come" (Hebrews 13:14). Saint Paul says, "Now we know that if the earthly tent we live in is destroyed, we have a building from God, an eternal house in heaven, not built by human hands" (2 Corinthians 5:1). Because of God's protection, our temporary tents are more secure than the houses of the wicked.

Most people believe there is a God. Most also feel they are on the right path to heaven, by earning their way with their good deeds. This is the way "that seems right to a man, but in the end it leads to death" (verse 12).

Pointing to his way, Jesus says: "Enter through the narrow gate. For wide is the gate and broad is the road that leads to destruction, and many enter through it. But small is the gate and narrow the road that leads to life, and only a few find it" (Matthew 7:13,14).

Verse 13 is also sad. Even on a happy occasion there are tinges of sadness. We might be sad over the loved one who couldn't be there or over the recent heartache of some friend. Life in this fallen world is like that. And if all we had was this world, every joy would end in the sadness of death.

Jesus tells us that it can go the other way as well: "Now is your time of grief, but I will see you again and you will rejoice, and no one will take away your joy" (John 16:22).

Granted, even wise King Solomon did not know these words. He and the other Old Testament believers could look forward to the promised Savior, but they did not have the full revelation we enjoy in the New Testament. Yet, even amid Solomon's melancholy, we see the God-given awareness that the future of the godly is far different and better than that of the wicked.

Proverbs 14:14-19

Personality patterns

¹⁴ **The faithless will be fully repaid for their ways,**
and the good man rewarded for his.

¹⁵ **A simple man believes anything,**
but a prudent man gives thought to his steps.

¹⁶ **A wise man fears the LORD and shuns evil,**
but a fool is hotheaded and reckless.

¹⁷ **A quick-tempered man does foolish things,**
and a crafty man is hated.

¹⁸ **The simple inherit folly,**
but the prudent are crowned with knowledge.

¹⁹ **Evil men will bow down in the presence of the good,**
and the wicked at the gates of the righteous.

The wicked are repaid. Some get their just deserts already in this life at the hands of other people. In the end, no matter what they get away with in this world, they must all face God's judgment.

Sometimes the good are recognized and honored in this life. More often, they must wait. As for God's rewarding the good man, we might wonder how this fits with God's grace. The Lord does see our good deeds and lovingly rewards us. But it is a reward of grace, in that Christ has won our salvation for us. He has paid the complete price for our sins. (See Ephesians 2:1-10.)

If one still wants to go the way of the world, verses 15 to 18 offer guidance on various ways to become a fool:

- Be gullible (verse 15). Believe anything. Avoid being prudent and thoughtful.
- Be hotheaded and reckless (verse 16). Pay no heed to the Lord, and don't avoid evil. Instead, boldly rush right into it.

Proverbs 14:20,21

- Be quick-tempered, and add to that a touch of craftiness (verse 17). If people hate you for it, so much the better. It shows they respect you.
- Don't waste time learning when there's so much to enjoy (verse 18). Let the wise have their knowledge. Worry about that later.

But know this, if you're going to play the fool, in the end you'll be humbled and the good will be exalted (verse 19). "At the gates of the righteous" may refer to the righteous being in the place of honor, while the wicked are left outside. The ancient city gates were the place at which the leaders met; the outcasts remained outside the city walls.

At the final judgment, everyone will bow before and acknowledge Jesus Christ as Lord. The righteous will be glad to do it, even as they bow before him now. The wicked will have no choice but to bow before their judge. (See Philippians 2:9-11.)

Neighbors

> [20] **The poor are shunned even by their neighbors,**
> **but the rich have many friends.**
>
> [21] **He who despises his neighbor sins,**
> **but blessed is he who is kind to the needy.**

In two brief lines (verse 20), Solomon describes what fair-weather friends are all about. One commentator speaks of it as "a part of the dark side of human nature." It's when we're down and out that we discover who our true friends are. As Solomon says later, "A friend loves at all times" (17:17).

Verse 21 says we should be sure not to be a fair-weather friend, who despises his needy neighbor. While the world couldn't care less, God, who is kind toward the needy, is

Proverbs 14:22-28

watching. Other proverbs tell us how to express that kindness—by sharing food with the poor (22:9), helping them financially (28:8), and defending their rights (31:9). God sees this kindness, and he blesses it.

General advice and observations

²² **Do not those who plot evil go astray?**
But those who plan what is good find love and
faithfulness.

²³ **All hard work brings a profit,**
but mere talk leads only to poverty.

²⁴ **The wealth of the wise is their crown,**
but the folly of fools yields folly.

²⁵ **A truthful witness saves lives,**
but a false witness is deceitful.

²⁶ **He who fears the LORD has a secure fortress,**
and for his children it will be a refuge.

²⁷ **The fear of the LORD is a fountain of life,**
turning a man from the snares of death.

²⁸ **A large population is a king's glory,**
but without subjects a prince is ruined.

We reap what we sow. Those who plot evil can expect evil results (verse 22). God said it this way through the prophet Micah:

> Woe to those who plan iniquity, to those who plot evil on their beds! . . . They covet fields and seize them, and houses, and take them. They defraud a man of his home, a fellowman of his inheritance. Therefore, the LORD says: "I am planning disaster against this people, from which you cannot save yourselves." (Micah 2:1-3)

The evil are led astray by their own wickedness and bring God's wrath upon themselves. But the righteous "plan what

Proverbs 14:22-28

is good." In return, they receive love and faithfulness from many sources.

The poverty spoken of in verse 23 is not that of verses 20 and 21. This poverty is brought about by laziness. It is the poverty described by Saint Paul when he spoke of idle "busybodies," people who didn't work themselves but stood around talking and bothering others. Paul wrote, "Such people we command and urge in the Lord Jesus Christ to settle down and earn the bread they eat" (2 Thessalonians 3:12).

Commentator Robert Alden notes three classes of poor in Proverbs:[10]

- The destitute or lonely poor: 13:8,23; 17:5; 18:23; 19:4,7,22; 22:2,7; 28:3,6,27; 29:13; 31:20
- The oppressed poor: 3:34; 13:23; 15:15; 22:22; 30:14; 31:5,9
- The lazy poor: 6:11; 11:24; 21:5,17; 22:16; 24:34; 28:22

The wise realize benefits from their wisdom, whether those benefits be monetary or other (verse 24). The foolish produce nothing but more foolishness.

Tell the truth (verse 25). Especially when we share the truth of God's grace can it be said that we are saving lives. Deceit destroys, instead of saves.

Verses 26 and 27 describe the fear of the Lord in two picturesque ways—as a fortress and as a fountain of life. Believers find refuge in God. He protects us from the onslaughts of Satan (see 1 Corinthians 10:13), and he sees to it that nothing will happen that is not for our ultimate good (see Romans 8:28). As our fountain of life, he has created us and also given us the gift of eternal life. With assurances such as these, we can face life, death, and eternity brimming with confidence.

Proverbs 14:29-33

"What good is a kingdom if there's nobody in it?" asks verse 28. Mere outward show of royalty is empty. Similarly, all outward pretense without real substance behind it is emptiness.

The results of wise living

**²⁹ A patient man has great understanding,
    but a quick-tempered man displays folly.**

**³⁰ A heart at peace gives life to the body,
    but envy rots the bones.**

**³¹ He who oppresses the poor shows contempt for
        their Maker,
    but whoever is kind to the needy honors God.**

**³² When calamity comes, the wicked are brought down,
    but even in death the righteous have a refuge.**

**³³ Wisdom reposes in the heart of the discerning
    and even among fools she lets herself be known.**

Patience is one of the characteristics of the sevenfold fruits of the Holy Spirit (Galatians 5:22,23). Everywhere, the Bible commends and encourages it. The quick-tempered man is neither encouraged nor commended. James comments, "My dear brothers, take note of this: Everyone should be quick to listen, slow to speak and slow to become angry, for man's anger does not bring about the righteous life that God desires" (1:19,20).

In verse 30 Solomon again stresses the tremendous influence that our inner spiritual life has on the rest of life, including our physical health. The heart at peace stands in contrast to the quick-tempered man of the previous verse. The peace that only God can give rules in a believer's heart. This peace of sins forgiven and assurance of God's love brings life and vitality. Its counterpart, envy, eats away at one like a deadly cancer.

136

Proverbs 14:34,35

Poverty can be the result of laziness (see verse 23 and 24:30-34). Often, however, circumstances beyond people's control lead to their poverty. Along with poverty, they suffer injustice (13:23) and loneliness (19:4,7). To add to their misery is to show contempt for God himself. In his parable of the last judgment, Jesus addresses our accountability to those in need: "I tell you the truth, whatever you did not do for one of the least of these, you did not do for me" (Matthew 25:45). But to help those in need is to honor God: "I tell you the truth, whatever you did for one of the least of these brothers of mine, you did for me" (Matthew 25:40).

What a word of comfort believers have in verse 32! When calamity comes, the wicked have nothing to fall back on. Their hopes are in this world and the things of this world. But death itself cannot overwhelm God's people. They still have refuge in the almighty God.

The Bible's teaching of the future life is not different in the Old Testament than in the New. Although not as fully revealed in the Old, it is there. This proverb is one passage of hope. There are others scattered throughout the Old Testament, such as Psalm 49:15, "God will redeem my life from the grave; he will surely take me to himself." And Psalm 73:24, "You guide me with your counsel, and afterward you will take me into glory."

Verse 33 is striking. This rare proverb says that on occasion even fools are able to recognize wisdom. They can't see the wisdom within a wise person's heart. Yet by his actions they see something they themselves lack. Perhaps by the life he leads, a wise man can help a fool step over to the other side, to that of wisdom.

Righteous ruling

34 Righteousness exalts a nation,
but sin is a disgrace to any people.

Proverbs 15:1-7

**³⁵ A king delights in a wise servant,
but a shameful servant incurs his wrath.**

Verse 34 is one of those proverbs that seem to rise above the rest in catching our attention. Its few words speak volumes about world history and current events.

The word "nation" applies to groups of people. God judges nations not by their economics, military power, or natural resources. He weighs them on the scales of sin and righteousness. Because of the wickedness of its king and rulers, the mighty empire of Babylon was brought down swiftly and unexpectedly (Daniel 5). Modern America faces God's judgment because of its sins, which have become a national disgrace—the breakdown of the family, abortion, materialism, moral indifference.

Wherever we may live, we need to promote righteousness. This includes civic righteousness, by which basic ethical standards are honored and applied. It includes the righteousness of Christ, as well. Through the gospel of Christ, not only are nations brought from the brink of destruction, but individual souls are saved for eternity.

"Rulers hold no terror for those who do right, but for those who do wrong," says Paul in his famous passage on government (Romans 13:3). That thought is similar to what Solomon says in verse 35. While it's true that good people at times suffer under unjust governments, the general principle still applies. Those rulers and governments that make a habit of punishing good citizens and favoring the wicked will not stand much longer.

Effective words

15 **A gentle answer turns away wrath,
but a harsh word stirs up anger.**

**² The tongue of the wise commends knowledge,
but the mouth of the fool gushes folly.**

Proverbs 15:1-7

³ **The eyes of the LORD are everywhere,**
    keeping watch on the wicked and the good.

⁴ **The tongue that brings healing is a tree of life,**
    but a deceitful tongue crushes the spirit.

⁵ **A fool spurns his father's discipline,**
    but whoever heeds correction shows prudence.

⁶ **The house of the righteous contains great treasure,**
    but the income of the wicked brings them trouble.

⁷ **The lips of the wise spread knowledge;**
    not so the hearts of fools.

Our sinful human nature likes to answer insults or anger with more anger. When someone steps on our toes, our first impulse might be to get back at that person. Though such responses come naturally, they only stir up anger. A gentle answer diffuses anger and turns it away. So, the next time you're tempted to snap back at someone, bite your tongue and remember this proverb: "A gentle answer turns away wrath, but a harsh word stirs up anger."

Verse 2 asserts that the wise are thoughtful in their speech. The fool has nothing to say but says something anyway. If we find ourselves feeling as if we have to state our opinion on every topic under the sun, it may be time to sit back and listen to what others have to say.

Verse 3 is a good proof text for the omniscience of God. He is all-knowing. The fact that God sees everything is a warning to the wicked; they won't get away with anything. It's also a comfort to the good; God's people have the assurance that he sees and cares about our burdens and will in his good time deliver us.

The mention of God's "eyes," by the way, is an anthropomorphism. That big word means that sometimes the Bible attributes human characteristics to God, as when it speaks of his eyes or hands. Since "God is spirit" (John 4:24), this ref-

Proverbs 15:8,9

erence to his eyes simply is a way of saying that he knows what is going on.

A deceitful tongue crushes a person's spirit (verse 4). It is disheartening when one is lied about and slandered. But kind words uplift and revive one's spirit. The "tree of life" brings back images of Eden. The tongue that shares the gospel is a tree of life in the fullest sense, as it shares the good news of paradise regained through Christ.

Verse 5 is one of many passages in Proverbs that deal with discipline. Others include 10:17; 12:1; 25:12; 29:1. Outside of Proverbs, the Bible also has many passages on the subject. One is Luke 17:3: "If your brother sins, rebuke him, and if he repents, forgive him." Scripture's frequent treatment of correction and discipline indicates how vital it is. The fool resents it; the person of good sense accepts it.

Often the righteous aren't rich materially, but their houses always contain "great treasure." The material possessions they do have are cause for thankfulness, and since they are not ill-gotten they cause no anxiety. They also enjoy the riches of God's love, a love reflected in their houses. The wicked have trouble along with their incomes—perhaps in worry over losing them or in troubled consciences.

In verse 7 Solomon sets "lips" and "hearts" in parallel lines. The connection between the two is close. The heart motivates what we say; the lips reflect what's in the heart. When they speak, the wise share knowledge, because they have it stored up in their hearts. Since fools don't have it inside, it can't come out in speech.

What the Lord loves

**⁸ The Lord detests the sacrifice of the wicked,
but the prayer of the upright pleases him.**

Proverbs 15:8,9

**⁹ The Lord detests the way of the wicked
but he loves those who pursue righteousness.**

In verse 3 we read that the Lord sees everything. Verses 8 and 9 teach that he is interested in everything. Contrary to the popular notion of God as a vague force "out there" somewhere, the Bible teaches that God takes a deep interest in human activity on earth.

He is interested in our religious activities. The sacrifices of the wicked were those sacrifices offered without faith. For some it was a mere formality to bring their sacrifices to God's altar. We think of Cain's offering as an example: "On Cain and his offering he [the Lord] did not look with favor" (Genesis 4:5). The prophets often spoke against Israel's halfhearted sacrifices. For instance, "'When you bring injured, crippled or diseased animals and offer them as sacrifices, should I accept them from your hands?' says the Lord" (Malachi 1:13).

The Lord is pleased with the prayer of the upright, often offered together with a sacrifice. (God isn't saying that prayers are acceptable but sacrifices aren't.) "The prayer of a righteous man," says James, "is powerful and effective" (5:16).

As verse 3 asserts, God watches our entire lives. We can't compartmentalize life into the religious part (which interests God) and the secular part (in which we can do as we please because he doesn't care). The Lord is Lord over our entire lives.

The wicked do not please God. He looks into their hearts and sees no faith or love toward him but only sinful and selfish motives, no matter how fine some of their outward actions might appear. The righteous, however, live by faith, without which "it is impossible to please God" (Hebrews 11:6). God loves the righteous, not because they deserve it but purely because he is gracious.

141

Proverbs 15:10-12

As an aside, it is noteworthy how often Solomon refers to God as "the LORD" throughout Proverbs. He uses the more general term *God* only about half a dozen times. In the wisdom literature of Ecclesiastes and Job, the word *God* predominates. In fact, the name "the LORD" does not occur in Ecclesiastes.

The name "the Lord" distinguished him as the God of free and faithful grace. (See Exodus 33:19; 34:5-7.) It was God's special covenant name, used with his chosen nation Israel. Yet wisdom literature was of a general nature and did not deal specifically with Israel. Proverbs contains only a few passing allusions to Israel (such as the mention of the fellowship offering in 7:14). This makes the frequent mention of "the Lord" all the more striking.

The consequences of foolishness

¹⁰ Stern discipline awaits him who leaves the path; he who hates correction will die.

¹¹ Death and Destruction lie open before the LORD— how much more the hearts of men!

¹² A mocker resents correction; he will not consult the wise.

To stray from God's paths invites correction. Sometimes God sends suffering into our lives as a corrective. Hebrews 12:1-13 offers an extended treatment on the topic of God's disciplining his children. It's always for our good. "No discipline seems pleasant at the time, but painful. Later on, however, it produces a harvest of righteousness and peace for those who have been trained by it" (12:11).

But some hate such correction, harden themselves against it, and bring about their own destruction.

Verse 11 speaks of "Death and Destruction"—Hebrew *Sheol* and *Abaddon*. The term *sheol* represents the afterlife

Proverbs 15:13-15

and can refer to death, the grave, or hell. *Abaddon* is decay or destruction. In the book of Revelation, *Abaddon* is personified as the king of destruction: "They had as king over them the angel of the Abyss, whose name in Hebrew is Abaddon" (9:11). In our Proverbs verse, the two words are personified, so the NIV capitalizes them as proper names.

The point is that if God can see into the depths of "Death and Destruction," surely it's an easy matter for him to look into human hearts! As he says elsewhere, "I the LORD search the heart" (Jeremiah 17:10).

These constant reminders that God sees and knows everything about us ought to move us to repentance. In spite of God's reminders, invitations, warnings, and loving discipline, mockers continue to resent correction and refuse to listen to God's spokespeople (verse 12). No wonder Jesus wept over Jerusalem (Luke 19:41). Nothing is more tragic than unbelief.

The joyful heart

> ¹³ **A happy heart makes the face cheerful,**
> **but heartache crushes the spirit.**
>
> ¹⁴ **The discerning heart seeks knowledge,**
> **but the mouth of a fool feeds on folly.**
>
> ¹⁵ **All the days of the oppressed are wretched,**
> **but the cheerful heart has a continual feast.**

When our hearts are happy, our faces light up. But broken hearts drain us of energy and confidence. Notice that Solomon does not speak of outward circumstances. Those circumstances could be favorable or not. What really affects us is what's inside of us, in our hearts.

Throughout, Proverbs deals with behavior. Time and again it takes us back to the source of what we do—the heart. God's Word always aims at the heart. Laws and

143

Proverbs 15:16,17

rewards can bring forth a degree of outward conformity. But the heart must be renewed for a true change to take place. That's why we regularly pray in our church services, "Create in me a pure heart, O God, and renew a steadfast spirit within me" (Psalm 51:10).

The heart that has been touched by God will seek to grow in godly knowledge (verse 14). So it longs for a daily diet of wisdom from the Scriptures. The fool just keeps feeding on spiritual and mental junk food.

The contrast in verse 15 is not between the wealthy and the poor. Rather, it's between the contented and those who are dissatisfied. In the next two verses, Solomon shows that one can be poor and happy or rich and unhappy:

The better things in life

**¹⁶ Better a little with the fear of the LORD
than great wealth with turmoil.**

**¹⁷ Better a meal of vegetables where there is love
than a fattened calf with hatred.**

The hymn writer expressed this thought beautifully when he said:

Many spend their lives in fretting
Over trifles and in getting
Things that have no solid ground.
I shall strive to win a treasure
That will bring me lasting pleasure
And that now is seldom found. (CW 421:3)

That lasting treasure, of course, is the wisdom of knowing God and his love.

The fattened calf represented luxury or a special meal, not unlike our juicy steak (perhaps with lobster). In Jesus' parable

144

Proverbs 15:20

of the lost son, when the son returned home, his father had the servants prepare a fattened calf for the happy occasion (Luke 15:23). Where there is no love, however, even the best meal isn't enjoyable.

Differing dispositions

> ¹⁸ **A hot-tempered man stirs up dissension,**
> **but a patient man calms a quarrel.**
>
> ¹⁹ **The way of the sluggard is blocked with thorns,**
> **but the path of the upright is a highway.**

Quarrels, or lack of them, depend more on the attitudes of people than on the actual subject being discussed. We've probably all been in situations in which a seemingly trivial remark set off a heated debate. Somebody was itching for an argument. We may also have seen the opposite—someone calmly defusing a very volatile situation. May God help us be more like that patient man who "calms a quarrel."

The picture in verse 19 is of a path lined with a thorny hedge, on which the traveler keeps snagging his clothes. It's not that the sluggard has more obstacles to face. Rather, he makes more obstacles because of his laziness. He also has a penchant for imagining difficulties that aren't really there.

While the upright encounter many difficulties along life's way, with the Lord's help, they are able to meet and overcome those problems.

A wise son

> ²⁰ **A wise son brings joy to his father,**
> **but a foolish man despises his mother.**

Variations on this theme occur throughout Proverbs. The opening verse in this First Collection of Solomon's Proverbs states, "A wise son brings joy to his father, but a foolish son grief to his mother" (10:1).

Proverbs 15:21-23

In verse 20 Solomon takes it a step further. Not only does the son bring grief to his mother, but he actually "despises" her! Grieving one's parents by sinful behavior is a hateful thing to do. A loving child will seek to honor his father and mother and make them happy.

Fun and delight

²¹ **Folly delights a man who lacks judgment,**
   but a man of understanding keeps a straight course.

²² **Plans fail for lack of counsel,**
   but with many advisers they succeed.

²³ **A man finds joy in giving an apt reply—**
   and how good is a timely word!

Folly in the book of Proverbs carries moral overtones. It's not merely an intellectual matter. The person who lacks judgment will instinctively incline toward the leanings of his sinful nature, that is, toward folly.

In order to develop one's ability to make judgments, training in the Scriptures is a must. It's the difference between keeping a straight course through life or being "tossed back and forth by the waves, and blown here and there by every wind of teaching and by the cunning and craftiness of men in their deceitful scheming" (Ephesians 4:14).

In our journeys through life, it's helpful to consult others as we make our plans (verse 22). When we marry or make career choices it's good to get the advice of our pastors and trusted Christian friends. The person who always acts alone, without the good advice of others, is bound to have some blind spots and to run into unnecessary failure.

The fool delights in folly (verse 21). The wise person delights in finding answers to life's problems and being able to help others with a timely word (verse 23). We shouldn't think that fools go through life having fun, while the wise are

Proverbs 15:24-27

always somber and stone faced. No, it's just that the wise find their joy in different, more fulfilling ways.

Destruction for the wicked; life for the upright

²⁴ **The path of life leads upward for the wise**
 to keep him from going down to the grave.

²⁵ **The LORD tears down the proud man's house**
 but he keeps the widow's boundaries intact.

²⁶ **The LORD detests the thoughts of the wicked,**
 but those of the pure are pleasing to him.

²⁷ **A greedy man brings trouble to his family,**
 but he who hates bribes will live.

Verse 24 pictures the path of life as going upward, toward heaven. It leads away from the grave and hell (Hebrew *sheol*). Old Testament believers did not have the full revelation we enjoy in the New Testament era. Yet their faith was in the promised Savior, whom we know by name and who has told us, "I am the way and the truth and the life" (John 14:6).

God tears down the proud man's house (verse 25). The house represents a person's family, not merely a physical structure. It also represents one's descendants; for instance, Jesus was from the "house" of David (Luke 2:4). Proud people, then, bring troubles and shame not only on themselves but on their families and descendants.

By contrast, the Lord guards the humble widow. Since property boundaries were marked by stones, it was relatively easy for wicked men to move the boundary stones of helpless widows and thus steal some of their property. God's Old Testament law was one way of protecting widows. That law declared: "Do not move your neighbor's boundary stone" (Deuteronomy 19:14). The Lord is always concerned about weaker, more vulnerable members of society.

In verses 8 and 9 of this chapter, we read that "the LORD detests" the "sacrifice" and the "way" of the wicked. Verse 26

147

Proverbs 15:28,29

adds that he also detests their "thoughts." Such passages do much to clear up misconceptions of God being indifferent toward sin. Happily, he isn't indifferent to his people either. He cares about them. Their thoughts and prayers please him.

Just as God is not indifferent toward evil, he expects that we feel the same. In an earlier chapter, we saw that "to fear the Lord is to hate evil" (8:13). Unlike the greedy man who brings all kinds of trouble to his family, the godly hates bribes, along with other forms of greediness. Content with his life, he enjoys his life.

Comparing the righteous and the wicked

**28 The heart of the righteous weighs its answers,
    but the mouth of the wicked gushes evil.**

**29 The Lord is far from the wicked
    but he hears the prayer of the righteous.**

Solomon says much about how the heart influences our speech. From the wicked heart comes evil speech (see Luke 6:45). In 1 Peter 3:15 we see what sort of answer comes from the mouth of God's children: "In your hearts set apart Christ as Lord. Always be prepared to give an answer to everyone who asks you to give the reason for the hope that you have. But do this with gentleness and respect."

"If I had cherished sin in my heart," says the psalmist, "the Lord would not have listened; but God has surely listened and heard my voice in prayer" (66:18,19). If we are clinging to pet sins, we shouldn't be surprised if our prayers go unanswered. The righteous are those who acknowledge their sin and trust in Christ, through whom they have their righteousness (see Philippians 3:7-9). When we who have such trust pray, Jesus tells us, "My Father will give you whatever you ask in my name" (John 16:23).

148

Proverbs 15:32,33

Good eyes and ears

> ³⁰ **A cheerful look brings joy to the heart,**
> **and good news gives health to the bones.**

> ³¹ **He who listens to a life-giving rebuke**
> **will be at home among the wise.**

Verse 30 is a reminder not to underestimate life's "little" things. A cheerful twinkle of the eyes can make someone's day. A bit of good news can make one feel good all over, down to his bones. "Health to the bones" is the opposite of "[drying] up the bones" (17:22).

Sometimes we cheer ourselves up by bringing joy to others. And what better "good news" can we share with anyone than the gospel, the good news of God's love in Christ?

"Life-giving rebuke" is that which turns one from sin and points the way to Christ. To listen to godly correction places one among the truly wise.

Discipline's value

> ³² **He who ignores discipline despises himself,**
> **but whoever heeds correction gains understanding.**

> ³³ **The fear of the LORD teaches a man wisdom,**
> **and humility comes before honor.**

We hear a lot today about self-esteem and self-love. True self-love, wrote Solomon long ago, comes not from self-indulgence but from self-discipline. To ignore discipline, especially that coming from God, is a form of self-hatred. It involves going the way that is most harmful to oneself.

When children are corrected and learn to accept it, they are gaining understanding. They will grow up with a better understanding of right and wrong, of self-control, and of how to relate to other people.

The fear of the Lord is the basic foundation of Proverbs (see 1:7). As we humbly bow before God and acknowledge

149

Proverbs 16:1-7

our sin and unworthiness, he uplifts us. Saint Peter says, "Humble yourselves, therefore, under God's mighty hand, that he may lift you up in due time" (1 Peter 5:6).

As we come to the end of chapter 15, we note a stylistic break between chapters 15 and 16. Up to this point in Solomon's First Collection, the verses were almost all antithetic parallelism (expressing contrasting thoughts). Although two such verses open chapter 16, they become rare after that. Hereafter, we'll see mainly synonymous (expressing the same thought) or synthetic (the second line building on the first) parallelism.

The sevenfold centrality of the Lord

16 To man belong the plans of the heart,
but from the LORD comes the reply of the tongue.

² All a man's ways seem innocent to him,
but motives are weighed by the LORD.

³ Commit to the LORD whatever you do,
and your plans will succeed.

⁴ The LORD works out everything for his own ends—
even the wicked for a day of disaster.

⁵ The LORD detests all the proud of heart.
Be sure of this: They will not go unpunished.

⁶ Through love and faithfulness sin is atoned for;
through the fear of the LORD a man avoids evil.

⁷ When a man's ways are pleasing to the LORD,
he makes even his enemies live at peace with him.

Who is the most important person in our lives? our spouses? our children? our parents? a friend? Or, is it God? The opening verses of Proverbs chapter 16 emphasize that the Lord is most important. He is central. And once we place him first, then we'll be able to see all other relationships in the proper perspective.

Proverbs 16:1-7

Verse 1 emphasizes the role of God in our planning. We can plan, but only he can enable us to carry out plans. "You ought to say, 'If it is the Lord's will, we will live and do this or that'" (James 4:15). Solomon's reference to the Lord supplying "the reply of the tongue" seems to be this: God alone can give us the gift of language to put our ideas into words and thus bring them to completion.

We all like to think we are good people (verse 2), and even criminals rationalize what they do. The writer William Saroyan noted: "Every man is a good man in a bad world— as he himself knows." Only God can look deeply into our hearts and see our motives, whether they are good or not. Rather than setting our own agendas, then, and trying to justify whatever we do, we ought to look at everything we do in the light of God's Word.

Committing whatever we do to the Lord (verse 3) means that we pray as Jesus prayed to his heavenly Father, "Yet not as I will, but as you will" (Matthew 26:39). We ask God's guidance, make our plans, commit them to God's will, and leave the results to him. In this way, our plans will always succeed, for God will always bring about the best results.

God is in control (verse 4). He uses everything for the ultimate good of his people: "We know that in all things God works for the good of those who love him, who have been called according to his purpose" (Romans 8:28). As for those who reject him, they are hurtling toward their day of disaster—judgment day.

"The LORD detests all the proud of heart" (verse 5). Strong words, indeed! They remind us that God is a God of judgment as well as of grace. The proud in heart are those who don't see their own sin. They are like the Pharisee in Jesus' parable, who prayed, "God, I thank you that I am not like other men—robbers, evildoers, adulterers" (Luke 18:11).

151

Proverbs 16:8,9

Though he may not recognize it, in God's sight such a person is in *worse* shape than other men. He is blinded to his own sinful condition and need for repentance.

Verse 6 speaks of atonement through love and faithfulness. Strictly speaking, this is something no sinful human can achieve. It is only through Jesus' love and faithfulness that our sins are atoned for. His innocent blood atones for—that is, covers—our sins and washes them away. His undeserved grace moves us to respond in kind. Our fear of God, our great respect for him, motivates us to avoid evil. Again, what we do is but a response to what God has done for us.

Our ways can be pleasing to God only through faith, for "without faith it is impossible to please God" (Hebrews 11:6). When we live God-pleasing lives, God blesses us with peace. During the reigns of the godly kings Asa and Jehoshaphat of Judah, God gave their whole country peace from their surrounding enemies (2 Chronicles 14:6,7; 17:10).

Honesty and planning

> ⁸ **Better a little with righteousness**
> **than much gain with injustice.**
>
> ⁹ **In his heart a man plans his course,**
> **but the LORD determines his steps.**

We all know of rich people who are unhappy and of people who have little money but are content. Particularly when riches have been gained dishonestly, their possessor will live in constant unrest. As we go about our work, the bottom line should be, How can I use my God-given gifts, and not, How can I get rich by any means?

This same principle holds true when it comes to our planning. We all make plans. But how often aren't those plans upset! We plan a vacation but can't go because someone gets sick. We plan to go to college but have to get a

Proverbs 16:10-15

job and earn some money instead. Exactly how our plans turn out is beyond our control. It is God who controls the outcome, and he who gives us strength to walk the way we should go. The psalmist reminds us, "If the LORD delights in a man's way, he makes his steps firm" (37:23).

That's why, when we make plans and go about our work, God should be a part of everything we do.

Kings

> ¹⁰ **The lips of a king speak as an oracle,**
> **and his mouth should not betray justice.**
>
> ¹¹ **Honest scales and balances are from the LORD;**
> **all the weights in the bag are of his making.**
>
> ¹² **Kings detest wrongdoing,**
> **for a throne is established through righteousness.**
>
> ¹³ **Kings take pleasure in honest lips;**
> **they value a man who speaks the truth.**
>
> ¹⁴ **A king's wrath is a messenger of death,**
> **but a wise man will appease it.**
>
> ¹⁵ **When a king's face brightens, it means life;**
> **his favor is like a rain cloud in spring.**

In these verses Solomon focuses on kings and their function (see also 25:2-7). What he says about kings applies to rulers and officials in general.

The Hebrew word translated "oracle" in verse 10 usually had a negative connotation, the "divination" condemned in Deuteronomy 18:10 and elsewhere. Here, however, we see the term lined up with "justice." God establishes kings and governments (see Romans 13:1-7). Just as it is incumbent upon citizens to honor their government, so God expects rulers to act as his representatives, speaking in civil matters as his mouthpiece and ruling justly.

Like other men, kings have to answer to God, the King of kings. This underscores an important difference between the

153

Proverbs 16:10-15

Old Testament view of kings and that of the pagan nations around Israel. The biblical view was that kings were not some sort of divine beings who created the laws, as other nations believed, but were subject to the laws of God.

The Lord expects honesty of rulers. They cannot create scales, balances, and weights to suit their own fancy (verse 11). The "weights in the bag" refer to stones used as measuring weights; merchants carried these stones in bags.

What establishes a king, then, is his standing with God. When rulers detest wrongdoing and follow righteous ways, God establishes them (verse 12). That is, he makes them secure. Such rulers also take pleasure in honesty (verse 13) and will surround themselves with truthful advisors.

Ancient despots held an awesome power of life and death. All they had to do was say the word and they could have a person put to death. The Bible gives many examples of this. Several come from the book of Esther. Queen Esther herself had to be careful how to approach the king, lest she incur his disfavor (Esther 5:1-3); and when the king became angry with Haman, a high-ranking official, he had him hanged (7:8-10). Wise men knew how to appease a king's anger.

The brightening of one's face (verse 15) signified that that person was looking on you with favor. When the king shows you favor, your life improves. Most important, however, is that the King of glory shows you his favor. The Aaronic blessing says, "The LORD bless you and keep you; the LORD *make his face shine* upon you and be gracious to you; the LORD turn his face toward you and give you peace" (Numbers 6:24-26). We use similar terminology when we talk of someone's face beaming or glowing with happiness or pride. As for the rain in spring, without it there would be no crops and no life. Similarly, without God's favor there can be no life—either physical or spiritual.

Proverbs 16:18,19

Wisdom's highway

¹⁶ **How much better to get wisdom than gold,**
to choose understanding rather than silver!

¹⁷ **The highway of the upright avoids evil;**
he who guards his way guards his life.

Verse 16 reiterates a thought from earlier chapters of Proverbs: "[Wisdom] is more profitable than silver and yields better returns than gold" (3:14; see also 8:10,19). In his day, Solomon was wealthier than all other kings; even all his goblets and household articles were gold, and he "made silver as common in Jerusalem as stones" (1 Kings 10:27). Yet what he treasured above all was wisdom.

Wisdom is the highway through life for the upright, and it protects us. Wisdom is a priceless gift from God; it cannot be bought.

Pride

¹⁸ **Pride goes before destruction,**
a haughty spirit before a fall.

¹⁹ **Better to be lowly in spirit and among the oppressed**
than to share plunder with the proud.

The proud person wants to usurp for himself what belongs to God, namely, the glory. Psalm 115:1 declares, "Not to us, O LORD, not to us but to your name be the glory." To raise ourselves up instead of God is to be proud. Such haughtiness is but for a moment, as God brings down the proud.

It seems apparent that many of today's ills stem from the fact that our society encourages aggressiveness and pride. "You're number one." "You deserve the best." The urge to put oneself forward easily leads to putting others down.

True humility is still the best way, even if it means being among the oppressed. This humility does not mean burying

Proverbs 16:20-24

one's talents. But it does mean recognizing that all we have comes from God and should be used in God-pleasing ways. Godly humility also recognizes our continuous need for the Lord's mercy and help. Then it proceeds to live boldly, confident of God's sustaining love.

Words that give understanding

> [20] **Whoever gives heed to instruction prospers,**
>   **and blessed is he who trusts in the LORD.**
>
> [21] **The wise in heart are called discerning,**
>   **and pleasant words promote instruction.**
>
> [22] **Understanding is a fountain of life to those who have it,**
>   **but folly brings punishment to fools.**
>
> [23] **A wise man's heart guides his mouth,**
>   **and his lips promote instruction.**
>
> [24] **Pleasant words are a honeycomb,**
>   **sweet to the soul and healing to the bones.**

We prosper as we trust in the Lord and follow his instructions. He promises that he will bless us. Just how those blessings come is up to God. We cannot dictate to him. He may bless us with friends, happy families, honor, wealth, steadfastness, or countless other gifts. It's in his hands.

Being a man of discernment (verse 21) means being able to sift out what is good from what is not, to distinguish the wheat from the chaff. "Pleasant" instruction is helpful toward becoming such a wise person. God isn't opposed to education being an enjoyable or fun experience.

At times the Bible likens spiritual blessings to a fountain (verse 22). For example, the Lord calls himself "the spring of living water" (Jeremiah 2:13). And Jesus promises, "To him who is thirsty I will give to drink without cost from the spring of the water of life" (Revelation 21:6). To pursue folly, however, brings misery and not God's blessings.

Proverbs 16:25-30

The wise man is thoughtful in his speech. His words are pleasant, both to the soul and the bones; that is, to the entire person.

Negative personality types

> [25] **There is a way that seems right to a man,**
> **but in the end it leads to death.**
>
> [26] **The laborer's appetite works for him;**
> **his hunger drives him on.**
>
> [27] **A scoundrel plots evil,**
> **and his speech is like a scorching fire.**
>
> [28] **A perverse man stirs up dissension,**
> **and a gossip separates close friends.**
>
> [29] **A violent man entices his neighbor**
> **and leads him down a path that is not good.**
>
> [30] **He who winks with his eye is plotting perversity;**
> **he who purses his lips is bent on evil.**

Test everything by God's Word. Sometimes what appears the best way isn't good at all—an unscriptural divorce to escape an unhappy marriage, an abortion to be rid of an unplanned pregnancy, a series of lies to cover a mistake, a little cheating to get through a tough class, following a religious leader who has something new and different to offer. What leads away from God's Word leads toward death.

Even if the task is drudgery, hunger drives a man to work. In this way "the laborer's appetite works for him" (verse 26). It's his motivation. Christians have a higher motivation: "Do it all for the glory of God" (1 Corinthians 10:31).

James takes up the imagery of verse 27: "The tongue also is a fire. . . . It corrupts the whole person, sets the whole course of his life on fire, and is itself set on fire by hell" (James 3:6). What damage the tongue can do! Verse 28

Better a patient man than a warrior

Proverbs 16:31-33

furnishes an example of that damage, the dissension that gossip can cause.

Modern newscasts not infrequently tell of murderers who enticed their victims into a trap. In a violent age like ours, verse 29 gives warning. Take care with whom you make friends.

Facial expressions (verse 30) sometimes say more than words. Slanderers make use of a knowing wink, implying that much more could be said, and bite or purse their lips, implying the same.

General advice and observations

31 Gray hair is a crown of splendor;
it is attained by a righteous life.

32 Better a patient man than a warrior,
a man who controls his temper than one who takes
a city.

33 The lot is cast into the lap,
but its every decision is from the LORD.

In Bible times gray hair symbolized more than old age. It also represented respect. Old people were looked upon as favored by God with long life and wise because of their years of experience. Among the laws for the Israelites was this: "Rise in the presence of the aged, show respect for the elderly and revere your God" (Leviticus 19:32). Sadly, in our day, disrespect for the elderly has often taken the place of respect. Christian children can learn God's will and respect the aged.

One quality that often comes with age is patience. God values patience and self-control more than the strength and energy displayed by a warrior, especially if that fighting man can't even control his own temper. We see our share of young athletic types who can win championships in their sport but can't keep a lid on their tempers. God is not

Proverbs 17:1-6

impressed. "Everyone should be quick to listen, slow to speak and slow to become angry, for man's anger does not bring about the righteous life that God desires" (James 1:19,20).

The casting of lots was a common way to make decisions. The disciples, for instance, cast lots to see who would replace Judas, but only after they prayed (Acts 1:23-26). The disciples recognized—as all believers do—that God holds the future in his hands. Our every decision should be made with this in mind.

When the disciples used lots, it was the last scriptural reference to this practice and, significantly, the last event before Pentecost. While lots are not forbidden, we are more likely to use other avenues. Today we might pray, read worthwhile advice, and discuss our plans with fellow believers, before moving ahead and entrusting the outcome to God.

17 Better a dry crust with peace and quiet
than a house full of feasting, with strife.

² A wise servant will rule over a disgraceful son,
and will share the inheritance as one of the brothers.

³ The crucible for silver and the furnace for gold,
but the LORD tests the heart.

⁴ A wicked man listens to evil lips;
a liar pays attention to a malicious tongue.

⁵ He who mocks the poor shows contempt for their Maker;
whoever gloats over disaster will not go unpunished.

⁶ Children's children are a crown to the aged,
and parents are the pride of their children.

Verse 1 presents a truism with which few would argue. Who would choose riches, if he could have peace instead? Simple choice? Seemingly, it is. Yet many people are so enamored of wealth that they will seek it even at the cost of having a loveless home. Pray to God for contentment. Then a dry crust will be as inviting as a sumptuous feast!

160

Proverbs 17:1-6

Among the ancients, a thankful master could grant his servant full freedom and take him into the family as a son. He could even disinherit a son and transfer the inheritance to the servant. Among prominent Old Testament servants was Abraham's trusted Eliezer. At one time, before he had a son, Abraham was prepared to give his inheritance to Eliezer (Genesis 15:2). The point of the proverb in verse 2 is that a good servant can rise to higher honor than a disgraceful son. What matters is not the position we are born into but what we do with the lives we have.

A crucible was a container that could resist great heat (verse 3). Silver and gold were melted down and refined in crucibles and furnaces (see also 27:21). While men have the ability to refine metals in this way, only God can test the heart.

God uses life's trials and suffering as a way to refine his people, making them stronger and purer. He says: "This third [a remnant of the people] I will bring into the fire; I will refine them like silver and test them like gold. They will call on my name and I will answer them; I will say, 'They are my people,' and they will say, 'The LORD is our God'" (Zechariah 13:9). Saint Peter encourages us to accept sufferings, since they are for our good: "These [trials] have come so that your faith—of greater worth than gold, which perishes even though refined by fire—may be proved genuine and may result in praise, glory and honor when Jesus Christ is revealed" (1 Peter 1:7).

We have a saying: Birds of a feather flock together. Verse 4 underscores that. In this case, it is the evil who flock together. Those who deal in lies and wicked speech listen to others like themselves.

Verse 5 hits home. How much of our humor isn't at someone else's expense! To make fun of the down-and-out is to

161

Proverbs 17:7-10

show contempt for God himself. He owns everything. If he should distribute less to some than to others, that is not cause for mockery. Rather, it is an opportunity God gives us to show love by sharing our gifts with those in need. Likewise, to mock those on whom the Lord has allowed disaster to fall is also to invite God's punishment.

The Bible often describes old age as a blessing. Proverbs 16:31 spoke of the "splendor" of old age. In verse 6 we see that part of the splendor is that the elderly live to see their grandchildren. This was a blessing the psalmist pronounced upon "all who fear the LORD. . . . May you live to see your children's children" (128:1,6).

Not only do parents rejoice to see their children grow up and have families of their own, but children are proud of their parents as well. Without using the words, Solomon has described the love and joy of a God-fearing family.

The consequences of being a fool

⁷ **Arrogant lips are unsuited to a fool—
how much worse lying lips to a ruler!**

⁸ **A bribe is a charm to the one who gives it;
wherever he turns, he succeeds.**

⁹ **He who covers over an offense promotes love,
but whoever repeats the matter separates close friends.**

¹⁰ **A rebuke impresses a man of discernment
more than a hundred lashes a fool.**

Although no one should be haughty, arrogant speech is especially unsuited to a fool. Even more, lies are not fitting on the lips of a ruler. While people might overlook an arrogant fool, a lying ruler isn't easily ignored. The higher the ruler or leader, the more serious are the consequences of his deceit.

The words of verse 8 are simple. Understanding them is not so easy. God's civil laws forbade the giving and taking of

Proverbs 17:11-15

bribes (Exodus 23:8; Deuteronomy 16:19), and elsewhere in Proverbs it is condemned (15:27; 17:23). How can verse 8 seem to recommend what is wrong?

There are several ways we can understand verse 8. Some see it as a sad, but true, commentary on the way things are in this world. Solomon is not recommending the bribe but simply stating a reality. Others translate the word "bribe" as "gift," since it can also mean that. In this case, it's a legitimate way of dealing with people. The last possibility is that while the bribe seems to be a charm and bring success, in the end the briber will suffer. While the others are not without merit, we favor the first approach. Several times Solomon discusses bribes, and each time he presents them as a sad reality of life.

To cover an offense promotes love (verse 9). We may know of some embarrassment in the life of another. Perhaps a neighbor or a friend spent some time in prison. Love says, let it be. This is not to overlook sin, but simply not to bring it up when it need not be brought up. To repeat the matter is a sure way to ruin friendships. On a daily basis, many slights, faults, and offenses come our way. How do we deal with them? In his great chapter on love, Saint Paul reminds us: "Love is patient. . . . It keeps no record of wrongs" (1 Corinthians 13:4,5). Solomon speaks of that same kind of love.

Verse 10 is easy to understand but difficult to accept. Who of us likes to be corrected for something we've done wrong? Yet a man of understanding will appreciate it and learn from it, more than a fool will from a hundred lashes across the back!

The consequences of evil living

> **¹¹ An evil man is bent only on rebellion;**
> **a merciless official will be sent against him.**

Proverbs 17:11-15

¹² **Better to meet a bear robbed of her cubs**
than a fool in his folly.

¹³ **If a man pays back evil for good,**
evil will never leave his house.

¹⁴ **Starting a quarrel is like breaching a dam;**
so drop the matter before a dispute breaks out.

¹⁵ **Acquitting the guilty and condemning the innocent—**
the LORD detests them both.

Some people can't be talked out of a wrongful course of action. The man "bent only on rebellion" is such a person. When he runs into the "merciless official"—policeman, the military—he'll stop. But not until then. The apostle Paul writes: "He who rebels against the authority is rebelling against what God has instituted. . . . If you do wrong, be afraid, for he [the government authority] does not bear the sword for nothing. He is God's servant, an agent of wrath to bring punishment on the wrongdoer" (Romans 13:2,4). The necessity of force is a harsh reality in our fallen world.

The fool is another harsh reality of life (verse 12). A bear robbed of her cubs will attack you and tear you apart; the fool in his mad folly is just as dangerous. Interestingly, God uses this same image of himself and his anger against a rebellious people: "Like a bear robbed of her cubs, I will attack them and rip them open" (Hosea 13:8).

Repaying evil with evil is wrong (see 1 Peter 3:9). How much worse it is to repay *good* with evil (verse 13)! Evil will never leave that person's house; that is, his family. Solomon himself came from just such a family. David killed the devoted Uriah and took Uriah's wife, Bathsheba, for himself. Solomon was the son of this union. Because of his sin, God told David, "The sword will never depart from your house" (2 Samuel 12:10).

164

Proverbs 17:16-24

All it takes is a little hole in a dam and the whole structure eventually begins to crumble. When someone is upset, all it takes is one little word to set off a quarrel. Be sensitive, says Solomon. Don't start the argument; you might start more than you can handle. A dam that has burst has tremendous force.

So often the innocent little guy seems to lose out, while the criminal who can hire the best lawyers gets away with murder. The famous lawyer Clarence Darrow remarked, "There is no such thing as justice—in or out of court." So it often appears. But God takes note and does not forget.

The language in these five verses has been strong—a merciless official, a bear robbed of her cubs, a bursting dam. Solomon has not minced words in describing evil and its consequences.

The mind of a fool

¹⁶ **Of what use is money in the hand of a fool,**
since he has no desire to get wisdom?

¹⁷ **A friend loves at all times,**
and a brother is born for adversity.

¹⁸ **A man lacking in judgment strikes hands in pledge**
and puts up security for his neighbor.

¹⁹ **He who loves a quarrel loves sin;**
he who builds a high gate invites destruction.

²⁰ **A man of perverse heart does not prosper;**
he whose tongue is deceitful falls into trouble.

²¹ **To have a fool for a son brings grief;**
there is no joy for the father of a fool.

²² **A cheerful heart is good medicine,**
but a crushed spirit dries up the bones.

²³ **A wicked man accepts a bribe in secret**
to pervert the course of justice.

Proverbs 17:16-24

**²⁴ A discerning man keeps wisdom in view,
but a fool's eyes wander to the ends of the earth.**

The idea behind verse 16 seems to be that even if a fool could buy wisdom (or pay for schooling), it wouldn't do him any good. He lacks the qualities necessary to make good use of wisdom. Those qualities would include such virtues as self-control and patience. First the fool must have a changed heart. Only then is he ready to learn.

The thought in verse 17 is that true friends and brothers are there to help at *all* times. They are not mere fair-weather friends. The verse is short, the thought simple. But this little proverb has a special brilliance, as it points to one of life's rarest and most excellent gifts.

While a true friend or brother is always there, we ought not try to take advantage of others. Verse 18 describes a situation in which one neighbor asks another to back him in some financial endeavor. Solomon dealt with this at length back in 6:1-5. His advice there was the same: Turn down such requests. Don't get involved.

A hot-tempered person falls into many sins. The connection between loving to quarrel and sin is close (verse 19, see also 29:22). Building a high gate alludes to being proud. It's akin to our trying to "keep up with the Joneses." If the neighbor has a gate in front of his house, we'll build a higher one. Although aimed toward self-aggrandizement, this attitude eventually leads to abasement. Once again, "Pride goes before destruction" (16:18).

Here again (verse 20), as so often in the middle of a grouping of proverbs, Solomon draws our attention to the heart—the inner center of emotions, thought, and spiritual life. While people with perverse or wicked hearts might prosper in this life, they do not enjoy God's spiritual bless-

Proverbs 17:16-24

ings. When they vent their twisted ideas in speech, it will lead them into trouble.

Verse 21 expresses the hard reality that children can grieve their parents. After they've done all they are able to, parents need to recognize that children can go off in their own direction. Sometimes it's a phase children go through; sometimes it lasts longer. Obviously, Solomon is speaking of good parents. If they were not good, they would not be grieved by their children's sinful behavior. They probably wouldn't care.

For godly parents to see a child go astray is perhaps the closest human beings come to knowing how our heavenly Father grieves over our rebelliousness. In love, he sent his Son to save us. In love, parents keep praying for that wayward child.

In verse 22 we see how the inner life affects us physically. David expressed how grief drains one of strength, when he wrote, "When I kept silent, my bones wasted away through my groaning all day long" (Psalm 32:3). "A crushed spirit"—whether it be crushed because of unacknowledged sin, pent-up grief, or anger—is debilitating. Long before the advent of modern psychology with its insights into the emotions, the Bible spoke of depression.

In contrast to a crushed spirit, joy invigorates. From Christ, the Great Physician, we have the medicine of forgiveness and peace with God. And the best part is, it's free!

These truths should alert us to the importance of being able to share our griefs and joys with fellow Christians. We need to share our griefs and joys, so that we can uplift and strengthen one another. The Bible urges us, "Rejoice with those who rejoice; mourn with those who mourn" (Romans 12:15).

In contrast to real concern, we see the man who tries to bribe others to win them over (verse 23). Motives are impor-

Proverbs 17:25

tant in gift giving. If the motive is to win favor or to pervert justice, then the gift becomes a bribe. (See also verse 8.)

One of the cardinal rules in sports is to keep your eye on the ball. That's so basic, and yet, in the heat of a game, it's easily forgotten. In life it is imperative that we keep focused (verse 24). The fool's eyes wander in every direction. "He is a double-minded man, unstable in all he does" (James 1:8). We need to keep our eyes, our attention, on our families, our marriages, our work, and, above all, on the Lord. Amid the heated trials of life, we easily turn our eyes away from where they need to be focused. When we do, we become fools. The writer to the Hebrews says, "Let us fix our eyes on Jesus, the author and perfecter of our faith" (12:2).

That's being the "discerning man," who "keeps wisdom in view." That's keeping our eyes on the ball.

A foolish son

²⁵ **A foolish son brings grief to his father
and bitterness to the one who bore him.**

This verse reiterates verse 21. Here both parents are more specifically designated, "the one who bore him" of course being the mother. The word "bitterness" is related to the word used in Exodus 15:23. As the Israelites traveled in the desert, "when they came to Marah, they could not drink its water because it was bitter. (That is why the place is called Marah.)" Bitterness spoils the taste of food or drink, and bitterness in life takes away all joy.

With a terse proverb, Solomon captures the heartache of many a parent. After Solomon's death, his own son Rehoboam was to bring bitterness and ruin to the kingdom of Solomon.

Amid life's bitter experiences, however, we can always find sweet joy in the unfailing love of our Savior.

Proverbs 17:28

Self-control

> ²⁶ **It is not good to punish an innocent man,**
> **or to flog officials for their integrity.**

> ²⁷ **A man of knowledge uses words with restraint,**
> **and a man of understanding is even-tempered.**

In verse 26 Solomon presents another of life's cruel twists, as he has done so frequently in the proverbs of this present chapter. Verse 15 expressed similar thoughts.

God's law called for beating, with up to 40 lashes, the guilty man in a dispute (Deuteronomy 25:2,3). But the wicked have often overturned justice so that good people are unfairly and cruelly punished. The book of Jeremiah records how the prophet Jeremiah was beaten and put in stocks (20:2). The gospels relate how Pontius Pilate released the "notorious prisoner" Barabbas and "had Jesus flogged" (Matthew 27:15-26).

Over against such injustice, Solomon describes the man of restraint and understanding. He is not quick to accuse others. His self-control is poles apart from the unbridled injustice of the previous verse. By placing such sharp distinctions side by side, Solomon skillfully portrays life in our fallen world. Amid all the injustice, we are to stand for what is God pleasing. In a world of darkness, Christians are the light of the world (Matthew 5:14-16).

About fools

> ²⁸ **Even a fool is thought wise if he keeps silent,**
> **and discerning if he holds his tongue.**

This is a commonly expressed thought, often with a touch of humor. As long as we keep silent, people don't know just how ignorant or foolish we really are. But there's more involved here than pulling the wool over people's eyes, until one finally opens his mouth and they see the truth. By taking

Proverbs 18:3-5

time to listen to others, the fool is taking the first steps toward ceasing to be a fool.

As the "man of knowledge uses words with restraint" (verse 27), so the road toward wisdom starts with less talking and more listening. Above all, listen to God's Word. Fear him; stand in awe of him. After a while, people won't just think you are wise—you'll actually be wise!

18 **An unfriendly man pursues selfish ends;
he defies all sound judgment.**

**² A fool finds no pleasure in understanding
but delights in airing his own opinions.**

The loner cuts himself off from communication with others. He has no access to their sound judgment, as he pursues his selfish ends. Consequently, he goes against the best interests of the majority and defies sound judgment. We might apply this to church life, in which we often see the sorry end of those who go it alone, without the fellowship of the rest of the congregation.

The fool also engages in another form of antisocial behavior. He doesn't physically cut himself off from others. Yet he cuts off communication by his unwillingness to listen. All he cares about is airing his ideas. We know this person. (Perhaps at times we've been this person!) Sometimes his opinions are pretty good; sometimes they are weird. In either case, we get to hear his opinions—and no one else's!

A reminder might be in place here—when we use the generic *he,* unless the context dictates otherwise, it applies to both sexes. Foolishness is not limited to the male gender, any more than wisdom is.

Aspects of wickedness

³ When wickedness comes, so does contempt,

Proverbs 18:6-8

and with shame comes disgrace.

**⁴ The words of a man's mouth are deep waters,
but the fountain of wisdom is a bubbling brook.**

**⁵ It is not good to be partial to the wicked
or to deprive the innocent of justice.**

Wickedness is never alone. Wherever it goes, contempt follows. Shame and disgrace are right there too. Actually all three words are synonyms. When Adam and Eve fell into sin, the first consequence was that they felt shame. (See Genesis 3:6-11.) We all live with a sense of shame, even as our consciences tell us we are sinners. Only in Christ is there release from this and sin's other results.

Most of the time we talk in "small talk." Far beneath the surface run our real thoughts and feelings, which can only be drawn out with difficulty. The wise man is able to express those words and to draw them out from others. In this way wisdom is a "bubbling brook" coming to the surface.

It's wrong to be partial to the rich. (See the comments on Proverbs 22:2.) It is also wrong to be partial to the wicked, whether out of fear or some other self-serving motive.

Rather than constantly calculating what we do and who's involved and what might happen, wisdom teaches us simply to do God's will and establish justice. And let the chips fall where they may.

A fool's mouth

**⁶ A fool's lips bring him strife,
and his mouth invites a beating.**

**⁷ A fool's mouth is his undoing,
and his lips are a snare to his soul.**

**⁸ The words of a gossip are like choice morsels;
they go down to a man's inmost parts.**

The fool in his stupidity, like the mocker in his wickedness

Proverbs 18:10,11

(22:10), gets into trouble when he opens his mouth. Without even being aware of it, he's asking for a beating. More than that, his mouth brings about his ruin. He can't speak wisely since he is not wise.

Most of us find gossip a temptation, perhaps more as receivers than as spreaders of it. That's because words of gossip are "like choice morsels." A juicy bit of gossip goes down easily. We enjoy it, because it makes us feel superior to the person who is the object of the gossip.

But gossip always has three victims: the one spoken about, the one speaking, and the one spoken to. And as delicious as it might be, the Bible strongly condemns gossip. It puts gossips in the same class as "God-haters" (Romans 1:29,30).

Gossip calls not for listening ears but for correction and repentance.

Laziness

> ⁹ **One who is slack in his work**
> **is brother to one who destroys.**

Just as gossip is a more serious sin than we might like to think, so is slothfulness. The lazy person is a brother to the destroyer. The one destroys property quickly by plundering and burning it. The other destroys more slowly by letting things fall apart.

Two types of safety

> ¹⁰ **The name of the LORD is a strong tower;**
> **the righteous run to it and are safe.**
> ¹¹ **The wealth of the rich is their fortified city;**
> **they imagine it an unscalable wall.**

This pair of verses speaks of true security. Where can we find it? Many mistakenly suppose they can find it in military

Proverbs 18:12-16

strength. "Some trust in chariots and some in horses," wrote the psalmist, "but we trust in the name of the LORD our God" (20:7).

Solomon addresses another form of false security— riches. When he speaks of "the rich," most of us could apply that word to ourselves. We enjoy a standard of living that most of the world's population only dreams of. And we have refined financial planning to a science. We have our Social Security programs, pension plans, life insurance, tax sheltered annuities, individual retirement accounts, the stock market, mutual funds. The list goes on.

If we trust in this kind of thing as our "fortified city," our imaginations have gotten the best of us. What good is any of that when we stand naked before our Maker?

God is our "strong tower." He is "our refuge and strength, an ever-present help in trouble" (Psalm 46:1). He saves us from sin, death, and damnation.

Human attitudes

¹² **Before his downfall a man's heart is proud,**
   but humility comes before honor.

¹³ **He who answers before listening—**
   that is his folly and his shame.

¹⁴ **A man's spirit sustains him in sickness,**
   but a crushed spirit who can bear?

¹⁵ **The heart of the discerning acquires knowledge;**
   the ears of the wise seek it out.

¹⁶ **A gift opens the way for the giver**
   and ushers him into the presence of the great.

The first line of verse 12 reflects Proverbs 16:18. The word "heart," or "hearts," occurs almost one hundred times in Proverbs, indicating how often Solomon directs our atten-

173

Proverbs 18:12-16

tion to the inner life. What's in our hearts influences our outward behavior. But God looks straight past the outward appearance and into the heart (see 1 Samuel 16:7).

When he sees a proud heart, he sees a heart that is not right. It is a heart that trusts not in its Maker but in itself. God brings down the person with a proud heart. The humble, however, recognize their unworthiness before God and ask his forgiveness. God honors the humble heart.

Did you ever find yourself so busy thinking about what you would say when the other person finished speaking, that you weren't even listening? It happens to all of us. But it's foolish and we should be ashamed of it. We all can work at being better listeners.

"Spirit" in verse 14 includes willpower and determination. The will to live enables people to come through severe physical hardships. But when the spirit is broken, the will to live goes too. May God grant us the "fighting" spirit of Saint Paul. He longed to be with the Lord. But if it was God's will for him to remain in this world and do more work, then he would give his all:

> I am torn between the two: I desire to depart and be with Christ, which is better by far; but it is more necessary for you that I remain in the body. Convinced of this, I know that I will remain, and I will continue with all of you for your progress and joy in the faith. (Philippians 1:23-25)

Oh, how the wise love to learn (verse 15)! With their ears they listen attentively to God's Word. Then they let it sink deeply into their hearts. Let us pray that we may never lose our love for hearing God's Word and taking it to heart.

In verse 16 we have another statement that describes life as it is in this world. The "gift" here looks pretty much like

Proverbs 18:17-19

a bribe. If the only way to get into the presence of "the great" is through gifts, then maybe the great aren't so great after all.

Lest we become cynical about all gift giving, however, the Bible certainly doesn't condemn it. The very center of Scripture is God's great gift to the world, the Savior. In Christlike love God's people gladly give to others. While such generosity may eventually lead one into the society of great people, that is not the Christian's motivation. Rather, we give as God has given us.

Contentions

¹⁷ **The first to present his case seems right,**
till another comes forward and questions him.

¹⁸ **Casting the lot settles disputes**
and keeps strong opponents apart.

¹⁹ **An offended brother is more unyielding than**
a fortified city,
and disputes are like the barred gates of a citadel.

We shouldn't form hasty opinions. Jumping to conclusions before hearing the entire case is similar to speaking before listening (see verse 13). If we only hear one side of the case, we might come to the wrong conclusion.

When Jesus was crucified, the Roman soldiers cast lots for his clothing (John 19:23,24). This was a common method of settling disputes among the ancients. Today we might flip a coin. The point is that we can agree on a way to come to terms, short of heated arguments and all-out battles.

We need to realize that when Solomon tells us to settle disputes, he is not calling on us to compromise the truth. He is speaking of areas in which there is room for give and take. "If it is possible, as far as it depends on you, live at

Proverbs 18:20,21

peace with everyone" (Romans 12:18).

Although invisible, the walls we build between one another are as formidable as a "fortified city" or the "barred gates of a citadel." That's why we ought to settle disagreements before walls are built. Try to work things out before a day goes by.

Some of the deepest and longest lasting arguments develop between brothers or other close relatives. Because he received the blessing Esau expected, Jacob had to flee for his life from his brother, Esau, and for many years there was no reconciliation. "Esau held a grudge against Jacob because of the blessing his father had given him" (Genesis 27:41).

Happily, the two finally did reconcile. This is God's will, as he says, "How good and pleasant it is when brothers live together in unity!" (Psalm 133:1). God desires us to live in peace.

Talking

20 From the fruit of his mouth a man's stomach is filled; with the harvest from his lips he is satisfied.

21 The tongue has the power of life and death, and those who love it will eat its fruit.

Verse 20 is a colorful way of saying that we reap the rewards or punishments of what we say. Our speech is likened to a farmer planting crops. Whenever we speak, we are planting. The hundreds and thousands of words that go out of our mouths each day are like seeds. Later we will reap the harvest and have to eat the fruit.

Maybe we should examine our own speech. Are we planting positive, loving words? or sarcasm and cutting words? Are we sowing kindness? or bitterness?

In verse 21 the sage emphasizes the positive fruit of speech. The tongue has tremendous power. When we share

176

Proverbs 18:22-24

the gospel of Christ, for example, we are planting seeds that spring up to life eternal. With God's help, may our speech produce life-giving fruit.

Companions

> [22] **He who finds a wife finds what is good**
> **and receives favor from the LORD.**
>
> [23] **A poor man pleads for mercy,**
> **but a rich man answers harshly.**
>
> [24] **A man of many companions may come to ruin,**
> **but there is a friend who sticks closer than a brother.**

Although he does not explicitly say it, the context makes it clear that Solomon is speaking of a *good* wife here. He reminds us what a blessing she is. She is a life-long companion, a lover, a mother. Elsewhere, Solomon discusses the tragedy of an unhappy marriage (12:4; 19:13; 21:9). The last chapter of Proverbs offers a detailed description of the ideal wife (31:10-31).

In contrast to the happily married man is the poor man who receives harsh treatment from the rich. The placement of this harsh reality between the description of two blessings—a wife and a close friend—shows life as it is. Side by side we see misery and joy.

We will recognize life's joys as gifts from God. Moreover, we will see the sorrows all around us as opportunities to reach out to the needy with a Christlike love.

If our friends are shallow friends, they aren't going to be around when we really need them. One true, devoted friend is more valuable than many superficial friends. That true friend is even closer than a brother. The word translated "a friend" is, literally, "one who loves." We could translate it as "a loving friend."

Such a friend, like a loving spouse, is a special blessing

Proverbs 19:1-4

from above. In choosing friends or a spouse, we need to pray for God's guidance. When we find them, we have reason to be very thankful.

Poverty and knowledge; poverty and wealth

19 **Better a poor man whose walk is blameless
than a fool whose lips are perverse.**

² **It is not good to have zeal without knowledge,
nor to be hasty and miss the way.**

³ **A man's own folly ruins his life,
yet his heart rages against the LORD.**

⁴ **Wealth brings many friends,
but a poor man's friend deserts him.**

Remember that when the Bible's wisdom literature speaks of the fool, it does not necessarily mean a person of lower intelligence. Rather, it refers to the moral and spiritual condition of one who rejects God. Given this, fools often get ahead in the world. Even if a fool becomes rich through lying and deceit—which is what verse 1 implies—a poor man who trusts in the Lord is still better off than the fool is.

All the emotion and energy in the world can't make up for a lack of knowledge (verse 2). Paul lamented the condition of his fellow Jews: "They are zealous for God, but their zeal is not based on knowledge. . . . They did not know the righteousness that comes from God [through Christ] and sought to establish their own" (Romans 10:2,3). In spiritual matters and in every area of life, before we throw ourselves into something, it's best to know which way we're headed.

The reality expressed in verse 3 is all too common. We human beings make a mess of things, and then we blame God! James wrote: "When tempted, no one should say, 'God is tempting me.' . . . But each one is tempted when, by his own evil desire, he is dragged away and enticed" (1:13,14).

Proverbs 19:5-9

Picking up the pieces of a ruined life begins with the humble recognition that it's our own fault and that we need God's forgiveness and help.

Another sinful reality of life is that money can and does buy friends. When the money is gone, so are the friends. Aware of this, we will want to follow the words of our Savior, rather than the ways of the world. Jesus said, "It is more blessed to give than to receive" (Acts 20:35). More important than what we can get out of others is what we can bring to them.

Deception

⁵ A false witness will not go unpunished,
and he who pours out lies will not go free.

⁶ Many curry favor with a ruler,
and everyone is the friend of a man who gives gifts.

⁷ A poor man is shunned by all his relatives—
how much more do his friends avoid him!
Though he pursues them with pleading,
they are nowhere to be found.

⁸ He who gets wisdom loves his own soul;
he who cherishes understanding prospers.

⁹ A false witness will not go unpunished,
and he who pours out lies will perish.

Verses 5 and 9 are almost identical. The former says that the false witness "will not go free"—that is, he won't escape judgment. The latter says that he "will perish"—that is, will be punished. In both cases, it ultimately comes down to the judgment of God, since in this world perjurers often seem to get away with it. We think of the false witnesses against Naboth (1 Kings 21) and against our Savior (Matthew 26:59-63).

Verses 6 and 7 bring up a subject that Solomon deals

Proverbs 19:10-12

with a number of times, the connection between wealth and friendship and poverty and loneliness. A powerful ruler and someone who can dole out gifts have many "friends." On the other hand, even the family of a poor man shuns him.

If a poor man's own relatives avoid him, how much more will his "friends"! He can go running after them, but they want nothing to do with him. The line between being popular and unpopular in the world is often the same line that separates the rich from the poor.

In spite of this, remember what Solomon said in verse 1, that a poor but upright man is better off than a rich fool. Material poverty is miserable but not as bad as spiritual bankruptcy.

Moreover, given that worldly friendships are no more stable than one's investments in the stock market, many a rich person must feel more than a slight sense of insecurity.

To love godly wisdom (verse 8) is to love one's own soul. We can find a deep and lasting satisfaction in God's Word. This kind of prosperity stands in sharp contrast to the shaky grounds of relying on money and the things that money can buy.

Being near the fool, the wise person, and the king

**¹⁰ It is not fitting for a fool to live in luxury—
   how much worse for a slave to rule over princes!**

**¹¹ A man's wisdom gives him patience;
   it is to his glory to overlook an offense.**

**¹² A king's rage is like the roar of a lion,
   but his favor is like dew on the grass.**

The reason that it's "not fitting for a fool to live in luxury" is that it may confirm him in his foolishness. If his foolishness rewards him with a life of ease, why shouldn't he continue to pursue that lifestyle? When one considers the lives of the rich

Proverbs 19:13,14

and famous, that is often exactly what happens.

When a slave gains power, it often leads to injustice. Filled with resentment, the former slave becomes a tyrant. When the czar lost power in Russia and the Communists took over, instead of uplifting the people, they made things even worse.

Patience (verse 11) is part of "the fruit of the Spirit" (Galatians 5:22,23). Patience will lead us to overlook offenses against us. There are times when Christian concern compels us to go and speak to the brother who "sins against you" (Matthew 18:15). Yet if we were to follow through on every offense that comes along, we'd have time for nothing else. It is the natural, sinful thing to store up these offenses in feelings of resentment that eventually break forth into angry outbursts. It is the godly, glorious thing to overlook them.

As we know, a raging lion (verse 12) can tear us apart. Such is the power of earthly rulers against those who rebel. The Lord, our heavenly King, likened himself to a lion raging against his rebellious people: "I will be like a lion to Ephraim, like a great lion to Judah. I will tear them to pieces" (Hosea 5:14). Yet, when a ruler shows favor, he can be as soft and gentle as the dew. Similarly, the Lord in his grace is like life-giving dew: "I will heal their waywardness and love them freely, for my anger has turned away from them. I will be like the dew" (Hosea 14:4,5).

As citizens of an earthly government, we will seek to be good citizens, enjoying our rulers' favor. As citizens of a heavenly kingdom, we will thank God for his gracious favor, though we have deserved his wrath.

Home life
¹³ A foolish son is his father's ruin,

Proverbs 19:15,16

and a quarrelsome wife is like a constant dripping.
¹⁴ Houses and wealth are inherited from parents,
but a prudent wife is from the LORD.

Family relations can be the source of life's greatest joy
. . . or life's greatest miseries. Several proverbs speak of
the grief that a foolish son brings to parents. The first
proverb in this large collection of Solomon's proverbs
deals with the topic (10:1).

A quarrelsome wife is another source of grief. An old
Arab proverb says that three things make a house intolerable: the leaking through of rain (*altakk*), the contention of
a wife (*alnakk*), and bugs (*albakk*). Her constant quarreling is like a leaky roof or a dripping faucet.

While we inherit material wealth from our parents, to
have a good wife is a gift from the Lord. It is not mere "luck."
Those who are not yet married should look beyond outward
appearances as they carefully and prayerfully choose godly
spouses. Those who are married will want to seek the guidance of God's Word in becoming better spouses.

In the case of both the child and the spouse, Solomon
does not say that the situation can't be changed. By God's
power, foolish sons and quarrelsome wives have been trans-
formed into dutiful sons and loving wives.

Proverbs directs most of its attention to fathers, husbands, and sons. As heads of households and future leaders
in ancient Israel, males received the focus of this piece of
wisdom literature. We must remember, of course, that much
of what Solomon says applies to both sexes. Husbands, just
as much as wives, can be quarrelsome; they too need God's
guidance and correctives.

Laziness and life
¹⁵ Laziness brings on deep sleep,

Proverbs 19:17-22

and the shiftless man goes hungry.

**¹⁶ He who obeys instructions guards his life,
but he who is contemptuous of his ways will die.**

One commentator labels verse 15 "the creeping spread of sloth." Laziness breeds more laziness. Perhaps you've had it happen on occasion that you've gotten more sleep than usual and still feel tired. With the sluggard, inactivity becomes habitual. As time goes by, the habit becomes more difficult to break. Eventually it will lead to hunger. Perhaps that will drive the sluggard to work, since nothing else has done it.

"Do your own thing!" we're told. That's the modern way. The old way of God's wisdom says, "Do God's thing!" The "instructions" of verse 16 are, literally, "commands," or "laws"—that is, the law of God. We are to follow him and not be "contemptuous of his ways." ("His" again refers to God.)

Many have found to their sorrow that following their own way does not lead to fulfillment. It brings frustration, takes one away from God, and ultimately leads to eternal death. The only safe way through life is to listen to God's Word and in faith "do what it says" (James 1:22).

Good advice

**¹⁷ He who is kind to the poor lends to the Lord,
and he will reward him for what he has done.**

**¹⁸ Discipline your son, for in that there is hope;
do not be a willing party to his death.**

**¹⁹ A hot-tempered man must pay the penalty;
if you rescue him, you will have to do it again.**

**²⁰ Listen to advice and accept instruction,
and in the end you will be wise.**

**²¹ Many are the plans in a man's heart,
but it is the Lord's purpose that prevails.**

²² What a man desires is unfailing love;

Proverbs 19:17-22

better to be poor than a liar.

When we lend to people, we expect they will pay us back. God says we can lend to him. We do this by being kind to the poor. Whatever we give to those in need, God considers as something we have lent to him. Although the poor can't pay us back, the Lord will. Jesus put it this way:

> When you give a luncheon or dinner, do not invite your friends, your brothers or relatives, or your rich neighbors; if you do, they may invite you back and so you will be repaid. But when you give a banquet, invite the poor, the crippled, the lame, the blind, and you will be blessed. Although they cannot repay you, you will be repaid at the resurrection of the righteous. (Luke 14:12-14)

Verse 18 urges parents not to give up disciplining their children. If a child is difficult, there still is hope for correction as long as you continue to apply firm discipline. The second line of this verse lends itself to two understandings: (1) don't overdo the physical discipline and beat your child to death; (2) don't underdo it and contribute to the child's self-destruction through an undisciplined life. Either fits the wording, and both fit with biblical teaching. Firm and loving discipline is the way to go. As Luther put it, keep the apple next to the rod.

A hot-tempered person (verse 19) has a way of getting into hot water over and over again. You can help him or her out of it, but be prepared to do it again. Rather than continually dealing with the symptom, it's better to help cure the disease. It's a matter of getting the heart right with God—confessing sins and asking forgiveness in Jesus' name. Once we work on the heart, then we can start to think about changing the behavior.

Verse 20 is a quick reminder that Proverbs and all other divine advice will do no good unless we *listen* to it and *accept* it.

We make many plans, but God decides what will happen (verse 21). That's why, when we plan, it's always wise to consult God's Word, seek the advice of trusted Christian friends, and offer the prayer that God's will be done. Then we can be sure that however our plans turn out, it is for the best.

At first glance, the two lines of verse 22 may not seem to fit together. Upon closer reflection the connection becomes clearer. We all have a yearning for love that won't let us down. A deceitful friend or spouse might pretend to love us, only to leave us in the lurch. It's better to be steadfast in love and poor than to be rich and unfaithful. Moreover, a wealthy person might wonder if others are loyal to him only because they're interested in his money.

No matter how good a relationship might be, no human being is perfect in "unfailing love." Only God gives us that kind of love. There is no pretense to his love, for we have done nothing to deserve it. Yet he declares, "I have loved you with an everlasting love" (Jeremiah 31:3). He has demonstrated his perfect love in sending his Son to be our Savior.

Contrasting harm and benefit

[23] **The fear of the LORD leads to life:**
Then one rests content, untouched by trouble.

[24] **The sluggard buries his hand in the dish;**
he will not even bring it back to his mouth!

[25] **Flog a mocker, and the simple will learn prudence;**
rebuke a discerning man, and he will gain knowledge.

The fear of the Lord brings fullness of life in this world and everlasting life in the world to come. When the Lord also promises that we will be untouched by harm, he is not saying that we will never suffer. We know that's not the case. But he does promise to deliver us from anything that will harm us spiritually, and he uses life's sufferings for our

Proverbs 19:26,27

eternal good.

Verse 24 blends a touch of humor with sarcasm. We can imagine a person becoming so lazy that it's too much effort for him to lift his hand from the plate to his mouth. The humor in verse 24 only serves to underscore the seriousness of the sin of sloth.

Proverbs frequently mentions various types of fools and evil people—the simple, the fool, the mocker, the wicked. Verse 25 indicates that a mocker is more hardened than the simple. In observing the hardened mocker being flogged, the simple might gain some understanding—namely, that evil results in punishment. The wise person doesn't need such a harsh object lesson. A word of rebuke is enough for him.

In society, schools, the church, and the home, there are many types of people at various levels of understanding. Wise parents, teachers, and leaders recognize this and make the proper application to each situation.

A foolish son

**²⁶ He who robs his father and drives out his mother
is a son who brings shame and disgrace.**

**²⁷ Stop listening to instruction, my son,
and you will stray from the words of knowledge.**

Who would think of robbing one's own father and driving out his mother? There are those who actually assault and "kill their fathers or mothers" (1 Timothy 1:9). We read about it in the papers from time to time. There are other, less crass ways of mistreating our parents. Neglect, indifference, and taking advantage of them without giving in return are more subtle ways. Christians will seek to follow the Fourth Commandment: "Honor your father and your mother" (Exodus 20:12).

Learning is an ongoing process. We need to feed on

Proverbs 20:1-8

God's Word regularly, just as we daily need to eat food to stay alive. When we begin to stay away from public worship and avoid reading the Bible, we are bound to stray.

Mockers

> ²⁸ **A corrupt witness mocks at justice,**
> **and the mouth of the wicked gulps down evil.**
>
> ²⁹ **Penalties are prepared for mockers,**
> **and beatings for the backs of fools.**

Verse 28 is interesting in that it pictures evil both as coming out of the mouth and being taken in through the mouth. Anyone who is a false witness makes a mockery of justice; evil in the form of lies is coming from that person's mouth.

In another sense, those who take in a steady diet of wickedness through what they see and read and hear are drinking in wickedness. In the book of Job, Eliphaz pictures a wicked man as one "who drinks up evil like water" (15:16).

The wicked, then, are pictured in this terrible way, as people who have a steady flow of wickedness coming in and going out of them.

With some people, says Solomon, instruction simply does not sink in. Penalties and beatings might be the only way to get through. In a day when physical punishment is frowned on, Solomon's words strike us as harsh. Nevertheless, we live in a very sinful world, and some people do become hardened in wickedness. They may require harsh measures to counter their wickedness.

It is also true, however, that God's law and gospel can break through and change even the hearts of mockers and fools.

From a king's point of view

Proverbs 20:1-8

20
Wine is a mocker and beer a brawler;
   whoever is led astray by them is not wise.
² A king's wrath is like the roar of a lion;
   he who angers him forfeits his life.

³ It is to a man's honor to avoid strife,
   but every fool is quick to quarrel.

⁴ A sluggard does not plow in season;
   so at harvest time he looks but finds nothing.

⁵ The purposes of a man's heart are deep waters,
   but a man of understanding draws them out.

⁶ Many a man claims to have unfailing love,
   but a faithful man who can find?

⁷ The righteous man leads a blameless life;
   blessed are his children after him.

⁸ When a king sits on his throne to judge,
   he winnows out all evil with his eyes.

The overuse of wine and other alcoholic drinks is a terrible problem today, as is the abuse of drugs. Is complete abstinence the answer? Proverbs gives the wisest answer: we may drink, but not to the point of being "led astray." Jesus himself drank wine, and Paul urged Timothy, "Stop drinking only water, and use a little wine because of your stomach and your frequent illnesses" (1 Timothy 5:23). But used to excess, alcohol will dull one's moral sensitivity, making him into a mocker, a brawler, and a fool. In calling wine and beer a mocker and brawler, Solomon attributes to the drinks the effects they have on the drinker.

Several proverbs broach the subject of the "king's wrath" (verse 2). (See, for example, 16:14.) In ancient times a king could issue the death sentence for the slightest provocation. Tactful speech was a must in the presence of royalty. Today's monarchs don't hold that kind of life-and-death power, although rulers in some totalitarian countries still have it. Yet the principle remains that God our heavenly

Proverbs 20:1-8

King wants us to respect those in authority.

Only a foolish person would get into an argument with a king. But whether dealing with kings or not, fools of all times have the tendency to be quick to quarrel. A man of honor will seek to avoid strife—not out of cowardice but out of a godly desire for peace.

Jesus teaches us, "Do not worry about tomorrow" (Matthew 6:34). That does not mean, "Do not plan for tomorrow." The sluggard is too lazy to plow his fields and plant them (verse 4). When the time for harvesting comes, he has nothing. Working and saving money for retirement or for our children's education can be God-pleasing endeavors. In a word, do your work today, get ready for the future, and then leave it all in the hands of God.

Proverbs 18:4 used the metaphor of "deep waters." We find the expression again in verse 5. Many human emotions and thoughts lie deep within the heart. A man of understanding knows human nature well enough that he can draw out from people these "deep waters." Much of modern psychology has focused its attention on just this endeavor. Wise men of all ages have studied and delved into man's inner life. Only the all-knowing God sees everything. He alone sees to the bottom of the waters.

Many a young lover promises eternal love. Many a friend says, "I'll be there if you need me." But time goes by and the lover finds another, or the friend is too busy. So Solomon asks, "A faithful man who can find?" In seeking companions, we will ask God's help. He can bring that rare person into our lives. Until he does, and afterward, we can be sure we have the most faithful friend of all—the Lord himself.

We've seen much in Proverbs about wise and foolish sons and about the importance of parental discipline. Verse 7 adds another dimension to parent-child relationships—that of

Proverbs 20:9-13

example. Words, correction, and discipline are important. But none of that will matter if parents don't follow their own advice. Actions speak louder than words is a cliché, but that doesn't make it any less true. Children who can observe their parents teaching *and living* Christian lives are doubly blessed.

As in Bible times, in the Middle East today, farmers separate the good grain from the worthless husks, or chaff, by winnowing. This involves using a pitchfork to throw the threshed grain into the air so that the light chaff blows away, while the heavier grain falls straight down. Verse 8 speaks of a discerning king, who watches his kingdom and can judge between the good and the evil there. King Solomon himself was known for his wisdom in judging cases brought before him. (See 1 Kings 3:16-28.)

The almighty King also watches and judges. Speaking of Jesus, John the Baptist declared, "His winnowing fork is in his hand to clear his threshing floor and to gather the wheat into his barn, but he will burn up the chaff with unquenchable fire" (Luke 3:17). None escapes the eye of this King, who judges all.

Inner aspects of life

9 **Who can say, "I have kept my heart pure;
I am clean and without sin"?**

10 **Differing weights and differing measures—
the LORD detests them both.**

11 **Even a child is known by his actions,
by whether his conduct is pure and right.**

12 **Ears that hear and eyes that see—
the LORD has made them both.**

13 **Do not love sleep or you will grow poor;
stay awake and you will have food to spare.**

No one can say, "I have kept my heart pure." As often

Proverbs 20:9-13

as he has pointed to the importance of proper motivation coming from the heart, Solomon must conclude that the heart is not pure and clean and without sin. The words of David are the Christian's constant prayer: "Create in me a pure heart, O God" (Psalm 51:10).

Because of Christ's sacrificial death on the cross, we can be sure that God answers that prayer. "The blood of Jesus, his Son, purifies us from all sin" (1 John 1:7). This is the center of all Bible teaching. To this great sacrifice, Old Testament believers looked forward in hope. And we New Testament believers look back with thanks.

"God is love" (1 John 4:16). That's a Bible truth we all love to hear. The other side of this truth is that God can also hate. Verse 10 mentions two practices that bring out his hatred—"differing weights and differing measures." Ancient merchants might have tampered with their weights, balances, and measures to cheat the buyer. Modern business-people might use more sophisticated means to juggle books and swindle the unsuspecting. What God hates is the sin behind such practices—dishonesty.

Already in childhood, we begin to reveal traits that remain distinguishing features of our personalities throughout life. Verse 11 says that, and more. Although they do not have an adult's understanding, children are moral creatures. They have consciences. They also are sinners, already from the time of conception and birth (Psalm 51:5). They too need the Savior, and by God's grace can believe and be saved.

All of our abilities are from God, our Maker. The Lord said to Moses: "Who gave man his mouth? Who makes him deaf or mute? Who gives him sight or makes him blind? Is it not I, the LORD?" (Exodus 4:11). Though we often take these gifts for granted, we should reflect on them and thank the Lord. We should also use whatever gifts we have

Proverbs 20:14-19

to his glory.

Verse 13 expresses a warning against sloth. It leads to poverty. Laziness is especially reprehensible if it affects not only oneself but his family as well: "If anyone does not provide for his relatives, and especially for his immediate family, he has denied the faith and is worse than an unbeliever" (1 Timothy 5:8).

The mouth in action

> 14 "It's no good, it's no good!" says the buyer;
>   then off he goes and boasts about his purchase.
>
> 15 Gold there is, and rubies in abundance,
>   but lips that speak knowledge are a rare jewel.
>
> 16 Take the garment of one who puts up security for
>   a stranger;
>   hold it in pledge if he does it for a wayward woman.
>
> 17 Food gained by fraud tastes sweet to a man,
>   but he ends up with a mouth full of gravel.
>
> 18 Make plans by seeking advice;
>   if you wage war, obtain guidance.
>
> 19 A gossip betrays a confidence;
>   so avoid a man who talks too much.

In the Near East, much shopping still involves bartering. The buyer offers a lower price than that which the seller is asking. "Why should I pay that much? This item isn't any good!" the buyer says. Once he gets the price down, he goes and tells his friends what a great deal he got! This practice illustrates the human desire to get the better of others. (Both buyer and seller are playing a game of wits.) The Lord doesn't say we can never barter for anything. But he does not want us to cheat or take unfair advantage of others.

One reason precious metals and jewels are so valuable is that they are so rare. They are also beautiful, and to give

"It's no good, it's no good!" says the buyer

Proverbs 20:14-19

them to another is a sign of love and friendship. Even more rare is a person who speaks with true knowledge. Just as there is dime store jewelry and fool's gold, there is a lot of talk that is not genuine. We can offer a priceless gift to others if we speak wisely and share the knowledge of salvation in Jesus Christ.

Verse 16 speaks of action against someone who has co-signed a loan for a stranger. Under Old Testament law, a person's garment could be taken as security (see Deuteronomy 24:10-13). The proverb says something like this: If someone is dumb enough to back a complete stranger on a loan, by all means take his garment. If he does it for a wayward woman, who is known to be untrustworthy, by all means hold onto that garment.

Verse 17 contrasts with 9:17. There, folly called out the bold lie, "Stolen water is sweet; food eaten in secret is delicious." While it may taste that way at first, forbidden fruit turns to gravel in the mouth. The food referred to here could be anything we have gotten through deceit. Initially, we might feel satisfaction in having gotten away with something. When we are found out, we'll live with remorse. And even if no human rebukes us for the sin, our consciences tell us that God has seen everything.

When we make plans, it's wise to seek the advice of others. For military leaders to wage war without consulting their advisors would be foolhardy. Jesus used a similar illustration: "Suppose a king is about to go to war against another king. Will he not first sit down and consider whether he is able with ten thousand men to oppose the one coming against him with twenty thousand?" (Luke 14:31). What applies for large-scale military operations applies to individuals as well. It makes good sense to plan and get advice.

Verse 19 is self-explanatory. If a gossip betrays the secrets

Proverbs 20:20-27

of others, he'll probably betray yours too. We might add—not only avoid a gossip but avoid *being* such a person yourself.

Good and bad judgment contrasted

²⁰ **If a man curses his father or mother,**
  his lamp will be snuffed out in pitch darkness.

²¹ **An inheritance quickly gained at the beginning**
  will not be blessed at the end.

²² **Do not say, "I'll pay you back for this wrong!"**
  Wait for the Lord, and he will deliver you.

²³ **The Lord detests differing weights,**
  and dishonest scales do not please him.

²⁴ **A man's steps are directed by the Lord.**
  How then can anyone understand his own way?

²⁵ **It is a trap for a man to dedicate something rashly**
  and only later to consider his vows.

²⁶ **A wise king winnows out the wicked;**
  he drives the threshing wheel over them.

²⁷ **The lamp of the Lord searches the spirit of a man;**
  it searches out his inmost being.

The laws that Israel received from God at Mount Sinai included the injunction, "Anyone who curses his father or mother must be put to death" (Exodus 21:17). The snuffing out of the lamp represents death. We tend to think that children owe parents respect only if the parents deserve it. (We feel the same about officials, church leaders, and others in authority.) The Bible, however, teaches that we owe some people honor simply because God has placed them over us and tells us to honor them.

When an inheritance is quickly gained (verse 21), it probably won't be appreciated. Jesus' parable of the lost son is a good example of this (Luke 15:11-32). The son wasted

Proverbs 20:20-27

his inheritance in wild living. Parents are not doing their children a favor by making things too easy for them. Valuable lessons in hard work, patience, and appreciation will not be learned. And "at the end," the inheritance won't bring the blessings that everyone had hoped it would.

Saint Paul's words to the Roman Christians expound on the thought of verse 22: "Do not repay anyone evil for evil. Be careful to do what is right in the eyes of everybody. If it is possible, as far as it depends on you, live at peace with everyone. Do not take revenge, my friends, but leave room for God's wrath, for it is written: 'It is mine to avenge; I will repay,' says the Lord" (Romans 12:17-19).

Even in religious matters, we sometimes think it is up to us to act as God's avengers. We must get the last ounce of punishment out of those who have done wrong. No, God calls on us to forgive. In his own good time, he will take revenge where necessary.

Verse 23 reiterates verse 10. That verse spoke of God detesting differing weights and measures. This one speaks of differing weights and dishonest scales. The sinful human heart is always looking for loopholes. In case anyone, after reading verse 10, was thinking, "Ah, but he didn't mention anything about scales!" God adds the other verse. The Lord does not give us a legal system so that we can play games trying to get around this or that rule. God calls for a loving attitude in the heart—an attitude that loathes the very idea of taking advantage of another, whether with weights, measures, scales, or any other means.

Verse 24 is quite profound. It reminds us that God is in control. We make our plans. We grope around trying to figure out which way to go. At times, we go against God's will. Meanwhile, behind the scenes, the Lord is working out his purposes.

He even uses the wickedness of men to serve his ends.

Proverbs 20:20-27

For example, Solomon's son Rehoboam did not listen to the people's complaints but went his own willful way. "The king [Rehoboam] did not listen to the people, for this turn of events was from the LORD, to fulfill the word the LORD had spoken" (1 Kings 12:15). God used the king's action to bring about what the Lord had promised to do.

The Lord knows what we are doing better than we ourselves do. And he directs our lives. For the believer this is a great source of faith and confidence.

Verse 25 warns against making rash vows. This is similar to what Solomon expounded on elsewhere:

> When you make a vow to God, do not delay in fulfilling it. He has no pleasure in fools; fulfill your vow. It is better not to vow than to make a vow and not fulfill it. Do not let your mouth lead you into sin. And do not protest to the temple messenger, "My vow was a mistake." Why should God be angry at what you say and destroy the work of your hands? (Ecclesiastes 5:4-6)

When we make promises, we should take them seriously. God does.

Verse 26 mentions the matter of winnowing out the wicked. We discussed this in verse 8. In verse 26 there is the added imagery of the threshing floor. In much threshing an ox would pull a heavy sled or wheel to crush the grain and break the kernels loose from the straw. After this was done, the grain was tossed into the air (winnowed) so that the chaff would blow away. Solomon uses this imagery to show how a good king crushes the wicked and gets rid of them like chaff. As we noted previously, it is a picture of divine judgment as well.

That God sees deep within us is the idea of verse 27. He knows everything about us. This often-repeated truth of

197

Proverbs 20:28-30

Proverbs is a reminder to the ungodly that they will not escape God's judgment. It is a comfort to God's people that he knows all our burdens and weaknesses and will be there to help.

Kings, good people, and evil people

**²⁸ Love and faithfulness keep a king safe;
through love his throne is made secure.**

**²⁹ The glory of young men is their strength,
gray hair the splendor of the old.**

**³⁰ Blows and wounds cleanse away evil,
and beatings purge the inmost being.**

One would think that a ruler secures his throne by might. Yet God says that love must be at the center of government. The more a king cares about his people, the more secure he will be.

Verse 29 declares that each age has its own glory. For the young it is their strength and energy; for the elderly it's their gray hair and the wisdom it represents. One of the tragedies of our day is that while the strength and glories of youth are extolled, the wisdom of old age is ignored or considered irrelevant.

Yet our greatest glory is not in our age and accomplishments but in the Lord. Through the prophet Jeremiah, God declares:

> This is what the LORD says: "Let not the wise man boast of his wisdom or the strong man boast of his strength or the rich man boast of his riches, but let him who boasts boast about this: that he understands and knows me, that I am the LORD, who exercises kindness, justice and righteousness on earth, for in these I delight," declares the LORD. (9:23,24)

Outward blows are able to drive away evil from within

Proverbs 21:1-8

(verse 30). By punishment at the hands of others, as well as by the blows that life itself inflicts, one can be humbled and mellowed. Yet the complete cleansing that we need from sin will never come from blows we receive. That must come completely from another source outside of us.

Only the sinless son of God, suffering in our place, could bring us that cleansing from sin. The prophet Isaiah said:

> Surely he took up our infirmities and carried our sorrows, yet we considered him stricken by God, smitten by him, and afflicted. But he was pierced for our transgressions, he was crushed for our iniquities; the punishment that brought us peace was upon him, and by his wounds we are healed. (Isaiah 53:4,5)

The ways of life

21 **The king's heart is in the hand of the LORD;**
       he directs it like a watercourse wherever he pleases.

² **All a man's ways seem right to him,**
    but the LORD weighs the heart.

³ **To do what is right and just**
    is more acceptable to the LORD than sacrifice.

⁴ **Haughty eyes and a proud heart,**
    the lamp of the wicked, are sin!

⁵ **The plans of the diligent lead to profit**
    as surely as haste leads to poverty.

⁶ **A fortune made by a lying tongue**
    is a fleeting vapor and a deadly snare.

⁷ **The violence of the wicked will drag them away,**
    for they refuse to do what is right.

⁸ **The way of the guilty is devious,**

Proverbs 21:1-8

but the conduct of the innocent is upright.

As the Lord controls nature with its rivers and streams, so he controls human affairs, including the dealings of mighty kings. The word "watercourse" could also refer to irrigation canals that farmers dig to control the flow of water into their fields. In that case, we would understand the proverb: As farmers control their irrigation channels, so God controls . . .

Through the Persian King Cyrus, God saw to it that his people Israel were returned to their homeland from their exile in Babylon. Through the Lord's planning, the Roman Emperor Caesar Augustus held a worldwide census, and Jesus was born in the town of Bethlehem, as God promised. Even the heathen King Nebuchadnezzar had to admit about the Lord Most High: "He does as he pleases with the powers of heaven and the peoples of the earth. No one can hold back his hand or say to him: 'What have you done?'" (Daniel 4:35).

It's not that the rulers of the world have consciously tried to follow God's plans. Rather, the omnipotent and omniscient Lord controls them for his eternal purposes.

Proverbs 16:2 is almost exactly the same as 21:2. The former spoke of motivation; this one speaks of the heart. By stating the same truth in slightly different wording, God brings home his teachings. On judgment day God "will bring to light what is hidden in darkness and will expose the motives of men's hearts" (1 Corinthians 4:5). He "weighs" the hearts, seeing whether they have faith or unbelief.

Verse 3 repeats almost verbatim the words of the prophet Samuel to Saul, the first king of Israel. Saul had disobeyed God and then tried to cover up by saying he was going to offer a sacrifice to the Lord (1 Samuel 15:22). The outward rite of sacrifice could not gloss over an unbelieving, disobedient heart. Similarly, for us to put large amounts

Proverbs 21:1-8

of money in the church offering plate will not be God pleasing, if we are living in unrepented sin.

In line with verse 4, Jesus said: "Your eye is the lamp of your body. When your eyes are good, your whole body also is full of light. But when they are bad, your body also is full of darkness. See to it, then, that the light within you is not darkness" (Luke 11:34,35).

The Bible seems to speak of the eyes as a lamp that shines two ways—both into the body and out from the body. If your spiritual eyes are bad, they are not bringing any light into one's soul. Moreover, if one is full of darkness inside, no light will shine out from the eyes. Haughty eyes (along with a sinful heart) indicate the darkness of sin within a person. To a degree, then, we can see into a person through his eyes.

Careful planning leads to success, while haste leads to mistakes and, as a result, to poverty (verse 5). Our saying, Haste makes waste, is similar to this proverb.

The term "fleeting vapor" (verse 6) refers to a breath, as when we see our breath on a cold day, and it quickly disappears. The fortune built through lies is just that solid! Not only that, but such a fortune is also a deadly snare. The dishonest person will get caught in the very lies he used to make himself rich.

Just as the lies of the deceitful eventually will come back to haunt them, so will violence turn back upon the wicked. Those who "refuse to do what is right" (verse 7) will learn this truth the hard way. Over and over in Proverbs we have seen these realities. People never get away with sin; sooner or later it comes back to them. Superficial attempts to buy God off with sacrifices (verse 3) don't work. The only real solution for sin lies outside of human capabilities. In Christ, God has paid for the sins of all. In Christ, he gives us strength to fight against the devil's temptations to sin.

Proverbs 21:9-13

As do other passages in Proverbs, verse 8 describes life as a path we are walking. In following their personal thoughts, ambitions, and lusts, the wicked lurch in one direction and then in another. Their way is "devious," or as some translate it, "crooked." The prophet Isaiah spoke of the wicked's walk through life in similar terms:

> Their *feet* rush into sin; they are swift to shed innocent blood. Their thoughts are evil thoughts; ruin and destruction mark their *ways*. The *way* of peace they do not know; there is no justice in their *paths*. They have turned them into *crooked roads;* no one who *walks* in them will know peace. (Isaiah 59:7,8)

The "conduct of the innocent" is not like that. It is "upright." The word translated as "upright" has the basic meaning of "straight." An upright person is one who walks a straight line. Because he is following God's direction rather than his own whims, the upright walks a straight path. With this in mind, we can make the psalmist David's prayer our own, "Teach me your way, O LORD; lead me in a straight path" (27:11).

Life with the wicked

⁹ Better to live on a corner of the roof
  than share a house with a quarrelsome wife.

¹⁰ The wicked man craves evil;
  his neighbor gets no mercy from him.

¹¹ When a mocker is punished, the simple gain wisdom;
  when a wise man is instructed, he gets knowledge.

¹² The Righteous One takes note of the house of
      the wicked
  and brings the wicked to ruin.

¹³ If a man shuts his ears to the cry of the poor,
  he too will cry out and not be answered.

Proverbs 21:9-13

Since the rooftops of Middle Eastern towns are flat, a man might go off in a corner there to escape his quarrelsome wife. This proverb occurs also in 25:24 and in a slightly altered form in 21:19. One commentator remarks, "Of all the proverbs that are repeated, this one in verse 9 seems least deserving."[11] We disagree. Since Proverbs is part of God's inspired Word, the Lord himself is behind the repetition. It underscores the importance God places on domestic tranquility.

Moreover, if it seems that the quarrelsome wife is singled out, we need to remember that the vast majority of proverbs describe wicked men. The wicked man thinks first, and last, of his personal advantage. He has no time for mercy toward others (verse 10). This proverb becomes especially disturbing when we consider that we live in the "Me" generation. Putting oneself first is encouraged at every turn. You've got to look out for yourself, we're told. And we read of "the virtue of selfishness."

Another disturbing note in verse 10 is that wickedness can become more than a weakness; it can develop into an actual craving. The wicked are past the point of trying to resist their sinful longings. They actively crave and pursue evil.

Verse 11 repeats the thought of 19:25. The simple can learn, although the motivation for that learning may not be ideal. When he sees the mocker being punished, fear of receiving the same punishment may be what makes the simple wiser.

This is partly what we mean when we speak of the moral law serving as a curb to prevent the widespread outbreak of evil. Many people live respectable lives, not out of deeply held conviction but simply because they don't want to pay fines or go to jail. A commonplace example of this kind of thing is when we see someone pulled over to the

Proverbs 21:14-19

side of the highway for speeding. Suddenly all traffic slows down to the posted speed limit!

The wise person loves knowledge for its own sake, not merely because it'll keep him away from punishments. We think of the 12-year-old Jesus in the temple, "sitting among the teachers, listening to them and asking them questions" (Luke 2:46). Although we and our children fall short of this ideal, we can cultivate a love for the Word of God.

"The Righteous One" in verse 12 can only refer to God. *Nothing* escapes his notice. In bringing the wicked to ruin, God often brings the entire household or family down with the wicked person himself. One of the most notorious kings in the entire Old Testament was King Ahab of Israel. Following the death of Ahab (1 Kings 22:37), his wife Jezebel and the "seventy sons of the house of Ahab" were also killed (2 Kings 9:30–10:17). The sons of his house probably included grandsons as well as his sons from his harem.

The point is that wicked people often bring disaster not only on themselves but on their household as well, especially when the family follows in the way of wickedness.

Like the other proverbs in this cluster, verse 13 has an alarming ring to it. Those who refuse to listen to the cries of the poor will someday be in the same situation. Jesus often spoke of hell as a place where there will be "weeping and gnashing of teeth" (Luke 13:28, for instance). The cries of the damned will go unheeded.

God has been so merciful to us. How can we turn our backs on the cries of those who need our help?

> **14 A gift given in secret soothes anger,**
> **and a bribe concealed in the cloak pacifies great wrath.**
>
> **15 When justice is done, it brings joy to the righteous**
> **but terror to evildoers.**

Proverbs 21:14-19

¹⁶ **A man who strays from the path of understanding**
comes to rest in the company of the dead.
¹⁷ **He who loves pleasure will become poor;**
whoever loves wine and oil will never be rich.

¹⁸ **The wicked become a ransom for the righteous,**
and the unfaithful for the upright.

¹⁹ **Better to live in a desert**
than with a quarrelsome and ill-tempered wife.

The topic of gifts and bribes has come up before, as in 17:8; 18:16; and 19:6. Without condoning the use of gifts as bribes, Solomon has shown that it is a way of life in this sinful world. In many countries today, bribes are almost part of government workers' salaries—to get an extension on a passport, to get out of a speeding ticket, to get favors in general. Verse 14 speaks of gifts soothing anger. This has been seen as a reference to gifts of charity, but it's more likely another example of the use of gifts to buy somebody off.

It seems that most of Solomon's references to gifts point to actual practices and let the readers draw their own conclusions. A gift might soothe someone's anger, but the wise person avoids unnecessary conflict in the first place.

If someone is angry at us because we have done wrong, we certainly aren't making things right by trying to pay off that person. Two wrongs don't make a right. If someone is angry at us because we have stood for what is right, then we willingly bear the brunt of that anger. (See 1 Peter 2:19-21.)

Before moving to the next verse, we ought not do so with the impression that we are to avoid all gift giving. When a husband, wife, or friend gives a gift to help make up after an argument, it can be a sign of love and need not be understood as a bribe. With gifts, as with many other areas of life, so much depends on the motivation.

Verse 15 presents a bold contrast. One man, the righteous,

205

Proverbs 21:14-19

rejoices when he sees justice done. Another, the evildoer, is *terrified* by it. Saint Paul spoke of the same phenomenon in his famous passage on the role of government: "Rulers hold no terror for those who do right, but for those who do wrong" (Romans 13:3).

We might drive our car off the road and get stuck in a ditch. We could even have a serious or fatal accident. Straying from God's road is much more serious (verse 16). The devil might tempt us to think that rejecting the Bible is the road to a full and free life. The fact is that the disobedient man gets the opposite of what he expects. Instead of freedom of movement, he "comes to rest." Instead of a fuller life, he ends up "in the company of the dead." This is not just physical death but spiritual death and, unless repented of, eternal death.

Wine was associated with feasting (verse 17). Expensive oil was used in lotions and perfume. The person addicted to these indulgences might lack the dedication needed to work hard and get rich. Or, because of his devotion to pleasure, he might lose what wealth he had.

There is another startling twist in verse 17. Earlier (verse 15), Solomon had indicated that the person who looks for justice gets that and more. He also gets "joy." In verse 17 he says that the person who makes "pleasure" his goal won't find it. The words translated "joy" and "pleasure" are the same in Hebrew. To put it another way, when we seek satisfaction in the things of this world, we won't find it. When we seek first the things of God, he will also give us contentment, satisfaction, and blessings here on earth as "frosting on the cake."

In verse 18 Solomon presents one more strange twist. Usually, wicked people hold good people ransom. Here it's the opposite. The thought is that although for a time the

Proverbs 21:20,21

wicked are in control and hold power over the righteous, the tables will be turned. The Bible contains numerous turnabouts like this. For instance, Jesus says, "Indeed there are those who are last who will be first, and first who will be last" (Luke 13:30). Often, what we see is not the way things really are, or the way they turn out.

Verse 19 is similar to verse 9, except that in the second passage Solomon says it would be better "to live in a desert," instead of simply a corner of the roof. There is an obvious increase in intensity from the first to the second statement of the proverb.

The wealth of the wise

²⁰ In the house of the wise are stores of choice food and oil, but a foolish man devours all he has.

²¹ He who pursues righteousness and love finds life, prosperity and honor.

When wisdom is our priority, other blessings come as well. These verses are not unlike the promise God gave to Israel as the people were about to enter the Promised Land. He told them that if they followed his decrees, he would bless them in their new home.

Included among the many blessings enumerated were "grain, new wine and oil" (see Deuteronomy 7:7-16). These terms represented the produce from fields, vineyards, and olive groves. Oil was used in perfumes, lotions, and on the hair. In many ways, oil was a symbol of prosperity.

Verse 20 states that the foolish man "devours"—squanders—his possessions, but the wise take care of what they have. The wise recognize their possessions as gifts from God. But verse 21 quickly adds, the wise man's heart is not with those possessions. It's with the spiritual

207

Proverbs 21:22-24

values of righteousness and love. The rest is secondary.

The wise man versus pride

²² **A wise man attacks the city of the mighty
and pulls down the stronghold in which they trust.**

²³ **He who guards his mouth and his tongue
keeps himself from calamity.**

²⁴ **The proud and arrogant man—"Mocker" is his name;
he behaves with overweening pride.**

As far as God is concerned, wisdom is superior to physical strength. This wisdom includes mental, but especially moral, strength. Elsewhere Solomon declared, "Wisdom is better than strength" (Ecclesiastes 9:16).

History shows that civilizations tend to forget this basic truth. Mighty Babylon fell when in its prime (see Daniel 5). Because of Babylon's wickedness, her strong walls were of no avail. In today's world high-tech armies and awesome weapons arsenals are not going to help the nation that has lost a basic sense of justice and morality.

The spiritual power of God's Word is stronger by far than any earthly power. The apostle Paul said:

> Though we live in the world, we do not wage war as the world does. The weapons we fight with are not the weapons of the world. On the contrary, they have divine power to demolish strongholds. We demolish arguments and every pretension that sets itself up against the knowledge of God, and we take captive every thought to make it obedient to Christ. (2 Corinthians 10:3-5)

Because wise people trust in God and not in their own strength, they are careful in their speech (verse 23). They avoid boasting and making rash promises beyond their

Proverbs 21:27-29

power to keep. Such care keeps them from calamities they might otherwise fall into.

While the wise "guards his mouth," the proud rushes right in. He boasts, scoffs at things holy, and behaves in an overbearing way. Some people might be impressed with Mr. Mocker. The wise surely aren't. Nor is God.

The lazy person

²⁵ **The sluggard's craving will be the death of him,**
    because his hands refuse to work.

²⁶ **All day long he craves for more,**
    but the righteous give without sparing.

This is another rare case of back-to-back proverbs in Solomon's collection that form a continuous thought.

The sluggard craves for a life of ease. Because all he does is sit around and dream of the easy life, he gets no work done. Not having done any work, he doesn't have food and ends up starving.

Meanwhile, as the sluggard spends his time daydreaming, the righteous are filled with energy for doing good. Not only do they provide for themselves, but they generously give to others as well!

The way of the wicked and the upright

²⁷ **The sacrifice of the wicked is detestable—**
    how much more so when brought with evil intent!

²⁸ **A false witness will perish,**
    and whoever listens to him will be destroyed forever.

²⁹ **A wicked man puts up a bold front,**
    but an upright man gives thought to his ways.

When wicked people brought sacrifices to the Lord's altar, it was hateful to God. It was hypocritical and made a

Proverbs 21:30,31

mockery of worship. How much worse when the sacrifice itself was brought "with evil intent"! That intent may have been to impress others with a false display of piety or to buy God off for some sin. A picture that might immediately come to mind is that of modern politicians who visit one church after another to win votes, when their personal morality and convictions are far removed from anything the churches stand for.

An NIV footnote offers an alternate translation for the second line of verse 28: "but the words of an obedient man will live on." This seems preferable. In contrast to the false witness who perishes, a wise person listens to advice, follows it, and is able to speak words worth remembering.

"A wicked man puts up a bold front"—literally, "he hardens his face." The wicked have no choice but to put on masks of false bravado. Their consciences accuse them. The natural knowledge of God reminds them they will someday have to meet their Maker.

The righteous man does not need to put on any front. He thoughtfully considers God's will and confidently follows that way.

The Lord is over everything

> **30 There is no wisdom, no insight, no plan**
> **that can succeed against the LORD.**
>
> **31 The horse is made ready for the day of battle,**
> **but victory rests with the LORD.**

Many have tried to defy God, only to fail. Pharaoh could not keep God's people from leaving Egypt when the Lord said it was time for them to go. Roman emperors tried to stamp out the early Christian church through persecutions, only to see it grow stronger. Worldly philosophers such as Voltaire, Friedrich Nietzsche, and Bertrand Russell scoffed at

Proverbs 22:2-10

the Bible but never could disprove it. Rationalists have tried to replace mysteries such as the Trinity with more reasonable beliefs, but millions humbly continue to acknowledge the biblical truth that God is three in one.

Mighty empires of days gone by, with their warhorses and chariots, have come and gone. The Lord raised them up and brought them down as he determined.

Given that no human power can triumph over the Lord and that no one succeeds without him, it is foolish and dangerous to trust in anything or anyone but the Lord. "Woe to those who go down to Egypt for help, who rely on horses, who trust in the multitude of their chariots and in the great strength of their horsemen, but do not look to the Holy One of Israel, or seek help from the LORD" (Isaiah 31:1).

A good name

22 A good name is more desirable than great riches;
to be esteemed is better than silver or gold.

A good reputation is priceless. In Ecclesiastes, Solomon declares, "A good name is better than fine perfume" (7:1). The good name of which he speaks is not that of the hypocrite, who keeps up a facade of goodness. It is the reputation that comes from selfless service to God and man. It is priceless because it opens to its owner channels of love and communication that money cannot buy.

General advice and observations

² **Rich and poor have this in common:**
The LORD is the Maker of them all.

³ **A prudent man sees danger and takes refuge,**
but the simple keep going and suffer for it.

⁴ **Humility and the fear of the LORD**
bring wealth and honor and life.

Proverbs 22:2-10

⁵ **In the paths of the wicked lie thorns and snares,**
   but he who guards his soul stays far from them.
⁶ **Train a child in the way he should go,**
   and when he is old he will not turn from it.

⁷ **The rich rule over the poor,**
   and the borrower is servant to the lender.

⁸ **He who sows wickedness reaps trouble,**
   and the rod of his fury will be destroyed.

⁹ **A generous man will himself be blessed,**
   for he shares his food with the poor.

¹⁰ **Drive out the mocker, and out goes strife;**
    quarrels and insults are ended.

Someone remarked that the rich are just like the rest of us, except that they have more money. Before God, the rich and poor have much in common. He made them both (verse 2). Both depend on their Creator for life and breath. Both must die and meet their Maker. When they die, the rich take no more with them than the poor. Job said, "Naked I came from my mother's womb, and naked I will depart" (1:21). Both are lost without the Savior.

These facts should keep us from treating rich or poor people differently. "If you really keep the royal law found in Scripture, 'Love your neighbor as yourself,' you are doing right. But if you show favoritism, you sin and are convicted by the law as lawbreakers" (James 2:8,9).

Wisdom helps us avoid physical and spiritual dangers (verse 3). The person who has not grown in God's Word doesn't see dangers and ends up suffering.

This is why it's foolish for people to think they can resist temptations and make godly decisions in life, when they never grow in the Word. The person who has never advanced beyond an eighth-grade understanding of Scripture won't be up to facing the challenges of marriage, raising children, witnessing, being a good steward of possessions, and generally

Proverbs 22:2-10

avoiding spiritual pitfalls. He won't even see them coming!

Verse 4 is one of many passages about "the fear of the LORD." These passages connect fearing the Lord with many blessings—in this case, with wealth, honor, and life. Humility goes naturally with fear of the Lord, since such fear is simply standing before God in humble respect and trust.

The thorns and snares in the wicked's way (verse 5) are the problems that sin creates in life. Think of the snares the dishonest man makes for himself . . . or the murderer, the adulterer, the thief, the liar. We avoid all that by guarding our souls with God's Word.

Verse 6 may well be the most quoted verse in Proverbs. Pastors and teachers point to it as God's guarantee that when children receive Christian training, they will never lose it or, if they do, will return to it when they are old.

Several possible interpretations center around the phrase "the way he should go." Since the words literally mean "according to his way," some understand the verse as a recommendation to encourage the child in his natural gifts and inclinations. This could end up good or bad. He may get locked into bad habits for the rest of his life. Or the early discipline of his special skills will give him a head start toward excellence. Certainly the Lord wants parents to help develop their children's gifts. Early training will ensure that they use those gifts for a lifetime to the glory of God.

But Proverbs focuses more on spiritual matters. It's most likely that "his way" is the way that God wants him to go. The verse, then, does contain a beautiful assurance. One's childhood training in the Bible is never entirely forgotten. It's always there as a reminder, a corrective, and a directive on the path to heaven.

Verse 7 simply states a fact of life. Money gives people

Proverbs 22:11,12

power over others. When Solomon states a bare fact such as this, we can apply it to our Christian lives. Although many might use money to control other human beings, with God's help, we won't. Rather, should we be blessed with material riches, we will use them to benefit those in need.

The Almighty will not let the wicked oppress others forever (verse 8). God will put down those who use their power—the rod, or scepter—to vent their anger. In their wickedness, they are sowing the seeds of their own destruction. In the words of the prophet Hosea, "They sow the wind and reap the whirlwind" (8:7).

Generosity does not come easily. We tend to fear that if we are generous, we won't have enough left over for ourselves. The Lord assures us that won't happen (verse 9). At the time of Moses (about 1400 B.C.), the Lord promised his people, "Give generously to him [the poor] and do so without a grudging heart; then because of this the LORD your God will bless you in all your work and in everything you put your hand to" (Deuteronomy 15:10). God continues to bless the generous—just as he promises.

When the mocker (verse 10) leaves the room, wisdom is able to get a hearing. It is difficult to converse with some people about important, spiritual topics. With the mocker, it's impossible. While we wouldn't use force, there are times when we might have to ask a mocker to leave so we can talk.

> **¹¹ He who loves a pure heart and whose speech is gracious will have the king for his friend.**
>
> **¹² The eyes of the LORD keep watch over knowledge, but he frustrates the words of the unfaithful.**

For one to rise in status with the king, two qualities are necessary: (1) a pure heart; that is, honest motives and (2) gracious speech; that is, an ability to express oneself.

Proverbs 22:13-16

Some might try to win a ruler's favor with insincere flattery or bribery, but sooner or later he'll see through this behavior. The Bible gives several examples of righteous people who rose to high government positions. Among them are Joseph in Egypt and Daniel in Babylon.

Having an earthly king for a friend is an honor. An even greater honor is to be called "God's friend," as Abraham was (James 2:23). This friendship is ours by faith.

The King of kings sees everything. "Nothing in all creation is hidden from God's sight. Everything is uncovered and laid bare before the eyes of him to whom we must give account" (Hebrews 4:13). No matter how clever and deceitful the wicked might be, the Lord knows. When he sees fit, he will bring their plans to ruin. But he watches over and protects those who know him as their God.

> **13 The sluggard says, "There is a lion outside!"**
> **or, "I will be murdered in the streets!"**
>
> **14 The mouth of an adulteress is a deep pit;**
> **he who is under the LORD's wrath will fall into it.**
>
> **15 Folly is bound up in the heart of a child,**
> **but the rod of discipline will drive it far from him.**
>
> **16 He who oppresses the poor to increase his wealth**
> **and he who gives gifts to the rich—both come to**
> **poverty.**

These closing verses of the First Collection of Solomon's Proverbs concentrate on some of the central warnings of the entire book of Proverbs. The warnings are against laziness, adultery, folly, oppression, and bribes.

The sluggard's excuses for not working sound preposterous (verse 13). And they are. He grasps at any reason, no matter how far-fetched, to avoid work. When we put off a task, getting at it becomes harder and harder until it takes on almost monstrous proportions. Don't be a sluggard; use

Proverbs 22:13-16

your God-given abilities.

Verse 14 is the first warning against adultery since the lengthy passage back in chapter 7. The adulteress' mouth with its kisses and smooth talk is the entrance to death and hell itself. To fall prey to her is a judgment of God upon the wicked.

By nature, we are all foolish—that is, turned away from God and toward our own sinful desires. Children also are given to silly and foolish behavior. Christian parents will keep this in mind and apply loving but firm discipline in training their children.

The Lord denounces oppression of the poor and bribery of the rich. Both are sinful attempts to take advantage of others for one's personal gain. God detests both. Solomon has given us many encouragements to help the poor, and we are to deal impartially with the rich.

We have come to the end of the longest portion of Proverbs. The hundreds of short proverbs offer food for thought and direction for daily living. They contain more than enough material for a lifetime of sanctified living. We'll want to return to them many times as we live to serve our Savior.

216

PART FOUR

Appendixes to the First Collection
(22:17–24:34)

In 1923, an ancient Egyptian document entitled "The Instruction of Amenemope" was first published for the English-speaking world. The document has been dated as early as 1570 B.C. or as late as about 500 B.C. and is ascribed to an Egyptian official named Amenemope. It consists of 30 wise sayings that are in some ways similar in form to 22:17–24:22.

Some translations, such as the NIV, render 22:20, "Have I not written *thirty sayings* for you . . . ?" (It can also be translated, "Have I not written to you *previously* . . . ?") In addition, it's *possible* to divide 22:17–24:22 into 30 sayings that deal with advice for living. Given these facts, some scholars have seen a connection between the sayings of Amenemope and this section of Proverbs.

If there was borrowing involved, it's more likely that the lesser known Amenemope would have borrowed from Solomon, who was famous for his wisdom, rather than the other way around.

While such comparisons are of historical interest, they affect neither the inspiration nor the meaning of this section of Proverbs. The Holy Spirit oversaw the composition and gathering of the Holy Scriptures, which make us "wise for salvation through faith in Christ Jesus" and which are "useful for teaching, rebuking, correcting and training in righteousness" (2 Timothy 3:15,16).

We continue with Sayings of the Wise:

Proverbs 22:17-21

Sayings of the wise

> ¹⁷ Pay attention and listen to the sayings of the wise;
>   apply your heart to what I teach,
> ¹⁸ for it is pleasing when you keep them in your heart
>   and have all of them ready on your lips.
> ¹⁹ So that your trust may be in the LORD,
>   I teach you today, even you.
> ²⁰ Have I not written thirty sayings for you,
>   sayings of counsel and knowledge,
> ²¹ teaching you true and reliable words,
>   so that you can give sound answers to him who sent you?

The opening line indicates that we are now in a new section of Proverbs. Verses 17 to 21 form an introduction into this new section.

Some feel that Solomon collected the following proverbs from various other wise men, and that is why he calls them "the sayings of the wise." ("Wise" in verse 17 is plural in the Hebrew; we find the same expression in 1:6.) Or it could be that the phrase "the sayings of the wise" indicates that Solomon is now getting into more advanced instruction, for those who are further along in wisdom. We favor this understanding.

If he collected the sayings from others, he refined them, improved them, and made them his own. After all, Scripture tells us he was "wiser than any other man" (1 Kings 4:31). The fact that the second line refers to "I" indicates that Solomon is still speaking here. The sayings are his.

The sayings that follow are to be kept within the heart, and they are to be repeated "on your lips." Verse 18 sounds much like a pastor assigning a list of Bible passages for his confirmation class to memorize and recite. The purpose is not merely to learn them mechanically and then mindlessly recite them. Rather, taking these truths into one's heart will lead to a deeper trust in the Lord (verse 19).

218

Proverbs 22:22-25

Verse 20 spells out what lies ahead—"thirty sayings." The NIV has a footnote stating that the phrase might also be translated: "Have I not formerly written" or "Have I not written excellent sayings." A slight change of one consonant in the word makes the difference.

Even if the phrase is translated as "thirty," there is disagreement as to whether or not the following verses (22:22–24:22) can be divided into 30 sections, and if so, just what they are. As mentioned above, some see a connection with the 30 sayings of Amenemope. But while there are some similarities to the Egyptian sayings, there are also differences.

We don't mean to get lost in these technicalities. Since they come up in most commentaries, however, and appear as footnotes in many translations, they deserve mention.

In summary, while it's possible to translate verse 20 as "thirty sayings" and to see a connection with an Egyptian document, these are matters of conjecture. None of this affects the material itself, which is a part of the Old Testament Scriptures and, as such, a part of God's inspired Word. That there is an occasional difficult word in translation should not surprise us. Nor should we be surprised that from time to time ancient literature outside the Bible touches on similar subject matter, although, of course, that other literature falls far short when compared with Scripture.

The one "who sent you" in verse 21 is probably a parent or guardian, who sent the young man for instruction. The pupil would return to that person and show what he had learned.

Robbing the poor

²² **Do not exploit the poor because they are poor**
   and do not crush the needy in court,
²³ **for the LORD will take up their case**
   and will plunder those who plunder them.

Proverbs 22:22-25

**²⁴ Do not make friends with a hot-tempered man,
do not associate with one easily angered,
²⁵ or you may learn his ways
and get yourself ensnared.**

Once we get into the "sayings of the wise," we find them crisp, clear, and to the point.

The first proverb warns against taking advantage of the poor and weak. Given the sinfulness of human nature, there is a natural tendency to exploit whomever we can to our own advantage.

Many of us have been raised on biblical teachings and steeped in a culture influenced by Christian principles. We find the very thought of exploitation repulsive. Yet the history of our own recent times shows how cruel human beings can become, as witnessed in the concentration camps of Nazi Germany and the pogroms of Russia.

God has never approved of man's inhumanity toward man. Centuries ago he declared through the prophet Isaiah: "Stop doing wrong, learn to do right! Seek justice, encourage the oppressed. Defend the cause of the fatherless, plead the case of the widow" (Isaiah 1:16,17).

Verses 24 and 25 tell us to avoid the friendship of a hot-tempered man. If anyone has a tendency to exploit others, it's such a man. The main reason Solomon gives for avoiding the man is that "you may learn his ways." The people we associate with influence us. Given enough time, we become like them.

The last word, "ensnared," says much. Sinful behavior has a way of becoming habitual and even addictive. Once caught in wicked ways, there is no escape—except for the grace of God. To toy with sin in the first place is to run the risk of hardening oneself forever to that grace.

Proverbs 22:26-29

Concerning loans

²⁶ **Do not be a man who strikes hands in pledge**
 or puts up security for debts;
²⁷ **if you lack the means to pay,**
 your very bed will be snatched from under you.
²⁸ **Do not move an ancient boundary stone**
 set up by your forefathers.

²⁹ **Do you see a man skilled in his work?**
 He will serve before kings;
 he will not serve before obscure men.

To strike hands in pledge was equivalent to our hand-shake. Before you close a deal by shaking hands, think about what you are doing. The specific advice here is against agree-ing to pay someone's else's debt if he is unable to. You may not be able to pay either. Then you'll lose everything you have. Such carelessness with one's money could reflect a lack of concern for taking care of one's own family.

Putting up security for someone else's debt was unwise. Moving someone else's boundary stone was wicked. The boundary stones marked property lines in ancient Israel. That property was passed down from one generation to the next within the same family. God forbade the moving of stones on someone else's land in order to enlarge one's own land: "Do not move your neighbor's boundary stone set up by your pre-decessors in the inheritance you receive in the land the LORD your God is giving you to possess" (Deuteronomy 19:14).

Instead of handling money foolishly (verses 26,27) or stealing from others (verse 28), Solomon advocates a better way: Develop your God-given talents (verse 29).

As we use our gifts, the Lord will see to it that we will find a way to make a living. If one is unusually skilled, he or she may end up with recognition and wealth.

Christian parents will do what they can to help their children develop their skills. The motivation is not fame and fortune but to glorify God and be useful to others.

Proverbs 23:1-3

The food of a ruler

23 When you sit to dine with a ruler,
note well what is before you,
² and put a knife to your throat
if you are given to gluttony.
³ Do not crave his delicacies,
for that food is deceptive.

Some see this cluster of verses as a lesson in etiquette. Others say it is a warning to be careful when socializing with untrustworthy people. Still others see here advice that we not become too accustomed to luxury.

The three are not mutually exclusive. For example, the caution against gluttony is certainly good etiquette, as well as the reminder not to become addicted to luxury. Moreover, it's probably not the smartest thing to stuff oneself in the presence of an enemy.

The setting is that of a formal banquet in the presence of a ruler. As we've noted in other proverbs, tactful behavior serves one well in such circumstances. "Put a knife to your throat" seems to be a Hebrew idiom, meaning, "Stop before you make a pig of yourself."

Verses 1 and 2 reach a conclusion in verse 3. The reason for practicing self-control is that the "food is deceptive." When rulers invited someone to dine with them, they probably had ulterior motives. The meal was but a way to make the guest indebted to the host or to get some information from him. Instead of being taken in by the wining and dining, the wise person stays focused on saying and doing what is right. There is no free lunch.

While we may never be invited to eat with royalty, the underlying principle is the same. Don't lose sight of your Savior amid the tinsel and glitter of worldly pleasures.

Proverbs 23:4,5

Getting rich

⁴ **Do not wear yourself out to get rich;**
have the wisdom to show restraint.
⁵ **Cast but a glance at riches, and they are gone,**
for they will surely sprout wings
and fly off to the sky like an eagle.

Money can't buy happiness, so don't burn yourself out in accumulating it. "The love of money is a root of all kinds of evil," writes Saint Paul (1 Timothy 6:10).

Anyone who's lost money in the stock market or in other ways understands just how quickly it can fly away. Hebrews 13:5 urges, "Keep your lives free from the love of money and be content with what you have, because God has said, 'Never will I leave you; never will I forsake you.'"

It's foolish to build our lives around money. The wise person builds his or her life on God, who is always there in life and death, sickness and health.

The Egyptian saying that reflects these verses says:

Cast not thy heart in pursuit of riches. . . .
Do not strain to seek an excess. . . .
Their places may be seen, but they are not. . . .
They have made themselves wings like geese
and are flown away to the heavens.[12]

The fact that at some points, such as this, Egyptian wisdom literature parallels biblical wisdom tells us something. Using their natural knowledge of God and lacking his written revelation, people have been able to arrive at certain moral principles. Saint Paul says that "the requirements of the law are written on their hearts, their consciences also bearing witness" (Romans 2:15).

Only in the Bible, however, do we have the moral law in its purity, without human adulteration. And only Scripture

Proverbs 23:9

contains the gospel, the good news that although we fail to keep the law, God saves us through Jesus Christ.

Eating with selfish people

⁶ Do not eat the food of a stingy man,
   do not crave his delicacies;
⁷ for he is the kind of man
   who is always thinking about the cost.
"Eat and drink," he says to you,
   but his heart is not with you.
⁸ You will vomit up the little you have eaten
   and will have wasted your compliments.

An old college professor of the author used to say, "There are two reasons for everything—the reason people give and the real reason."

This cluster of verses warns against duplicity in social matters. Some people will be friendly and entertain you. But they have ulterior motives; their hearts really aren't with you. It's on the business deal they hope to get from you.

Such a "friend" is mentally counting up the cost of this business lunch or party and has no true concern for your enjoyment. You'll probably sense it, and the dinner will be sickening. On top of that, the compliments you feel you owe your host will be wasted.

Incidentally, the "stingy" man is, literally, the one with "an evil eye." He is selfishly looking out for his own welfare and his alone. If making money is your priority in life, you'll probably end up at quite a few of these dinners.

Talking to fools

⁹ Do not speak to a fool,
   for he will scorn the wisdom of your words.

A fool despises wisdom and discipline (1:7); he hates correction (12:1); he answers correction and rebuke with insult

Proverbs 23:10,11

and abuse (9:7); he finds no pleasure in understanding but only in airing his own opinions (18:2); sending a message by him is like cutting off one's feet (26:6); he returns to his folly like a dog returning to its vomit (26:11). Is it any wonder we are told not even to speak to him?

Protect the property of the fatherless

> **¹⁰ Do not move an ancient boundary stone**
> **or encroach on the fields of the fatherless,**
> **¹¹ for their Defender is strong;**
> **he will take up their case against you.**

Boundary stones marked property lines. To move these stones was, in effect, stealing land. No doubt the wicked found it tempting to take land from the fatherless (verse 10) or widows (15:25).

But even though their father or husband was dead, they still had a "Defender." The word *Defender* is the Hebrew word for *Redeemer* (*Goel*). This term referred to the closest relative who would be responsible for the widow and her children.

The Old Testament often applies the word to God himself. For example, in his suffering Job exclaimed: "I know that my Redeemer lives, and that in the end he will stand upon the earth. And after my skin has been destroyed, yet in my flesh I will see God" (19:25,26). God is our heavenly Father and our heavenly Bridegroom. He comes to the defense of his people. "A father to the fatherless, a defender of widows, is God in his holy dwelling," declared the psalmist (68:5).

What a threat to the ungodly! The Almighty will take up the cause of the downtrodden. And what a comfort to God's people! Jesus, our Redeemer-Defender, has stood upon this earth and will visibly return as judge of all. He promises, "I am with you always" (Matthew 28:20).

225

Proverbs 23:13,14

Disciplined living

**¹² Apply your heart to instruction
and your ears to words of knowledge.**

Disciplined living involves the whole person. Contrary to what many seem to think, it's not easily picked up. It takes study of the Bible, reading and listening to God's Word. Then that Word must sink deeply into our hearts and become a part of our lives.

Instruction comes not only as we have direct contact with the Bible. It also comes indirectly, through the advice and correction of Christian friends and teachers.

Child discipline

**¹³ Do not withhold discipline from a child;
if you punish him with the rod, he will not die.
¹⁴ Punish him with the rod
and save his soul from death.**

This is one of several passages dealing with the discipline of children. (Others are 13:24; 29:15,17.) We've just seen that godly adults are to seek instruction (verse 12, Hebrew *musar*); Christian parents should be prepared to apply discipline (Hebrew *musar*) to their children as well.

We cannot bow out from growing in God's Word by saying we are too old. Nor can we excuse ourselves from training the next generation by saying they'll learn that when they are older. Now is the time.

The discipline of children may call for an occasional spanking. Physical discipline can work spiritual good. Spoiling the child can lead to physical death because of a reckless lifestyle or spiritual death or both.

Luther comments on this passage:

226

Proverbs 23:15,16

> It is great cruelty, nay, horrible murder, when
> a father lets his child go unpunished; for this
> neglect amounts to killing him with his own
> hands. That is why Solomon says in Proverbs
> 23:13,14: "Withhold not correction from the
> child: for if thou beatest him with the rod, he
> shall not die. Thou shalt beat him with the
> rod and shalt deliver his soul from hell." . . .
> Solomon would say: If you do not chastise
> your son that he may stay alive, then you are
> his murderer; for you are helping your child
> to become a rogue, and then the executioner
> must punish him with the death-dealing rod.[13]

Notice that Luther translated the last word as "hell." The Hebrew term (*sheol*) refers to the afterlife and can mean death, grave, or hell. Notice also that the discipline of the rod is far different from child abuse, which is done in anger and not for the child's good and, at times, is fatal.

What makes a father rejoice

> [15] **My son, if your heart is wise,**
> **then my heart will be glad;**
> [16] **my inmost being will rejoice**
> **when your lips speak what is right.**

Alongside the rod of discipline, godly parents will keep the apple of praise. They let their children know how much they love them and how happy they are to see their children grow in maturity and wisdom. Sometimes we forget to praise children and think only in terms of correcting them. This, like neglecting discipline, is a mistake.

Our emotions for our children run deep. Children are blessings from God (see Psalms 127,128). What a heartfelt joy it is to see them grow spiritually! Can there be a greater

Proverbs 23:17,18

joy for parents than to hear their children "speak what is right," especially by expressing faith in the Savior?

Sin versus hope

¹⁷ Do not let your heart envy sinners,
   but always be zealous for the fear of the Lord.
¹⁸ There is surely a future hope for you,
   and your hope will not be cut off.

Psalm 37:1-11 has been called the classic passage among those telling us not to envy sinners. In verses 17 and 18 Solomon summarizes what his father, David, had expressed more at length in the psalm. The basic thoughts are:

- Don't envy sinners, even though for a while they seem to prosper.
- Continue following the Lord, for this is the only right way.
- In the end, the ungodly will be "cut off"; that is, destroyed.
- You can look forward to a happy future, as God promises.

We need to keep such basics before us, since in this world the ungodly often do prosper, while the righteous suffer. We have words of encouragement, such as those of David and Solomon. We also have the wonderful examples of believers who have gone before us (see Hebrews 11:1–12:13). Most important, we have our Savior, who suffered that we might live forever in heaven.

> Let us fix our eyes on Jesus, the author and perfecter of our faith, who for the joy set before him endured the cross, scorning its shame, and sat down at the right hand of the throne of God. Consider him who endured such opposition from sinful men, so that you do not grow weary and lose heart. (Hebrews 12:2,3)

Proverbs 23:22-25

Associating with drunks and gluttons

> ¹⁹ **Listen, my son, and be wise,**
> **and keep your heart on the right path.**
> ²⁰ **Do not join those who drink too much wine**
> **or gorge themselves on meat,**
> ²¹ **for drunkards and gluttons become poor,**
> **and drowsiness clothes them in rags.**

Envying the wicked (verses 17,18) can lead to indulgence in eating and drinking. While having an alcoholic drink is not sinful, drinking too much is. Our society encourages heavy drinking. Even the celebration of Jesus' birth is for many an excuse for drunkenness. We need to be careful. We need to know our limits and to ask that the Lord will help us keep within them.

While much of the world lives with starvation, most of the West enjoys plenty. We have more than enough food. And eating too much can become a way of life. Both drunkenness and gluttony can dull one physically and mentally. They can lead to poverty.

As we strive to walk God's way and keep away from these sins, we will want to avoid wrongfully judging others. The priest Eli wrongly judged Hannah as drunk because her behavior seemed unusual to him (1 Samuel 1:12-17). If we see someone we know having a drink in a restaurant, we ought not jump to conclusions. Nor should we think that anyone who seems a bit heavy is guilty of the sin of gluttony. We need to look to ourselves first, that we live moderately to the glory of God.

Parental advice

> ²² **Listen to your father, who gave you life,**
> **and do not despise your mother when she is old.**

Proverbs 23:26-28

²³ **Buy the truth and do not sell it;**
   get wisdom, discipline and understanding.
²⁴ **The father of a righteous man has great joy;**
   he who has a wise son delights in him.
²⁵ **May your father and mother be glad;**
   may she who gave you birth rejoice!

A life of self-control is God pleasing (verses 19-21). So is honoring our parents. God wants us to listen to our fathers' and mothers' advice. After all, through them God gave us the gift of life itself. Even when a mother grows old and perhaps too talkative, we should patiently listen.

The greatest wisdom parents can pass on to their children is the truth of God's Word. It is a pearl of great value (Matthew 13:45,46) and worth more than anything else. The wonderful surprise is that to buy this treasure costs nothing. It's free! Once we have it, we'll gladly share it, without ever losing it.

As we ourselves grow older, we'll appreciate our parents' wisdom more. Mark Twain said, "When I was seventeen my father was so ignorant that I could hardly stand to have him around, but when I became twenty-one, I was surprised at how much he had learned in those four years."

The parent-child relationship goes both ways. Children honor their parents, who in turn rejoice in their children.

Against prostitution

²⁶ **My son, give me your heart**
   and let your eyes keep to my ways,
²⁷ **for a prostitute is a deep pit**
   and a wayward wife is a narrow well.
²⁸ **Like a bandit she lies in wait,**
   and multiplies the unfaithful among men.

In Proverbs chapters 5 to 7, we heard extensive warnings against adultery. Now we have a warning against the

Proverbs 23:29-35

prostitute and "wayward wife." Proverbs' many warnings against sexual immorality show just how serious it is. In the New Testament, Paul writes:

> Do you not know that your bodies are members of Christ himself? Shall I then take the members of Christ and unite them with a prostitute? Never! Do you not know that he who unites himself with a prostitute is one with her in body? For it is said, "The two will become one flesh." But he who unites himself with the Lord is one with him in spirit. (1 Corinthians 6:15-17)

Proverbs 22:14 called the mouth of an adulteress a deep pit; now the wayward woman herself is referred to in that way. Her entire demeanor, along with her seductive words, leads into a deep trap. As if stuck in a narrow well, once you're in, it's impossible to escape without help. She "multiplies the unfaithful" points to her leading more and more astray.

Meanwhile, books and movies go on romanticizing promiscuity. And sexual sin continues to spread across our land. Along with unchastity, venereal diseases are rampant everywhere—the physical fruits of a spiritual sickness that destroys lives, families, civilizations, and souls.

The misery caused by drinking

²⁹ **Who has woe? Who has sorrow?**
     Who has strife? Who has complaints?
     Who has needless bruises? Who has bloodshot eyes?
³⁰ **Those who linger over wine,**
     who go to sample bowls of mixed wine.
³¹ **Do not gaze at wine when it is red,**
     when it sparkles in the cup,
     when it goes down smoothly!

231

Proverbs 23:29-35

> ³² **In the end it bites like a snake**
>   **and poisons like a viper.**
> ³³ **Your eyes will see strange sights**
>   **and your mind imagine confusing things.**
> ³⁴ **You will be like one sleeping on the high seas,**
>   **lying on top of the rigging.**
> ³⁵ **"They hit me," you will say, "but I'm not hurt!**
>   **They beat me, but I don't feel it!**
> **When will I wake up**
>   **so I can find another drink?"**

This is the longest section on a single topic since the earlier chapters of Proverbs (prior to chapter 10). That it follows immediately after the warning against sexual immorality indicates the relationship between the two sins. Drunkenness excites lust. Once one desensitizes himself with drink, he is more likely to wallow in sensuality.

The description of drunkenness is vivid. Were it not so tragic, it would border on the humorous. Solomon begins with a description of the misery drunkenness brings (verses 29,30). He continues with the allurement of alcohol—its inviting look and taste (verse 31). Then he turns to a graphic description of a drunken person (verses 32-35).

The mixed wine of verse 30 may refer to the practice of mixing wine with spices (Psalm 75:8; Song of Songs 8:2).

For the most part, Old Testament Israelites were not a seagoing people. Hence the comparison of drunkenness to seasickness (verse 34) would be especially nauseating.

The most tragic part of this description is the drunk's closing question: "When will I wake up so I can find another drink?"

Anyone who thinks lightly of this sin will think otherwise after reading this description. If this passage hits home, seek Christian help. For those struggling with alcoholism, God's

232

Proverbs 24:3,4

Word gives hope. "Do not get drunk on wine, which leads to debauchery. Instead, be filled with the Spirit" (Ephesians 5:18).

Wrong thoughts, wrong company

24 **Do not envy wicked men,
do not desire their company;
² for their hearts plot violence,
and their lips talk about making trouble.**

At times we are tempted to envy the wicked, especially when they seem to do whatever they please and get ahead in this world. This is how the psalmist Asaph felt: "I envied the arrogant when I saw the prosperity of the wicked" (73:3).

Solomon reminds us that the God-fearing cannot envy such people, simply because they are wicked inside ("their hearts") and outside ("their lips"). Although he doesn't mention it here, he frequently does point out that in the end they do not get away with evil.

Asaph too came to see this: "How suddenly are they destroyed, completely swept away by terrors!" (Psalm 73:19).

Spiritual building materials

**³ By wisdom a house is built,
and through understanding it is established;
⁴ through knowledge its rooms are filled
with rare and beautiful treasures.**

On occasion we've all probably driven through the wealthier neighborhoods in our communities. We like to look at the big, beautiful homes with their perfect landscaping and perhaps think about how nice it would be to live in such a house. Maybe some of us actually do live there.

Proverbs 24:5,6

God points to something that can make any house beautiful, no matter what neighborhood it's in. Wisdom builds the best houses—or, better, homes.

Notice the threefold use of nouns and verbs: wisdom . . . built; understanding . . . established; knowledge . . . filled. While we are not implying that this is a hidden reference to the Trinity, we're safe in saying that only the triune God can truly make a house into a loving home. His Word contains directives for husbands and wives (such as Ephesians 5:22-33) and for children and parents (Ephesians 6:1-4).

Most of all, he gives us the motivation and foundation for building a Christian home—the love of Christ. "Love each other as I have loved you," says Jesus (John 15:12).

With these rare and beautiful treasures, he fills each room.

Strategic planning

> ⁵ **A wise man has great power,**
> **and a man of knowledge increases strength;**
> ⁶ **for waging war you need guidance,**
> **and for victory many advisers.**

We can apply these verses in both a worldly and a spiritual way. Worldly knowledge often does lead to power. The person who has learned certain skills or knows the right people or has insights into human nature and how to lead others—this person may well be on the road to power.

Moreover, in time of war, the general does well to surround himself with many wise advisers.

Spiritual wisdom may not lead to worldly success. Solomon took note of this in the book of Ecclesiastes: "There is something else meaningless that occurs on earth: righteous men who get what the wicked deserve, and wicked men who get what the righteous deserve" (8:14). To be righteous, of course, is to be wise in God's sight. That doesn't mean

234

Proverbs 24:10-12

worldly power. But it does mean power with the Lord. "The prayer of a righteous man is powerful and effective" (James 5:16).

Ultimately, victory belongs with those who are wise in the Lord.

Foolish scheming

> ⁷ **Wisdom is too high for a fool;**
> **in the assembly at the gate he has nothing to say.**
>
> ⁸ **He who plots evil**
> **will be known as a schemer.**
> ⁹ **The schemes of folly are sin,**
> **and men detest a mocker.**

The protected city gate was where community leaders met and court was held in Bible times. The fool has nothing worthwhile to offer at such assemblies.

When one is constantly stirring up trouble, he will get a bad reputation. The mocker is the person who would rather make fun of others than offer constructive criticism; he too will come to be detested.

Fools, schemers, and mockers—they all end up turning people away.

Caring and its reward

> ¹⁰ **If you falter in times of trouble,**
> **how small is your strength!**
>
> ¹¹ **Rescue those being led away to death;**
> **hold back those staggering toward slaughter.**
> ¹² **If you say, "But we knew nothing about this,"**
> **does not he who weighs the heart perceive it?**
> **Does not he who guards your life know it?**
> **Will he not repay each person according to what**
> **he has done?**

Honey from the comb is sweet

Proverbs 24:13,14

This passage calls us to be courageous in defense of those in need. Some have applied it to the situation in Germany under the Nazis. While Jews and others were being led to slaughter, it was tempting for many Germans who knew better to pretend, "But we knew nothing about this." Many apply it to the abortion holocaust in the United States today— a million-and-a-half babies are being slaughtered each year. Few Christians can say, "But we knew nothing about this."

The verses apply to all situations that call for defending those in need. We can't fool God and pretend not to see what's going on. The Lord looks into our hearts.

The last two lines of verse 12 appear in one of David's psalms (62:12), not as a rhetorical question but as a statement: "Surely [he] will reward each person according to what he has done." Paul also uses these words in reference to judgment day (Romans 2:6).

The thought that God will hold us accountable can be frightening. But Solomon also encourages us. He speaks of the Lord as the one "who guards your life." Since God watches over us and guards us, he will surely give us the necessary boldness to speak up and stand up when necessary. He will give us strength, so that we do not "falter in times of trouble." With God's strength and Christ's forgiveness, we have boldness—even on the Last Day.

Honey and wisdom compared

> ¹³ **Eat honey, my son, for it is good;**
> **honey from the comb is sweet to your taste.**
> ¹⁴ **Know also that wisdom is sweet to your soul;**
> **if you find it, there is a future hope for you,**
> **and your hope will not be cut off.**

Verse 13 is more than dietary advice; it leads into the following verse. Solomon is saying, "As honey is sweet to the

Proverbs 24:17,18

taste, so wisdom is sweet to your soul. It's tasty and, what's more, it's nourishing."

Wisdom brings a hope that will never be cut off. When the Bible speaks of the hope believers have, it speaks of a positive, certain hope. This is not the kind of hope we have when we look at a cloudy sky and say, "I hope it doesn't rain." Rather, it is the hope that is ours in Christ.

The resilient righteous; the devastated damned

> [15] **Do not lie in wait like an outlaw against a righteous man's house,**
> **do not raid his dwelling place;**
> [16] **for though a righteous man falls seven times, he rises again,**
> **but the wicked are brought down by calamity.**

We've seen the warning against "lying in wait" before (1:11). While most people wouldn't think of lying in ambush (as in the old cowboy movies), there are more subtle forms of doing this. Any attempt to cheat or steal from another person is "lying in wait."

Because the Lord watches over the righteous, he will uphold and rescue them many times. Seven signifies a complete number, as if to say, "As many times as he needs to, God will rescue his people."

The wicked live—and die—without this assurance. They have no hope.

How to react to your enemies' misfortune

> [17] **Do not gloat when your enemy falls;**
> **when he stumbles, do not let your heart rejoice,**
> [18] **or the LORD will see and disapprove**
> **and turn his wrath away from him.**

Proverbs 24:21,22

God has just said that "the wicked are brought down" (verse 16). Now he says, "Don't gloat when you see it happen." Vengeance belongs to God, not us. We are to help our enemy when he is in need (25:21). Perhaps that enemy can become our friend and, more significantly, a friend of God.

The idea in verse 18 seems to be that if you gloat over your enemy's troubles, God will turn his wrath away from the enemy and toward you.

Levelheaded restraint

> ¹⁹ **Do not fret because of evil men**
> **or be envious of the wicked,**
> ²⁰ **for the evil man has no future hope,**
> **and the lamp of the wicked will be snuffed out.**

The first line of this passage echoes David's words in Psalm 37:1. It's interesting that Solomon quotes his father on this item. Every generation of believers struggles with the temptation to envy the wicked. And so each new generation must address the issue.

That hasn't changed today. The wicked continue to flourish, while the righteous struggle along. Or so it seems. But the end of the wicked hasn't changed either. "The evil man has no future hope."

His lamp being snuffed out signifies calamity or his life coming to an end. In contrast to this, in the last chapter of Proverbs we read of the noble wife whose "lamp does not go out at night" (31:18).

Godly traditions cushion misery

> ²¹ **Fear the LORD and the king, my son,**
> **and do not join with the rebellious,**
> ²² **for those two will send sudden destruction upon them,**
> **and who knows what calamities they can bring?**

239

Proverbs 24:23-26

"The fear of the LORD" appears at key places in Proverbs: the end of the Prologue (1:7), the second last verse of the entire book (31:30), and here, at the end of another section. These two verses bring to an end the Sayings of the Wise section, sometimes referred to as Thirty Sayings.

The only difference is that here "my son" is enjoined to fear not only the Lord but right along with him the king. In the New Testament, Peter refers to the first line of this passage when he writes, "Show proper respect to everyone: Love the brotherhood of believers, fear God, honor the king" (1 Peter 2:17).

Kings, like rulers in general, are God's representatives. We owe them respect. The apostle Paul writes:

> The authorities that exist have been established by God. Consequently, he who rebels against the authority is rebelling against what God has instituted, and those who do so will bring judgment on themselves. For rulers hold no terror for those who do right, but for those who do wrong. Do you want to be free from fear of the one in authority? Then do what is right and he will commend you. (Romans 13:1-3)

Further sayings of the wise

Partiality and fairness

²³**These also are sayings of the wise:**

To show partiality in judging is not good:
²⁴ **Whoever says to the guilty, "You are innocent"—**
peoples will curse him and nations denounce him.
²⁵ **But it will go well with those who convict the guilty,**
and rich blessing will come upon them.

Proverbs 24:27

**²⁶ An honest answer
is like a kiss on the lips.**

The opening line indicates another break into a new section of Proverbs. This is a short section, containing only a dozen verses.

"To show partiality" literally means to recognize faces. We humans tend to be influenced by a person's earthly position. But "God does not show favoritism" (Acts 10:34).

Everyone denounces an unjust judge. One commentator states, "Among no people is conscience so blunted, that he who absolves the crime and ennobles the miscarriage of justice shall escape the *vox populi* [voice of the people]."[14]

On the other hand, people respect those who stand for law and order. Blessings await them. When the Israelites were about to enter the Promised Land, God held out this promise: "Follow justice and justice alone, so that you may live and possess the land the LORD your God is giving you" (Deuteronomy 16:20).

Verse 26 uses a pleasant illustration to describe the sweetness of honesty. Like a kiss, honesty represents concern, love, respect, and friendship for another person.

Plan ahead!

**²⁷ Finish your outdoor work
and get your fields ready;
after that, build your house.**

Building the house is a metaphor for marriage and family life (see verse 3). In Ruth 4:11, Rachel and Leah, the wives of Jacob (Israel), are described as the women who "together built up the house of Israel." From that family the nation of Israel came. The proverb is saying, "Be ready for building a family; make your plans."

Proverbs 24:28,29

When so many people jump into marriage merely on the basis of their emotions, this is sound advice. Readiness includes finances, perhaps premarital counseling, open communication, sharing, and, above all, a common commitment to Christ and his Word.

Don't try to get even

**²⁸ Do not testify against your neighbor without cause,
or use your lips to deceive.
²⁹ Do not say, "I'll do to him as he has done to me;
I'll pay that man back for what he did."**

The first line refers to slander or libel against our neighbor; that is, our fellowman. Given the poetic parallelism of Proverbs, the second line speaks not of gossip in general but of false witness against the neighbor.

Sometimes the motive for lying is to get back at a person who has in some way hurt us. Verse 29 forbids this, as does 25:21,22.

The Old Testament takes testifying against another very seriously. We quote from Deuteronomy 19:15-21, where the subject is dealt with at length. (Notice the call for two witnesses, and recall how much difficulty Jesus' enemies had in meeting this criterion, Matthew 26:59-61.)

> One witness is not enough to convict a man accused of any crime or offense he may have committed. A matter must be established by the testimony of two or three witnesses.
>
> If a malicious witness takes the stand to accuse a man of a crime, the two men involved in the dispute must stand in the presence of the LORD before the priests and the judges who are in office at the time. The judges must make a thorough investiga-

Proverbs 24:30-34

tion, and if the witness proves to be a liar, giving false testimony against his brother, then do to him as he intended to do to his brother. You must purge the evil from among you. The rest of the people will hear of this and be afraid, and never again will such an evil thing be done among you. Show no pity: life for life, eye for eye, tooth for tooth, hand for hand, foot for foot.

Learn from the laziness of others

³⁰ **I went past the field of the sluggard,**
    past the vineyard of the man who lacks judgment;
³¹ **thorns had come up everywhere,**
    the ground was covered with weeds,
    and the stone wall was in ruins.
³² **I applied my heart to what I observed**
    and learned a lesson from what I saw:
³³ **A little sleep, a little slumber,**
    a little folding of the hands to rest—
³⁴ **and poverty will come on you like a bandit**
    and scarcity like an armed man.

This lesson about laziness comes from personal observation—"I went past . . ."

The sluggard is synonymous with the man who lacks understanding. He does not realize the necessity of work. Consequently, his property is in ruins.

Verses 33 and 34 are a repetition of 6:10,11. (The section of 6:6-11 offers an extensive treatment of laziness, and the subject comes up numerous times throughout the book.)

The folding of the hands is the position of what we might call a couch potato. The point is not that a little slumber and rest are wrong. Everyone needs rest and relaxation. But

Proverbs 24:30-34

the sluggard doesn't stop with a little. For him it starts with that and becomes a way of life.

The solution? Live for God. Use your God-given abilities to his glory and for the good of others.

PART FIVE

Second Collection of Solomon's Proverbs—Hezekiah's Collection
(25:1–29:27)

As with the First Collection of Solomon's Proverbs (10:1–22:16), the proverbs here are mainly of the two-line variety, and most of them are antithetic in form. A number of proverbs in this section are identical or similar to proverbs in the first collection. Scholar C. Hassell Bullock offers the following table:[15]

IDENTICAL OR SIMILAR PROVERBS	
First Collection	Second Collection
Identical	
21:9	25:24
18:8	26:22
22:3	27:12
20:16	27:13
Identical meaning with altered expression	
22:13	26:13
19:24	26:15
19:1	28:6
12:11	28:19
22:2	29:13
One line identical	
17:3	27:21
15:18	29:22

245

Proverbs 25:2-7

More proverbs of Solomon

25 These are more proverbs of Solomon, copied by the men of Hezekiah king of Judah:

Although he was not without his faults, the Bible tells us that for the most part King Hezekiah was a good, God-fearing king. In the next few chapters of Proverbs, we have one of the good results that came from his reign—namely, the collecting of more of Solomon's proverbs.

Hezekiah reigned from 729 to 700 B.C. (some historians say 715 to 686 B.C.), more than two centuries after King Solomon (970 to 931 B.C.). This collection of additional proverbs of Solomon indicates that while many of Solomon's proverbs had been kept through the years, considerable time passed before they were gathered into one document.

The word "copied" need not mean that Hezekiah's scribes copied written documents. It could also mean that they selected and put into writing proverbs that had been passed down simply by word of mouth.

The following collection represents another relatively small part of the total number of Solomon's proverbs. According to 1 Kings 4:32, Solomon "spoke three thousand proverbs." Perhaps to honor Solomon and Hezekiah, the scribes placed at the head of this collection a series of proverbs dealing with kings (verses 2-7):

In relation to kings

> ² It is the glory of God to conceal a matter;
>   to search out a matter is the glory of kings.
>
> ³ As the heavens are high and the earth is deep,
>   so the hearts of kings are unsearchable.
>
> ⁴ Remove the dross from the silver,
>   and out comes material for the silversmith;
>
> ⁵ remove the wicked from the king's presence,
>   and his throne will be established through righteousness.

Proverbs 25:2-7

⁶ Do not exalt yourself in the king's presence,
and do not claim a place among great men;
⁷ It is better for him to say to you, "Come up here,"
than for him to humiliate you before a nobleman.

Part of God's glory comes from the fact that he is mysterious, beyond our understanding. His working in nature and history is often hidden, which only makes him all the more awesome. Saint Paul describes this in a magnificent doxology in Romans 11:33-36:

> Oh, the depth of the riches of the wisdom
> and knowledge of God!
> How unsearchable his judgments,
> and his paths beyond tracing out!
> "Who has known the mind of the Lord?
> Or who has been his counselor?"
> "Who has ever given to God,
> that God should repay him?"
> For from him and through him and to him are all
> things.
> To him be the glory forever! Amen.

As for kings, their glory is to search out and discover. When he became king, Solomon asked God for "a discerning heart to govern your people and to distinguish between right and wrong" (1 Kings 3:9). To search out justice and enlightenment is to a ruler's glory.

Proverbs is full of sharp turns. Solomon just finished saying that it is to a king's glory to search out a matter and then, in verse 3, he describes the king's heart as "unsearchable." Rulers, in fact, often are anything but open. Who can follow the behind-the-scenes maneuvering of diplomats?

We also have here a warning against being taken in by the flattery of kings. It may not be sincere. We ought to be guided by higher motives than that of the outward approval of earthly potentates, whose praise can be quite fickle. Rather than

247

Proverbs 25:2-7

living to please the high and mighty of this world, we live by faith in the King of kings and let his Word direct our lives.

"The dross from the silver" refers to impurities that are taken out in the process of refining silver. Likewise, if wicked people (for example, self-serving advisors) are not surrounding the king, his will be a precious, righteous governing. The prophet Isaiah used the same imagery in lamenting the state of Israel in his day: "Your silver has become dross, your choice wine is diluted with water. Your rulers are rebels, companions of thieves; they all love bribes and chase after gifts. They do not defend the cause of the fatherless; the widow's case does not come before them" (Isaiah 1:22,23).

Sooner or later and one way or another, there will be a purifying. Sometimes God brings governments to their knees because they have become so corrupt. Isaiah went on to speak of this process: "Therefore the Lord, the LORD Almighty, the Mighty One of Israel, declares: 'Ah, I will get relief from my foes and avenge myself on my enemies. I will turn my hand against you; I will thoroughly purge away your dross and remove all your impurities'" (Isaiah 1:24,25).

In our day we have witnessed the overthrow of godless communist states. The Almighty raises up nations and rulers and brings them down as he sees fit.

The picture Solomon uses in verses 6 and 7 is that of a royal feast in which people are seated according to their social standing. Jesus used this same illustration when he attended a banquet and "noticed how the guests picked the places of honor at the table" (Luke 14:7-11). He said: "Do not take the place of honor, for a person more distinguished than you may have been invited. . . . For everyone who exalts himself will be humbled, and he who humbles himself will be exalted."

Some people feel that you've got to "blow your own horn." God says otherwise. We do not have to boast about

248

Proverbs 25:11-14

our gifts in order for others to see them. If we use our God-given talents well, discerning people will notice them.

Lawsuits, libel, and levelheadedness

> **What you have seen with your eyes**
> **⁸ do not bring hastily to court,**
> **for what will you do in the end**
> **if your neighbor puts you to shame?**
>
> **⁹ If you argue your case with a neighbor,**
> **do not betray another man's confidence,**
> **¹⁰ or he who hears it may shame you**
> **and you will never lose your bad reputation.**

Don't be in a hurry to get a lawyer, sue, and take someone to court. You may come out a loser. God wants us to try to settle matters in a personal way outside of court. Jesus said, "As you are going with your adversary to the magistrate, try hard to be reconciled to him on the way, or he may drag you off to the judge, and the judge will turn you over to the officer, and the officer throw you into prison" (Luke 12:58). The Bible always urges us to try to take the loving, forgiving, and peaceful way.

Not only should we try to avoid legal action against another, we should also avoid gossip. Several proverbs condemn gossip (see, for example, 11:13; 20:19). To betray another's confidence is to make a bad reputation for oneself. Who really wants to be friends with a gossip?

The word is like . . .

> **¹¹ A word aptly spoken**
> **is like apples of gold in settings of silver.**
> **¹² Like an earring of gold or an ornament of fine gold**
> **is a wise man's rebuke to a listening ear.**
> **¹³ Like the coolness of snow at harvest time**
> **is a trustworthy messenger to those who send him;**
> **he refreshes the spirit of his masters.**

Proverbs 25:15-17

**¹⁴ Like clouds and wind without rain
is a man who boasts of gifts he does not give.**

Having discussed wrongful talk—such as betraying the confidence of another—Solomon now points to the positive use of words. In an earlier chapter, wisdom exclaimed, "My fruit is better than fine gold; what I yield surpasses choice silver" (8:19). A word aptly spoken, then, is a word of godly wisdom.

When a wise man rebukes someone, he does so in a loving way. Though his words may sting, they are constructive and appropriate. The "listening ear" is that of another wise person, as an earlier proverb states, "He who listens to a life-giving rebuke will be at home among the wise" (15:31). The wise man's rebuke and the receptive ear combine to create a beautiful model of interaction, which Solomon compares to a golden earring or other piece of jewelry.

A snowfall at harvesttime would be a calamity. The cool snow in verse 13 has to refer to snow from the mountains, used for cooling drinks during the work of harvest. Peasants would store up mountain snow in rock clefts and in the warm months bring it out. A trusty messenger is refreshing to his masters, to those who send him. He is reliable and uplifts their confidence.

As Solomon does in verse 14, Jude, in the New Testament, likens wicked men to "clouds without rain" (verse 12). In hot lands such as Palestine, clouds without rain raise expectations and then let people down. So does the person who boasts, makes promises and, in the end, doesn't deliver.

Moderation in human relations

**¹⁵ Through patience a ruler can be persuaded,
and a gentle tongue can break a bone.**

**¹⁶ If you find honey, eat just enough—
too much of it, and you will vomit.**

**¹⁷ Seldom set foot in your neighbor's house—
too much of you, and he will hate you.**

Proverbs 25:18-20

Since they had absolute power, ancient rulers could be very arbitrary. In dealing with them, it was wise to be diplomatic, even to walk on eggshells. In our day too rude, angry behavior is likely to make those in authority become resentful, rather than opening them up to your suggestions. Be patient.

As for a gentle tongue breaking a bone, the idea is that soft speech is more likely to overcome stubborn opposition.

Verses 15 and 16 both urge us to practice moderation. "Honey," no doubt, refers not only to the food but is symbolic of good relationships. Moderation is good in every area of life. In eating, in recreation and working, in study and play—don't overdo it.

Neighborly friendships should exhibit moderation (verse 17). There is an old German proverb, "Let him who seeks to be of esteem come seldom." We have a saying, "Familiarity breeds contempt."

Children who are always at the neighbors' can get on their nerves. The homemaker who is always stopping in for coffee can do the same. Even husbands and wives might need a little space once in a while. It helps them appreciate each other all the more. Let relationships develop gradually, and then nurture them.

> ¹⁸ **Like a club or a sword or a sharp arrow**
> **is the man who gives false testimony**
> **against his neighbor.**
>
> ¹⁹ **Like a bad tooth or a lame foot**
> **is reliance on the unfaithful in times of trouble.**
>
> ²⁰ **Like one who takes away a garment on a cold day,**
> **or like vinegar poured on soda,**
> **is one who sings songs to a heavy heart.**

As children we used to say, "Sticks and stones can break my bones, but words can never hurt me!" That's not really

Proverbs 25:21,22

true. Words can and do hurt. They can batter like a club, cut like a sword, or pierce like an arrow. Especially hurtful are lying words that drag down one's reputation. If we have been guilty of speaking such words, we need to ask forgiveness of both God and our neighbor.

When everything else seems to be going wrong, the last thing you need is to break a tooth and have to visit the dentist. Nor, when someone needs to run to escape danger, does a bad foot help. Similarly, the last kind of friends you need when you're in trouble are unfaithful ones. They'll let you down just when you really need them most. Let's look for better friends than that. And let's not be that kind of friend to others!

"There is a time for everything," wrote Solomon in Ecclesiastes (3:1). A cold day is not the time to take off your coat. Pouring vinegar on soda (probably sodium carbonate) causes a fermentation; there are times you don't want this stirred-up reaction. There also are times when the heart is heavy, and any attempt to cheer it up only makes it more depressed. With God's help, wisdom discerns what is best to do—and when is the best time to do it.

> ²¹ **If your enemy is hungry, give him food to eat;**
> **if he is thirsty, give him water to drink.**
> ²² **In doing this, you will heap burning coals on his head,**
> **and the LORD will reward you.**

The "burning coals" represent the enemy's conscience. It will bother him when he receives kindness instead of retaliation for mistreating you. The burning is painful, yet at the same time beneficial. It helps him come to repentance. The reward from God is a clear conscience and, we would pray, the good will of a *former* enemy.

Contrary to the erroneous picture some have of the Old Testament as being full of revenge, this proverb is in keeping

Proverbs 25:23,24

with Mosaic Law: "If you come across your enemy's ox or donkey wandering off, be sure to take it back to him. If you see the donkey of someone who hates you fallen down under its load, do not leave it there; be sure you help him with it" (Exodus 23:4,5).

One's enemy might be a stranger, a neighbor, or even a family member. Whoever it happens to be, we are to treat him with forgiveness and love.

This proverb is quoted in Romans 12:20. There it is part of a wonderful passage in which the apostle Paul tells Christians not to repay evil with evil but to overcome evil with good.

> [23] **As a north wind brings rain,**
> **so a sly tongue brings angry looks.**
>
> [24] **Better to live on a corner of the roof**
> **than share a house with a quarrelsome wife.**

Verse 23 is somewhat problematic, because in Israel the north wind usually was dry. Rain came with the west wind, as Jesus noted, "When you see a cloud rising in the west, immediately you say, 'It's going to rain,' and it does" (Luke 12:54). The reference might be to a northwest wind. Or it may be that the proverb originated outside of Palestine.

At any rate, the point of the proverb is clear. A sly tongue with its gossip and slander is bound to stir up resentment and anger.

Fault finding is easy. It's especially easy when we know someone well, such as our spouses. A husband whose wife picks at him and puts him down is like a prisoner in his own house. He'd be better off, says Solomon, living on the roof! (In Israel the roofs are flat and at times are used for sleeping or storage.) Of course, it isn't always a one-way street; husbands can do the same to their wives.

253

Proverbs 25:25,26

How are we to treat our spouses? The Bible tells us, "Each one of you [husbands] also must love his wife as he loves himself, and the wife must respect her husband" (Ephesians 5:33).

This proverb is identical to 21:9.

> ²⁵ **Like cold water to a weary soul**
> **is good news from a distant land.**
> ²⁶ **Like a muddied spring or a polluted well**
> **is a righteous man who gives way to the wicked.**

We are told that "the spirit of their father Jacob revived" when he received evidence from Egypt that his beloved son Joseph was alive (Genesis 45:27). For years Jacob had lived with the sad burden of thinking Joseph was dead. The news about Joseph came like refreshing "cold water to a weary soul."

A letter or card from some old friend now living far away, a long-distance call from a loved one, greetings sent by way of mutual friends—how refreshing it can be, especially when we've been feeling down. Let's not forget those "little" kindnesses ourselves. Is there someone far away whom you could uplift with a bit of cheerful news?

A good person who gives in to the wicked becomes soiled. He becomes like muddied water. It can take a long time to clear up a polluted source of water. In the meantime, that water can poison and sicken those who drink it. Similarly, it can take a long time for a righteous man to get back on track. Meanwhile, he can pollute many others who drink in his advice or follow his example.

People who are righteous before God through faith in Christ will also want to live righteously. In this way we glorify God. Lives of integrity and good reputation are like clear, unpolluted, refreshing springs and wells!

Proverbs 26:1-3

²⁷ **It is not good to eat too much honey,**
nor is it honorable to seek one's own honor.

²⁸ **Like a city whose walls are broken down**
is a man who lacks self-control.

In verses 6 and 7, we were told not to seek our own honor. Here it is compared to eating too much honey. That would make us physically sick. Seeking one's own honor is harmful to our spiritual health.

In Bible times a city with broken down walls was defenseless. When the Assyrians were threatening Jerusalem, King Hezekiah prepared for the city's defense. Among other things, "he worked hard repairing all the broken sections of the wall and building towers on it. He built another wall outside that one and reinforced the supporting terraces" (2 Chronicles 32:5).

The man who can't control his impulses is constantly in danger of blindly following them and then paying the price. Those impulses might be anger, lust, drunkenness, ambition, or revenge. Our defense is the Lord who is our strength and, if we fall, our source of forgiveness.

The fool

26 **Like snow in summer or rain in harvest,**
honor is not fitting for a fool.

² **Like a fluttering sparrow or a darting swallow,**
an undeserved curse does not come to rest.

³ **A whip for the horse, a halter for the donkey,**
and a rod for the backs of fools!

Eleven of the next twelve verses (all except verse 2) deal with the fool. We have read about the fool in many passages, but this is the largest concentration of verses about him.

When it snows or rains out of season, we consider it inappropriate. It can also be destructive rather than beneficial.

255

Proverbs 26:4,5

A position of honor is inappropriate for a fool, and from that position he can do more harm than good. In our day superficial people often rise to positions of honor because of their looks, athletic ability, or popular music appeal. Their opinions on politics and religion, along with endorsements of everything from underwear to beer, reach the hearing of millions. This is not fitting.

Earlier, we've seen Solomon use the ant as an object lesson (6:6). Beginning with verse 2, he uses several more animals as illustrations in chapter 26: the sparrow, swallow, horse, donkey, dog, and lion. In keeping with his wide-ranging studies, Solomon "taught about animals and birds, reptiles and fish" (1 Kings 4:33).

As sparrows and swallows restlessly wander from their nests and back again, so a curse restlessly stays in the air once it's been uttered. The word *curse* has the root meaning of "be slight, of little account." To curse someone is to put that person down, although we often tend to think of cursing only in terms of the biggest put down, wishing someone damned. When we have been slighted—whether verbally or otherwise—it bothers us. Like a restless bird, it keeps fluttering overhead and won't go away. That's the nature of curses, in particular undeserved ones. Let's be careful, therefore, how we treat others and build them up instead of cursing them.

A horse needs a whip to keep moving in the right direction. A donkey, being more stubborn, needs a bridle. Like an animal, a fool needs a rod across his back, or as some might say, a good swift kick! The point is that some people—namely, fools—don't respond to words and reason. They need strong object lessons.

> **⁴ Do not answer a fool according to his folly,
> or you will be like him yourself.**

256

Proverbs 26:6-11

**⁵ Answer a fool according to his folly,
or he will be wise in his own eyes.**

For centuries, these back-to-back proverbs have given Bible scholars headaches. Some felt this to be an obvious contradiction, enough reason for Proverbs not to be a part of Scripture. When we think about it, however, it's highly unlikely that wise King Solomon or the scribes of Hezekiah's day would be so dense as not to see that these proverbs stand in opposition to each other! Obviously, they placed them side by side for a reason.

There are several possibilities as to what that reason was. (1) Some suggest that the pair of proverbs shows the impossibility of dealing with the fool. Whether you answer the fool or not, you'll look bad, simply for having dealt with him. (2) Others suggest that verse 4 applies to worldly matters and verse 5 to religious concerns. (3) Still another suggestion is that we are to answer a person, unless we know him to be a fool. In other words, give him the benefit of the doubt, until you discover that the person is a dyed-in-the-wool fool.

The second and third possibilities have this in common: both suggest that circumstances determine how one responds. With this in mind, we offer a fourth suggestion. Timing is central. "There is a time for everything," says the wise king (Ecclesiastes 3:1). While there is still hope of reaching the fool, do not answer "according to his folly" (verse 4). Rather than a foolish answer, give him a serious one. It may sink in. If he refuses to listen, then answer him "according to his folly" (verse 5). Give him a silly answer in keeping with his foolish state of mind.

**⁶ Like cutting off one's feet or drinking violence
is the sending of a message by the hand of a fool.**

Proverbs 26:6-11

⁷ **Like a lame man's legs that hang limp**
   is a proverb in the mouth of a fool.

⁸ **Like tying a stone in a sling**
   is the giving of honor to a fool.

⁹ **Like a thornbush in a drunkard's hand**
   is a proverb in the mouth of a fool.

¹⁰ **Like an archer who wounds at random**
   is he who hires a fool or any passer-by.

¹¹ **As a dog returns to its vomit,**
   so a fool repeats his folly.

"Drinking violence" is a phrase we've seen before (4:17). It has to do with wicked people's thirst for evil. Like cutting off one's feet, it depicts the kind of behavior that produces nothing but evil and pain. Solomon places the foolish messenger on a level with such horrors. The fool-as-messenger is likely to get the message wrong or in some way fail in his mission. The result: pain and evil consequences.

Continuing with the imagery of a lame man, Solomon compares the man's legs with a proverb in a fool's mouth. The lame man's legs are not able to carry him; a fool's mouth cannot properly convey a proverb. He can say the words, but because he lacks real understanding he misuses the words. He is unable to apply them to his life. On occasion one hears a politician blatantly misquoting a Bible passage in an attempt to show his knowledge of Scripture to Christian voters. On occasion one sees professing Christians living lives that blatantly contradict what their lips profess. Both illustrate the truth of verse 7.

With a stone he hurled from his sling, young David slew the giant Goliath (1 Samuel 17:48-50). That never would have happened if David had foolishly tied the stone into the sling! Honoring a fool is about as useless (verse 8).

258

Proverbs 26:6-11

Verse 9 uses a different illustration to express the same truth as verse 7. A drunkard holding a thornbush is bound to cut his hand, and he'll probably swing some branches around and cut somebody who's standing nearby. A fool will bring hurt to himself and others through his mishandling of wisdom. Saint Peter offers an interesting example of this, as he discusses how some misused the inspired writings of his fellow apostle Saint Paul:

> Bear in mind that our Lord's patience means salvation, just as our dear brother Paul also wrote you with the wisdom that God gave him. He writes the same way in all his letters, speaking in them of these matters. His letters contain some things that are hard to understand, which ignorant and unstable people distort, as they do the other Scriptures, to their own destruction. (2 Peter 3:15,16)

Those who take Scripture out of context and twist it to fit their own ideas are harming themselves and others. They are fools.

Care in the choice of workers is the theme of verse 10. An archer who shoots wildly is a dangerous person. It's a dangerous practice to hire anyone who comes along. The person may turn out to be a thief or lazy; your business may end in ruin. This is not to say we shouldn't give people the opportunity to work and earn a living. But care is necessary.

Peter quotes the first line of verse 11 and adds another proverb not in the book of Proverbs: "A sow that is washed goes back to her wallowing in the mud." He applies these proverbs to people who knew the "way of righteousness," only "to turn their backs on the sacred command that was passed on to them" (2 Peter 2:21,22). Without quoting from Proverbs, the writer to the Hebrews and the apostle John

Proverbs 26:13-16

also warn of falling from grace and back into sin (Hebrews 6:4-8; 1 John 2:19). The picture isn't pretty. Eating vomited food will only make the dog sick all over again. Forsaking God's wisdom and returning to sinful habits and unbelief is spiritually sickening, foolish, and destructive.

**¹² Do you see a man wise in his own eyes?
There is more hope for a fool than for him.**

This verse closes the proverbs concerning the fool with a reminder. Believe it or not, there is someone worse off than the fool! That's the person who proudly thinks he is wise. Pride is the most frightening of conditions, because it cuts one off from the Savior. Those who are wise in their own eyes are blind to their sin and their need for God's grace.

The attitude of the self-satisfied is far removed from that of the believer who humbly stands in fear of the Lord.

The lazy person

**¹³ The sluggard says, "There is a lion in the road,
a fierce lion roaming the streets!"**

**¹⁴ As a door turns on its hinges,
so a sluggard turns on his bed.**

**¹⁵ The sluggard buries his hand in the dish;
he is too lazy to bring it back to his mouth.**

**¹⁶ The sluggard is wiser in his own eyes
than seven men who answer discreetly.**

Immediately following a large cluster of proverbs concerning the fool, we have four proverbs about the sluggard. The connection is not accidental; laziness is a variety of foolishness.

Verse 13 is a variation of Proverbs 22:13. The Hebrew word for *lion* is different in each case. In passing, we note the sluggard's creativity—in his use of different terms and in his

Proverbs 26:17-19

variety of excuses. But when it comes right down to it, the lazy person is merely grasping for any excuse to avoid going out to work.

After offering an excuse, the sluggard rolls over in bed (verse 14). Not only does he roll over like a door turning on its hinge, but he is about as attached to his bed as a door is to its hinge.

Verse 15 is almost identical with Proverbs 19:24. Having listened to the sluggard offer excuses and having seen him lying in bed, we now watch him lazily sit down at the dinner table. Again, the picture is exasperating.

What's most exasperating of all is that the sluggard doesn't even realize his own pitiful condition (verse 16)! He is too lazy to acquire wisdom, and yet he considers himself wiser than those who are truly thoughtful and show it in the answers they give. The number 7 is a number signifying completeness. We might say, "several men," instead of "seven men."

Notice that the section on the sluggard, like the previous section on the fool, ends with a proverb against being wise in one's own eyes. The person who thinks he or she can't be taught is in the worst shape of all.

Concerning meddling

> ¹⁷ Like one who seizes a dog by the ears
>   is a passer-by who meddles in a quarrel not his own.
>
> ¹⁸ Like a madman shooting
>   firebrands or deadly arrows
> ¹⁹ is a man who deceives his neighbor
>   and says, "I was only joking!"

For people in ancient Israel, the dog usually wasn't a cute household pet. Rather, it was a dirty scavenger that ran wild in the streets. To grab a passing dog was to invite getting bit.

Proverbs 26:20-22

Solomon compares that with jumping into a quarrel between other parties. Granted, there is a time for being a peacemaker. Christian common sense will dictate when that is.

There's also a proper time for humor and a proper way to be humorous. To deceive someone and cause discomfort is not God pleasing, even if you are "only joking." Solomon speaks against the kind of humor that leads to misunderstandings and hurt feelings. He compares it with a madman shooting flaming, deadly arrows. Innocent people are bound to get wounded.

Godly humor maintains a gentleness and concern for others. It is the humor of love.

Avoid gossip

> ²⁰ **Without wood a fire goes out;**
> **without gossip a quarrel dies down.**
>
> ²¹ **As charcoal to embers and as wood to fire,**
> **so is a quarrelsome man for kindling strife.**
>
> ²² **The words of a gossip are like choice morsels;**
> **they go down to a man's inmost parts.**

Proverbs calls for self-control, over against the uninhibited venting of one's passions. Most people are able to control themselves enough physically so that they don't strike out and hit others. Controlling the tongue is another matter. Most people have a great deal of trouble in this area. Solomon offers three proverbs on tongue control.

The first two use imagery related to fire. The sage begins with an obvious statement: "Without wood a fire goes out." This is a fact of the material world. Solomon continues: "Without gossip a quarrel dies down." This is an ethical fact. Gossip is a fuel on which quarrels feed. The way to extinguish the fire is to remove the gossip. Instead, speak words of forgiveness and love.

262

Proverbs 26:23-28

Verse 21 likens quarrelsome people to the materials that keep fires burning. We use similar images to depict such persons: They have "fiery tempers," easily get "hot under the collar," and become involved in "heated arguments." In his inspired letter, James expressed it more strongly:

> Consider what a great forest is set on fire by a small spark. The tongue also is a fire, a world of evil among the parts of the body. It corrupts the whole person, sets the whole course of his life on fire, and is itself set on fire by hell. (3:5-7)

If we have such inclinations (and who can say he or she doesn't?), then we need to "cool it," step back, and pour some water on the fire. Jesus says that when a person has God's Word and the Holy Spirit, "streams of living water will flow from within him" (John 7:38). The Word is the extinguisher for the tongue's deadly fires.

Verse 22 is exactly the same as 18:8. In this present context, we might build on the fire imagery some more. If the fires of gossip never get started, those "choice morsels" will never get cooked.

The evils of lying

> 23 Like a coating of glaze over earthenware
> are fervent lips with an evil heart.
>
> 24 A malicious man disguises himself with his lips,
> but in his heart he harbors deceit.
>
> 25 Though his speech is charming, do not believe him,
> for seven abominations fill his heart.
>
> 26 His malice may be concealed by deception,
> but his wickedness will be exposed in the assembly.
>
> 27 If a man digs a pit, he will fall into it;
> if a man rolls a stone, it will roll back on him.

Proverbs 26:23-28

**²⁸ A lying tongue hates those it hurts,
and a flattering mouth works ruin.**

The clean, smooth outer surface of a ceramic cup conceals the common clay of which the pot is made. Jesus used the same picture in denouncing the hypocrites of his day: "Woe to you, teachers of the law and Pharisees, you hypocrites! You clean the outside of the cup and dish, but inside they are full of greed and self-indulgence. Blind Pharisee! First clean the inside of the cup and dish, and then the outside also will be clean" (Matthew 23:25,26). Cleaning the inside of the cup means praying with the psalmist: "Hide your face from my sins and blot out all my iniquity. Create in me a pure heart, O God" (51:9,10).

Verses 24 to 26 emphasize the fact that smooth speech is frequently a cover-up for a deceitful heart. For the "seven abominations," see Proverbs 6:16-19. Again, the number 7 represents completeness. It's a way of saying the heart is full of evil.

One might wonder, "If a deceiver is so smooth, how will I know he's a liar so that I do not believe him?" Sooner or later the truth will come out. Jesus says, "There is nothing hidden that will not be disclosed, and nothing concealed that will not be known or brought out into the open" (Luke 8:17). Often that exposure comes in this lifetime. Evidences of lying surface; a person's teaching or life does not square with what the Bible teaches. Where there is unrepented sin, Christians will carry out church discipline and bring the matter before "the assembly," the congregation. (See Matthew 18:15-20.) God has his ways of exposing the wicked.

Those who plan evil for others often have that very evil come back on them (verse 27). In the book of Esther, the fate of wicked Haman furnishes a vivid example of this truth. Haman had a large gallows built for the hanging of his enemy,

Proverbs 27:1,2

the Jew Mordecai, but ended up being hanged on that very gallows! (See Esther 7:9,10.) Often, people are destroyed in less direct ways by their schemes. One's anger toward another, for instance, can come back and consume. The illustration of one falling into his own pit occurs elsewhere in the Old Testament, as in Ecclesiastes 10:8 in which Solomon uses it.

In verse 28 the lying tongue and flattering mouth are given the characteristics of the person behind them: the tongue hates and the mouth ruins. A "flattering mouth" is, literally, a "smooth mouth." Smooth speech conceals the liar's real purpose, which is to harm the one he or she is flattering.

Once again in this cluster of proverbs, we are struck by how Solomon intertwines speech with motives and actions. The heart, the mouth, and the hand are to work together. We can't have one set of values in our hearts and then try to fake another with our outward behavior. It all goes together. It's all one package.

All of chapter 26 has dealt with negative subjects—things to avoid. We studied the fool (verses 1-12); the sluggard (verses 13-16); and the misuse of the tongue by meddling (verses 17-19), gossiping (verses 20-22), and lying (verses 23-28). Sanctified living always has two sides. On the positive side, God tells us what to do. On the negative, he tells us what not to do. Both are necessary, so that we get a complete picture of what it means to live as God's children.

General advice and observations

27 **Do not boast about tomorrow,
      for you do not know what a day may bring forth.**

**² Let another praise you, and not your own mouth;
      someone else, and not your own lips.**

James refers to Proverbs 27:1 as he teaches us to say, "If it is the Lord's will, we will live and do this or that"

Proverbs 27:3-8

(4:15). Since our times are in God's hands (Psalm 31:15), it is foolish to boast as if we control the future.

The rich fool in Jesus' parable made that mistake. He boasted: "I'll say to myself, 'You have plenty of good things laid up for many years. Take life easy; eat, drink and be merry.'" God's response was: "You fool! This very night your life will be demanded from you." (See Luke 12:16-21.)

Just as we ought not boast about the future, we are not to boast about ourselves either. Leave that to others. Whatever talents we have come from God. And whatever we accomplish in life happens only because he has enabled us. So, if there is to be praise, let that come from someone else.

Solomon's frequent warnings about the smooth talk of wicked people and about the fickleness of many "friends" should remind us not to put too much stock in human praise. Far more important than the praise of other human beings is the praise of God himself (John 12:43).

> ³ **Stone is heavy and sand a burden,**
> **but provocation by a fool is heavier than both.**
>
> ⁴ **Anger is cruel and fury overwhelming,**
> **but who can stand before jealousy?**
>
> ⁵ **Better is open rebuke**
> **than hidden love.**
>
> ⁶ **Wounds from a friend can be trusted,**
> **but an enemy multiplies kisses.**
>
> ⁷ **He who is full loathes honey,**
> **but to the hungry even what is bitter tastes sweet.**
>
> ⁸ **Like a bird that strays from its nest**
> **is a man who strays from his home.**

When a fool provokes others, it's a heavy burden. Because the fool cannot be reasoned with, he becomes all the more annoying. People who reject God and his Word are fools; they provoke the Lord. For example, we read that King Jeroboam

Proverbs 27:3-8

"provoked the LORD, the God of Israel, to anger" (1 Kings 15:30). As a judgment upon this wicked king, his entire family was destroyed.

As harsh as anger and fury are, jealousy is even more severe (verse 4). Often when the Bible speaks of jealousy, it speaks of the positive characteristic, such as God being jealous. In his intense love for us, he wants our devotion (see, for example, Exodus 20:5). He is jealous for us. Saint Paul wrote to the Christians in Corinth, "I am jealous for you with a godly jealousy" (2 Corinthians 11:2).

Besides jealousy *for* someone, there is jealousy *of* someone. Solomon speaks of this negative jealousy. In answer to his rhetorical question, no one can stand before this jealousy. It leads to the destruction of its object, and it consumes its possessor. If our hearts harbor such jealousy, we need to ask God's forgiveness and help to root it out.

The seven simple words of verse 5 speak volumes. For all the brashness of our present world, our society shies away from criticizing, especially on a person-to-person basis. It takes courage to confront, and there is always the danger that openness will result in hurt feelings and broken friendships. Yet open, loving, constructive rebuke is God's way. It is better than talking behind one's back or, out of love, saying nothing when something needs to be said.

Paul openly criticized Peter for "not acting in line with the truth of the gospel" (Galatians 2:14). It was the loving, God-pleasing, and helpful thing to do. At times Jesus rebuked his disciples. We need to ask God's help in this area—both to offer loving rebuke when necessary and to accept it when we need it. Hidden love, however, remains within the heart and neither rebukes nor warms the loved one with its fire.

No matter how tactfully they come, loving rebukes still sting. These are the "wounds from a friend" (verse 6). But

267

Proverbs 27:9,10

like good medicine that stings, such wounds are wholesome. The one who applies the medicine is trustworthy. As Judas betrayed Jesus with a kiss (Mark 14:44,45), however, enemies merely feign friendship and love.

They say that hunger is the best cook. When we have eaten a big meal, nothing looks inviting. When we're famished, anything does. Applying verse 7 to spiritual matters, we need daily to remember our sinfulness and our need for the Savior. Otherwise, we become self-satisfied and foolishly think we need nothing, when in reality we are starving to death.

The mother bird that strays from her nest must build another one. The person who strays from home must begin all over from scratch. Those who have physically wandered or been uprooted know what an overwhelming task it can be. The word picture Solomon paints in verse 8 is lonely and sad, especially when applied to our spiritual lives. Those who stray from the teachings of God's Word are spiritually homeless. They might build another home, but it will never be as good as what they left behind.

> ⁹ **Perfume and incense bring joy to the heart,**
> **and the pleasantness of one's friend springs from his earnest counsel.**
> ¹⁰ **Do not forsake your friend and the friend of your father,**
> **and do not go to your brother's house when disaster strikes you—**
> **better a neighbor nearby than a brother far away.**

Solomon appeals to the sense of smell in describing the joy of true friendship. The fragrances of perfume and incense please anyone who comes near. The "earnest counsel" of a friend is his deep-felt desire to help. It's one of life's finer pleasures to have a good friend who's willing to listen and offer loving advice.

Proverbs 27:11-16

Just as we want the benefits of friendship from others, we will want to be a friend as well. Be the kind of friend who nurtures lasting friendships, such as with longtime family friends. The second and third lines of verse 10 point out that a good friend can be more helpful than one's own brother, especially if that friend lives nearby. Sometimes one's own family members are far away not only in distance but also emotionally. What a joy it is to know that in Jesus we have the closest friend of all!

These two verses, like 18:24, emphasize the priceless value of good friends. Pray for that kind of friend and be one too.

> ¹¹ **Be wise, my son, and bring joy to my heart;**
> **then I can answer anyone who treats me with**
> **contempt.**
> ¹² **The prudent see danger and take refuge,**
> **but the simple keep going and suffer for it.**
> ¹³ **Take the garment of one who puts up security for**
> **a stranger;**
> **hold it in pledge if he does it for a wayward woman.**
> ¹⁴ **If a man loudly blesses his neighbor early in the morning,**
> **it will be taken as a curse.**
> ¹⁵ **A quarrelsome wife**
> **is like a constant dripping on a rainy day;**
> ¹⁶ **restraining her is like restraining the wind**
> **or grasping oil with the hand.**

It's a source of joy when the young accept the teaching of parents or teachers. Should critics question them or try to put them down, they can point to the young who have followed their teachings. Wise young people are proof of the value of their elders.

The sage goes on to point to one of the results of good instruction—"the prudent" are able to spot danger and avoid it.

Proverbs 27:17-22

But the simple, who have not been well instructed, naively walk into danger and suffer for it. One can think of many examples in our day of dangers about which to warn the young: premarital sex, drugs, drinking, unwise friendships, disrespect for authority. Christian parents, teachers, and church leaders will work together to guide and warn the young.

In verse 13 we see yet another of life's dangers to which the young might be especially susceptible—foolishly assuming someone else's debt. This verse is an exact repetition of 20:16.

Although not explicitly stated in verse 14, the implication is that the blessing is not sincere. The description of the blessing as being both "loud" and "early in the morning" indicates that it comes with vigor and energy. The point is that when a person comes across as too eager to be friendly, his overtures may well be met with suspicion. People think there must be ulterior motives behind the blessing.

While some might be overly eager to please, verses 15 and 16 portray a wife who is at the opposite end of the spectrum. Her complaining is constant—like dripping on a rainy day. Nor can one stop it—anymore than one can hold back the wind or grab hold of oil with his hand. Far from downplaying the role of wives in ancient society, these verses show the vital part they played in their husbands' lives. That still holds true. A wife can either make or break her husband. The only way to deal with the quarrelsome wife is to remove oneself until her mood has passed (see 21:9,19).

Scattered throughout Proverbs are verses describing the disagreeable wife. The book's closing verses, however, describe the wife of noble character (31:10-31).

> [17] **As iron sharpens iron,**
> **so one man sharpens another.**

Proverbs 27:17-22

¹⁸ **He who tends a fig tree will eat its fruit,**
and he who looks after his master will be honored.

¹⁹ **As water reflects a face,**
so a man's heart reflects the man.

²⁰ **Death and Destruction are never satisfied,**
and neither are the eyes of man.

²¹ **The crucible for silver and the furnace for gold,**
but man is tested by the praise he receives.

²² **Though you grind a fool in a mortar,**
grinding him like grain with a pestle,
you will not remove his folly from him.

When we share and learn with others, we sharpen one another, as iron sharpens iron. The rabbis of old held that studying with others leads to fuller and more accurate knowledge. When we do all of our learning alone, there is the possibility that, without the corrective of others, we will go off on tangents. Verse 17 is a good endorsement for attending Bible study at church, in addition to reading Scripture at home alone.

Along with the grapevine, olive trees, and palm trees, the fig tree receives frequent mention on the pages of Scripture. This slow-growing plant requires years of patient care. It was often planted with the grapevine, and its growth symbolized prosperity. For example: "During Solomon's lifetime Judah and Israel . . . lived in safety, each man under his own vine and fig tree" (1 Kings 4:25). Conversely, the failure or destruction of the fig tree represented national disaster. In light of all this, the person tending a fig tree in verse 18 is the person who through careful effort enjoys prosperity.

Solomon compares the hardworking farmer with a servant who faithfully works for his master and enjoys his favor. Saint Paul takes up the picture and applies it to the servant of the Lord Jesus Christ: "The hardworking farmer should be the

271

Proverbs 27:17-22

first to receive a share of the crops" (2 Timothy 2:6). And Jesus himself declares, "My Father will honor the one who serves me" (John 12:26). When our heavenly Master so rewards us, it is an undeserved reward of grace. For, as Jesus tells us elsewhere, we have to admit, "We are unworthy servants; we have only done our duty" (Luke 17:10).

Verse 19 compares the human heart to a reflection in water. We might understand the second line in two ways, both of which are fitting. (1) The heart reflects the true person. If you want to know what a person is really like, you'll need to know what's in his or her heart. (2) The reflection spoken of comes not from within our own hearts but from the heart of another. In other words, what is in our hearts is reflected in the heart of another. Our feelings and thoughts find reflection in the feelings and thoughts of others. Because of this, we are able to pour out our hearts to another, and that person will understand and sympathize, because his or her heart holds similar thoughts and feelings.

Earlier, we discussed the personification of "Death and Destruction." (See 15:11.) Never satisfied, they continually take in more and more (verse 20). The eyes of man, says Solomon, are like that. In Ecclesiastes the wise king speaks in a similar way: "The eye never has enough of seeing" (1:8), and the eye of a greedy man is "not content with his wealth" (4:8). Solomon is describing what the Bible elsewhere calls "the lust of the eyes" (1 John 2:16). The eye represents human covetousness and greed. Sinful man always wants more and is never content.

Ironically, the dust of the grave will finally fill the unsatisfied eye! There is, of course, another, better solution for the restless eye. Rather than fixing our eyes on the things of this world, which can never satisfy, let us fix them on Jesus. He brings peace, satisfaction, forgiveness, and victory over

272

Proverbs 27:23-27

"Death and Destruction." Saint Paul put it this way: "We fix our eyes not on what is seen, but on what is unseen. For what is seen is temporary, but what is unseen is eternal" (2 Corinthians 4:18).

The first line of verse 21 is the same as the first line of 17:3. There the second line reads, "But the LORD tests the heart." God tests the heart through trials; verse 21 shows that men test the heart in a different way. How we respond to whatever flattery we might receive is a test of our character. Jesus warned, "Woe to you when all men speak well of you, for that is how their fathers treated the false prophets" (Luke 6:26). If the praise of men is a major driving force in our lives, we'll tend to be less than honest and not so willing to speak up for and live the truth of God's Word.

Moreover, when praise comes, how do we deal with it? Do we let it "go to our heads"? Or do we keep focused on the One who gives us whatever abilities and success we have?

Akin to the thought of verse 22, an old Jewish saying goes, "Drunkards sober up, but fools remain fools." If even after grinding a fool down to powder in a mortar with a pestle, his foolishness remains—what hope is there? Humanly speaking, none. Only God, for whom nothing is impossible, can change the fool. By nature we are all fools. Through Christ, we become wise.

Rural routines

23 **Be sure you know the condition of your flocks,**
   give careful attention to your herds;
24 **for riches do not endure forever,**
   and a crown is not secure for all generations.
25 **When the hay is removed and new growth appears**
   and the grass from the hills is gathered in,
26 **the lambs will provide you with clothing,**
   and the goats with the price of a field.

Proverbs 27:23-27

²⁷ **You will have plenty of goats' milk to feed you
and your family and to nourish your servant girls.**

This little group of proverbs paints a rural scene. In Solomon's day young men were tempted to leave the rural life for the wealth and luxuries of the city. He depicts the simplicity and beauty of country life.

Instead of leaving the country, Solomon urges attention to the work at hand—taking care of the flocks and herds (verse 23). Young Israelites may have recalled the care that Jacob took while tending his father-in-law's sheep and goats (Genesis 31:38-40). Riches, even the crown of a king, are not secure (verse 24). Even if you amass them for yourself, you may not be able to pass them on to future generations. The implication is this: therefore, do not set your heart on them.

Part of the joy of rural life comes from observing the wonder of the changing seasons, in particular harvesttime (verse 25), which in Israel takes place in April. The "grass from the hills" refers to pasturage that was harvested somewhat later. The psalmist reminds us of the source of these blessings, when he declares, "[The LORD] makes grass grow on the hills" (147:8).

Then there are the animals (verses 26,27). Lambs provide wool, which the women would select and spin into clothing (see 31:13,19). Goats could be sold for purchasing a field (see 31:16), or their milk would feed the family as well as servants. To this day, goats' milk is commonly drunk in the Middle East.

This depiction of rural life is more than just a pretty picture. It also serves as an illustration of contentment with God's provision. We continue to rely on the produce of the country. And may we continue to thank a gracious God who sustains our lives, as he sends the rain and sunshine.

274

Proverbs 28:1-6

General advice and observations

28 The wicked man flees though no one pursues,
but the righteous are as bold as a lion.

² When a country is rebellious, it has many rulers,
but a man of understanding and knowledge
maintains order.

³ A ruler who oppresses the poor
is like a driving rain that leaves no crops.

⁴ Those who forsake the law praise the wicked,
but those who keep the law resist them.

⁵ Evil men do not understand justice,
but those who seek the Lord understand it fully.

⁶ Better a poor man whose walk is blameless
than a rich man whose ways are perverse.

We are still in the Second Collection of Solomon's Proverbs (25:1–29:27). From this point until the end of the collection, we note a difference. Almost all the proverbs from here on are of the antithetical type, expressing a contrast between the first and second lines. In this respect, they more closely resemble the large First Collection of Solomon's Proverbs (10:1–22:16). They express truths we have encountered before in our study of Proverbs.

"Thus conscience does make cowards of us all," wrote Shakespeare. Those who do not know God's grace must live not only with the awareness of their sin but also with the nagging awareness of judgment. There is the continual fear of getting found out by other people or caught by God himself.

When he wrote the second line of verse 1, Solomon may have been thinking of his father, David. Armed with a slingshot and the strength of the Almighty, David had boldly challenged and defeated the giant Goliath. In Psalm 18:32, David declared, "It is God who arms me with strength."

275

Proverbs 28:1-6

Throughout the centuries, believers have found that same lionlike courage, not in their own powers but in the righteousness of Christ.

Following Solomon's time, the Northern Kingdom of Israel changed dynasties nine times in a little more than two hundred years of existence. Because of the sinfulness of its rulers, each dynasty (except the first) began with the destruction of the previous one. As God said of them, "All their kings fall, and none of them calls on me" (Hosea 7:7). The Southern Kingdom of Judah, however, had only one dynasty during its almost 350 years; that was the family of righteous King David. In our day we continue to see a constant turnover of wicked rulers who invite rebellion and overthrow. But the Lord continues to bless godly countries and their rulers (verse 2).

As an NIV footnote indicates, verse 3 might also be translated, "A poor man." This seems preferable. When greedy poor people seize power, they can be more ruthless than anyone in oppressing other poor people. Like a driving storm, they destroy everything in sight. How unlike the eternal King described by Solomon in his messianic psalm: "He will be like rain falling on a mown field, like showers watering the earth" (72:6).

At times believers become discouraged when they observe how the world praises the ungodly, while it ignores or persecutes the righteous. Some might even be tempted to join ranks with the wicked. Verse 4, however, strengthens God's people. Rather than forsaking "the law," believers, with God's help, stand up against the wicked. The word for "law" in this verse (and in verses 7 and 9) is *torah*. This term refers not simply to the Law, as in the Ten Commandments, but to God's teachings in general. It is also the term designating the first five books of the Bible— the Pentateuch, the books of Moses. To keep the law means to hold to the teachings of Scripture.

276

Proverbs 28:7-10

The word "justice" in verse 5 is another interesting term. Justice is not merely a human attribute; its source is God, whose "ways are just" (Deuteronomy 32:4). Ultimately, it is "from the LORD that man gets justice" (Proverbs 29:26). This justice includes compassion toward the fatherless, widows, and aliens (Deuteronomy 10:18), as well as God's punishment of those who oppress his people (Deuteronomy 32:40-43). Only those who are connected by faith to the source of this justice really understand it. They seek God in his Word and reflect his justice in their lives.

Keeping God's law and understanding justice—such are the real issues in the eyes of the Lord. God looks for these qualities, not superficial matters, such as how much money someone has. Solomon drives this point home in verse 6.

When we see the word "blameless" here and elsewhere in Proverbs, it is not synonymous with *sinless*. Everyone sins. The blameless are those whose sins are forgiven and who live sanctified lives. Some translations use the word *integrity*.

> ⁷ **He who keeps the law is a discerning son,**
> **but a companion of gluttons disgraces his father.**
>
> ⁸ **He who increases his wealth by exorbitant interest**
> **amasses it for another, who will be kind to the poor.**
>
> ⁹ **If anyone turns a deaf ear to the law,**
> **even his prayers are detestable.**
>
> ¹⁰ **He who leads the upright along an evil path**
> **will fall into his own trap,**
> **but the blameless will receive a good inheritance.**

A wise son listens to and keeps God's Word. A wicked son is a disgrace. Verse 7 summarizes Proverbs' many passages concerning wise and foolish sons, especially 23:19-25.

Proverbs 28:7-10

Verse 8 contains the only reference in Proverbs to usury. Several Old Testament passages forbade Israelites charging interest of fellow Israelites (for example, Leviticus 25:35-37; Deuteronomy 23:19,20). We see this attitude expressed in the laws given at Mount Sinai:

> If you lend money to one of my people among you who is needy, do not be like a moneylender; charge him no interest. If you take your neighbor's cloak as a pledge, return it to him by sunset, because his cloak is the only covering he has for his body. What else will he sleep in? When he cries out to me, I will hear, for I am compassionate. (Exodus 22:25-27)

God's judgment on those who take advantage of the poor is that their wealth will eventually end up in the hands of those who use it to help the poor!

In verse 9 we again see the word "law" (see also verses 4 and 7). To "turn a deaf ear to the law" is, literally, "to turn one's ear from hearing the law"; that is, refusing to listen. This proverb is about as blunt as can be. Since the wicked refuse to listen to God, God will not listen to the wicked!

In and of itself, sinning is bad enough. It is even more terrible to lead others into sin. The wicked are preparing their own doom when they lead the upright into sin. Jesus talks about the severity of leading children into sin: "If anyone causes one of these little ones who believe in me to sin, it would be better for him to have a large millstone hung around his neck and to be drowned in the depths of the sea" (Matthew 18:6).

Peter speaks of Christians inheriting a blessing (1 Peter 3:9). And Jesus says that on judgment day, he will declare to those on his right, "Come, you who are blessed by my

Proverbs 28:11-14

Father; take your inheritance, the kingdom prepared for you since the creation of the world" (Matthew 25:34). Such is the "good inheritance" God has in store for his people. Unlike wages, which we earn, an inheritance is a gift—in this case, a gift of God's grace.

> ¹¹ **A rich man may be wise in his own eyes,**
> **but a poor man who has discernment sees through him.**
> ¹² **When the righteous triumph, there is great elation;**
> **but when the wicked rise to power, men go into hiding.**
> ¹³ **He who conceals his sins does not prosper,**
> **but whoever confesses and renounces them finds mercy.**
> ¹⁴ **Blessed is the man who always fears the LORD,**
> **but he who hardens his heart falls into trouble.**

In our day, as in Solomon's, wealth is often associated with wisdom. Because a person is good at making money, supposedly he is wise. We've seen enough of Proverbs to know that the materially rich can be spiritually foolish. The poor but discerning person sees through this. As one commentator puts it, "Wisdom is no respecter of rank."

This passage is troubling when we think of how eager churches can be to court the rich and place them on important committees and boards. Yet nowhere does the Bible hold up riches as a measure of wisdom. In listing qualifications for an elder, for instance, Paul says, "He must hold firmly to the trustworthy message as it has been taught, so that he can encourage others by sound doctrine and refute those who oppose it" (Titus 1:9). God distributes this kind of wisdom without regard for how much money a person has or doesn't have.

Verse 12 is similar to 11:10. Although the wicked often prosper, no one is elated when they gain power. Everyone knows—or soon finds out—that the wicked are inter-

279

Proverbs 28:15-17

ested only in themselves. They will step on anyone who gets in their way. During the reign of Israel's notorious King Ahab, one hundred prophets went into hiding (1 Kings 18:13). On the other hand, when the righteous come to power, people know that justice and mercy will prevail.

Verse 13 is a beautiful expression of the gospel. It brings to mind the words of the apostle John: "If we claim to be without sin, we deceive ourselves and the truth is not in us. If we confess our sins, he is faithful and just and will forgive us our sins and purify us from all unrighteousness" (1 John 1:8,9; see also Psalm 32). As long as we refuse to admit our sinfulness, we suffer—in our emotional lives, in our relationships with other people, and, above all, in relation to God. To confess sins is to know the joy of forgiveness. With repentance goes the sincere desire to renounce sin and, with God's help, amend our ways.

The fear spoken of in verse 14 is not the reverent fear usually associated with fearing the Lord. Rather, a different Hebrew word is used. The idea is one of fearing sin and its consequences. Along with godly fear, the Christian has a healthy fear of sin. We know what it can do. But the ungodly couldn't care less. He hardens his heart, boldly jumps into sin, and sooner or later faces the terrible consequences.

> ¹⁵ **Like a roaring lion or a charging bear**
> **is a wicked man ruling over a helpless people.**
>
> ¹⁶ **A tyrannical ruler lacks judgment,**
> **but he who hates ill-gotten gain will enjoy a long life.**
>
> ¹⁷ **A man tormented by the guilt of murder**
> **will be a fugitive till death;**
> **let no one support him.**

The prophet Amos asks the questions "Does a lion roar in the thicket when he has no prey? Does he growl in his den

Like a roaring lion . . . is a wicked man ruling

Proverbs 28:18-23

when he has caught nothing?" (3:4). Likewise, the wicked ruler roars and confidently charges forth when he knows he can dominate others. The devil is like that too. "Be self-controlled and alert. Your enemy the devil prowls around like a roaring lion looking for someone to devour" (1 Peter 5:8). The wicked are bullies who enjoy picking on the weak and unsuspecting.

The contrast in verse 16 is between the ruler who unfairly takes advantage of people and the righteous person who hates injustice. In his blind fury, the tyrant rashly oppresses the poor. In doing so, he sows the seeds of his own downfall. History is full of examples of tyrants who abused their power and were overthrown. The honest, hardworking person doesn't face that prospect. Rather, God blesses that person with a long, full life.

Verse 17 brings to mind Genesis 9:6, "Whoever sheds the blood of man, by man shall his blood be shed." In the Old Testament, murder was punishable by death. Those guilty of murder were destined to be on the run until caught by "the avenger of blood," a near relative of the victim. The cities of refuge in Israel afforded shelter for the person who accidentally killed another or who was wrongly accused of murder (see Numbers 35). But the proverb is not addressing such cases. It deals with the one guilty of murder. Supporting him was tantamount to condoning the crime.

> [18] **He whose walk is blameless is kept safe,**
> **but he whose ways are perverse will suddenly fall.**
>
> [19] **He who works his land will have abundant food,**
> **but the one who chases fantasies will have his fill**
> **of poverty.**
>
> [20] **A faithful man will be richly blessed,**
> **but one eager to get rich will not go unpunished.**

Proverbs 28:18-23

²¹ **To show partiality is not good—**
yet a man will do wrong for a piece of bread.
²² **A stingy man is eager to get rich**
and is unaware that poverty awaits him.
²³ **He who rebukes a man will in the end gain more favor**
than he who has a flattering tongue.

Outside of God's path there is no real safety. Money can't buy security. Worldly power and influence can't do it. Human relationships, no matter how close, aren't enough. Ultimately, any who take a way through life that does not follow the Savior are taking a perverse way, no matter how fine it might seem. Whether their "fall" comes in this life or in the hour of death, it will come. The "blameless" are those who walk with Christ, who is "the way" (John 14:6).

God calls on his people to work for a living (verses 19, 20). Our work is the channel through which he blesses us. Those who try to bypass God's Word on this matter will end up empty-handed. Our age has its share of "fantasies" appealing to those interested in getting rich quick. While we might joke about investing in swampland in Florida (or anywhere), many have found out the truth of this proverb by gambling away their money on countless other fantasies. There's no substitute for earning a living the old-fashioned way—working for it. Paul's words to Timothy form a fitting New Testament parallel to these two proverbs:

> But if we have food and clothing, we will be content with that. People who want to get rich fall into temptation and a trap and into many foolish and harmful desires that plunge men into ruin and destruction. For the love of money is a root of all kinds of evil. Some people, eager for money, have wandered from the faith and pierced themselves with many griefs. (1 Timothy 6:8-10)

Proverbs 28:24-28

Everyone is aware that it's not good to play favorites (verse 21). Yet in this corrupt world, some people will turn on you for the slightest bribe, even for "a piece of bread." Nor should we think that God's people have a higher price, as if we can be bought off for two pieces of bread. The Bible emphasizes that Christians are "to do nothing out of favoritism" (1 Timothy 5:21). When it came to our salvation, God showed no partiality; Christ died for all. "He is the atoning sacrifice for our sins, and not only for ours but also for the sins of the whole world" (1 John 2:2). We will want to show that kind of love for all.

Like several other verses in this chapter of Proverbs, verse 22 deals with our attitude toward money. The biblical principle is that generosity, not stinginess, leads to wealth. At times, this wealth may be of a material nature; often it comes in the form of other blessings. And while a stingy man may occasionally acquire the worldly wealth he covets, he won't find true riches, such as friendship and love.

Confronting someone can be difficult. We fear being rejected or hurting people's feelings and losing their friendship. We usually find it much easier to flatter people, even when we know they need to be corrected. In the long run, the person who rebukes gains respect, while the flatterer is dismissed as being insincere. So, while flattery may be easier for the moment, it doesn't accomplish what it's intended to, namely, win the favor of others. Although in the short run rebuke may appear to be harsh, it's actually the loving thing to do. It helps the other person. This rebuke, of course, is not to be confused with purely negative, heartless criticism. It involves loving concern for the welfare of others.

> **24 He who robs his father or mother**
> **and says, "It's not wrong"—**
> **he is partner to him who destroys.**

Proverbs 28:24-28

²⁵ **A greedy man stirs up dissension,**
　　but he who trusts in the LORD **will prosper.**

²⁶ **He who trusts in himself is a fool,**
　　but he who walks in wisdom is kept safe.

²⁷ **He who gives to the poor will lack nothing,**
　　but he who closes his eyes to them receives many curses.

²⁸ **When the wicked rise to power, people go into hiding;**
　　but when the wicked perish, the righteous thrive.

It's hard to imagine anyone robbing his father and mother and saying, "It's not wrong." Yet it happens all the time. In Jesus' day the Jews had a tradition that allowed them to get out of supporting their aged parents by giving a gift to the temple instead (see Mark 7:9-13). Today many children neglect the care of their parents—selfishly getting whatever they can but never returning any love or never visiting them. That's robbing parents of what they deserve. Such children may as well go and vandalize their parents' homes. What they do is just as bad, says Solomon.

Verse 25 sets the greedy man in contrast to the one who trusts in God. Greed, of course, is nothing other than a lack of trust. Since this person doesn't believe that God will provide, he needs to store up more and more possessions. In his mad pursuit for wealth (and the supposed security it brings), he tramples over others and stirs up dissension. In the end, the greedy man has caused a lot of trouble and still not found that peace that only the Lord can bring.

In the first line of verse 26, we have Solomon's definition of the fool. The line literally says, "He who trusts his own heart is a fool." (Since the heart represents the entire inner life of man, the translation "himself" is appropriate.) By nature, the human heart or self is full of sin. Jesus declares, "Out of the heart come evil thoughts, murder, adultery, sexual immorality, theft, false testimony, slander" (Matthew

285

Proverbs 29:1-7

15:19). To trust in one's own evil heart, then, is to make oneself into a fool. Clearly, Solomon's definition of fool fits many people who in the eyes of the world are very wise.

Those who trust in the Lord are the wise ones. Rather than looking within themselves for guidance along life's way, they look to God's Word. God keeps his people safe. With his angels watching over us, he delivers us from harm in this world and brings us safely to our heavenly home.

As we give to the needy, God blesses us (verse 27). Conversely, when we are stingy, we suffer. This is a truth of God's Word that we must take on faith. God challenges us, as he challenged the Old Testament believers to test him by bringing their tithes and offerings: "'Test me in this,' says the LORD Almighty, 'and see if I will not throw open the floodgates of heaven and pour out so much blessing that you will not have room enough for it'" (Malachi 3:10).

Like some sort of moral equation, verse 28 shows the relationship between righteousness in power and the prosperity of a land. As more and more of the wicked rise to positions of power, they use their power to suppress what is good. People are forced into hiding for fear of their lives and for the protection of their families. Sometimes this hiding is physical; sometimes it might mean that people must hide their convictions. Conversely, when the number of the wicked decreases, the righteous thrive (literally, increase). So the population of a land is not static. The righteous and the wicked are increasing and decreasing according to what the other side is doing.

Observing some patterns of life

29 A man who remains stiff-necked after many rebukes will suddenly be destroyed—without remedy.

Proverbs 29:1-7

² **When the righteous thrive, the people rejoice;**
   when the wicked rule, the people groan.

³ **A man who loves wisdom brings joy to his father,**
   but a companion of prostitutes squanders his wealth.

⁴ **By justice a king gives a country stability,**
   but one who is greedy for bribes tears it down.

⁵ **Whoever flatters his neighbor**
   is spreading a net for his feet.

⁶ **An evil man is snared by his own sin,**
   but a righteous one can sing and be glad.

⁷ **The righteous care about justice for the poor,**
   but the wicked have no such concern.

"Stiff-necked" was the Old Testament's vivid way of describing stubborn, willful people. During the Israelites' 40 years in the desert, God and his servant Moses often described them in this way. For example, Moses prayed, "Although this is a stiff-necked people, forgive our wickedness and our sin" (Exodus 34:9).

What a warning this proverb (verse 1) presents! God's patience wears out when people continually rebel against his will. There comes a point of no return.

Verse 2 is similar to 11:10. We can see from ancient history—such as that of the Israelites in Egypt (Exodus 2)—how difficult life can be under wicked rulers. There are also plenty of examples in our own day. We are reminded to work for and pray for righteousness among our officials and throughout our land.

Jesus is the perfect example of the wise son bringing "joy to his father" (verse 3). Of him God the Father declared, "With him I am well pleased" (Matthew 3:17). For an example of the negative line of the proverb, we think of Jesus' parable of the lost son who "squandered" his inheritance

Proverbs 29:1-7

with prostitutes (Luke 15:11-31). This proverb speaks both to fathers and sons. Fathers, raise your children in a way that someday you'll be proud of them. Sons, be the kind of child who will make your father happy.

The theme of just rulers (verse 4) has been treated before (16:12; 25:5). Its continued reoccurrence in Proverbs demonstrates the importance of the subject. This proverb shows how serious a matter bribes can be. Greedy officials who take bribes can destroy a country! The term translated "bribes" usually referred to parts of the sacrifices assigned to priests. For kings to dip into religious contributions was especially reprehensible.

Commentators have understood verse 5 in either of two ways. With his smooth talk the flatterer spreads a net for his neighbor's feet, or he spreads it for his own feet—that is, he gets caught in his own scheming. Both approaches fit with other passages in Proverbs. Solomon may intentionally have left this ambiguous. Flattery is wrong on both counts. Insincere flattery ends up hurting the flatterer or the neighbor or both.

Since verse 6 speaks of an evil man being snared in his own sin, we might be inclined to understand the previous verse in the same way—the flatterer getting caught in his own net. Wicked people are never really at ease. They live with troubled consciences and the awareness that at some time their evil will catch up with them. Not so the righteous man. Knowing God's grace, he sings God's praises and faces the future confidently.

Job was a righteous man; he said, "I was a father to the needy; I took up the case of the stranger" (29:16). The wicked think of themselves first . . . and last. A recent survey of US citizens found that 63 percent agreed that "when it comes right down to it, your first responsibility is to

Proverbs 29:8-14

yourself." How far the "me" generation has departed from what God's Word teaches (verse 7)!

> **⁸ Mockers stir up a city,**
> **but wise men turn away anger.**
>
> **⁹ If a wise man goes to court with a fool,**
> **the fool rages and scoffs, and there is no peace.**
>
> **¹⁰ Bloodthirsty men hate a man of integrity**
> **and seek to kill the upright.**
>
> **¹¹ A fool gives full vent to his anger,**
> **but a wise man keeps himself under control.**
>
> **¹² If a ruler listens to lies,**
> **all his officials become wicked.**
>
> **¹³ The poor man and the oppressor have this in common:**
> **The LORD gives sight to the eyes of both.**
>
> **¹⁴ If a king judges the poor with fairness,**
> **his throne will always be secure.**

Ungodly mockers "stir up a city"—literally, "fan a city [into a flame]." They are rabble-rousers who like to stir up dissension. But the wise seek peace, as Saint Paul says, "Live in peace with each other" (1 Thessalonians 5:13).

Remember that when Proverbs speaks of the fool, as in verse 9, it means the morally foolish person who is trying to live without God. Such a person can bluster and rage, like "a bear robbed of her cubs" (17:12). A wise person avoids legal entanglements with the fool.

Verse 10 makes a close connection between being bloodthirsty and hating integrity. Because bloody men commit murder, they can't stand the truth that exposes their evil. Or, because truthful people point out wicked men's sins, the wicked want to get rid of the upright. Hence, killing and deceit go hand in hand. God despises both, as the psalmist writes, "You [O LORD] destroy those who tell lies; bloodthirsty and deceitful men the LORD abhors" (5:6).

Proverbs 29:15-21

Jesus describes the devil himself as "a murderer from the beginning, not holding to the truth, for there is no truth in him" (John 8:44). Knowing the nature of Satan and of those who belong to him, if we are truthful we can expect to incur their wrath.

There is a healthy way to vent emotions. We can talk about how we feel and share our frustrations. The fool, however, doesn't exercise restraint (verse 11). He has a short fuse and lets his feelings take control of him.

Most officials will tell their leader what he wants to hear (verse 12). If he doesn't want the truth, but would rather hear lies and phony flattery, that's what he'll get. Since they don't have the backbones to tell the truth, his officials become liars and flatterers in the process.

The oppressor and the poor seem to be at opposite poles, since the former tends to take advantage of the latter (verse 13). But God can equalize things. The Lord can give the oppressor sight to see his sin and repent of it. To the poor he gives sight to find a way to endure his poverty.

The powerful of this world often despise the poor, frequently to their own undoing. When the poor can't take any more oppression, they eventually rise up against unjust rulers and overthrow them. The ruler who seeks to help the poor and treat them fairly doesn't face this danger (verse 14). So, while the poor may seem to be insignificant, they really are quite influential.

General truths

> ¹⁵ **The rod of correction imparts wisdom,**
> **but a child left to himself disgraces his mother.**
>
> ¹⁶ **When the wicked thrive, so does sin,**
> **but the righteous will see their downfall.**
>
> ¹⁷ **Discipline your son, and he will give you peace;**
> **he will bring delight to your soul.**

Proverbs 29:15-21

¹⁸ **Where there is no revelation, the people cast off restraint;**
but blessed is he who keeps the law.

¹⁹ **A servant cannot be corrected by mere words;**
though he understands, he will not respond.

²⁰ **Do you see a man who speaks in haste?**
There is more hope for a fool than for him.

²¹ **If a man pampers his servant from youth,**
he will bring grief in the end.

While the "rod of correction" can include spanking when called for, it can also refer to verbal correction. It does not include child abuse. The neglected child receives neither spankings nor verbal correction. *This* child may well grow up to disgrace his parents. Solomon could have written the proverb in verse 15 yesterday, since it speaks so directly to today's parents. When children are left by themselves at home night after night with nothing but television as their companion and a TV dinner to fix for themselves . . . You complete the story.

What a priceless gift children are! We have only a few years to train them before they grow up. How are we parents going to use that time? May God help us use it wisely!

In verse 16 Solomon repeats a theme he has treated several times. We can't have wicked people in positions of power in business, government, entertainment, and communication and not expect evil to spread throughout the land. But when God's people stand up for what is right, the Lord will bless their efforts (see 21:12).

Verse 17 describes one of the joys of raising children with loving discipline. Later in life they will bring peace, literally, "rest." That is, they'll take care of you and bring rest from anxiety. They will also make you very happy.

When Moses went up on Mount Sinai to receive the Ten Commandments, the Israelites built the golden calf and then

291

Proverbs 29:15-21

"sat down to eat and drink and got up to indulge in revelry. . . . The people were running wild" (Exodus 32:6,25). That's the kind of thing that happens where God's revelation is absent (verse 18). People will get out of control and lose themselves in self-indulgence.

As the Bible loses its influence across our land, we see that sort of lawlessness taking place. Violence, promiscuity, and immorality of every kind are breaking loose. Such indulgence does not bring God's blessings. It brings fear, disease, confusion, despair, and death. But to hold to God's Word brings all kinds of blessings: courage, forgiveness, peace, hope, and life.

Like sons (verses 15 and 17), servants also need discipline (verse 19). Reasoning alone is not enough. Imagine what an army would be like if an officer had to explain every order in the heat of battle! There are times when one in authority must simply lead, and the one under authority must accept that leadership.

In Proverbs only two kinds of people rank lower than the fool. One is the person who is "wise in his own eyes" (26:12). The other one is mentioned here in verse 20, the "man who speaks in haste." Why is speaking in haste such a serious wrong? Probably because this person never receives any input. He can't learn, since he is always blurting out whatever comes to his mind.

The thought in verse 21 is not far from that of verse 19. The thought of someone taking charge and being in authority may be difficult for people to accept in our day, when we tend to downplay authority and level out all role distinctions—whether at work, in the home, or in government. Nevertheless, authority is necessary. The person in authority is not to "pamper" the one under him. Carrying out discipline can and should be done in a firm yet caring way.

Proverbs 29:22-27

²² An angry man stirs up dissension,
   and a hot-tempered one commits many sins.

²³ A man's pride brings him low,
   but a man of lowly spirit gains honor.

²⁴ The accomplice of a thief is his own enemy;
   he is put under oath and dare not testify.

²⁵ Fear of man will prove to be a snare,
   but whoever trusts in the Lord is kept safe.

²⁶ Many seek an audience with a ruler,
   but it is from the Lord that man gets justice.

²⁷ The righteous detest the dishonest;
   the wicked detest the upright.

Earlier in this chapter, Solomon had warned against losing one's self-control (verse 11). Elsewhere he has spoken of the hot-tempered, angry man (15:18). As verse 22 indicates, many troubles and sins are connected with unbridled anger. Among them are dissension, cursing, violence, and revenge.

There is an old saying: He who runs after honor, honor flees from him; he who shuns honor, honor pursues him. Instead of thinking, "What's in it for me? How can I gain glory for myself?" we should think of doing God's will, using our God-given talents, and helping others. Then, let whatever honor there is to be take care of itself.

According to the Mosaic Law: "If a person sins because he does not speak up when he hears a public charge to testify regarding something he has seen or learned about, he will be held responsible" (Leviticus 5:1). Under this system, the "accomplice of a thief" (verse 24) was caught in a no-win situation. Even though he may not have actually committed the theft, he could not refuse to testify; and yet to testify would be to condemn himself. Getting ourselves involved with wrongdoers only puts us in no-win situations. It is wisdom to flee from evil.

293

Proverbs 29:22-27

The Lord assures his people: "I, even I, am he who comforts you. Who are you that you fear mortal men, the sons of men, who are but grass, that you forget the LORD your Maker, who stretched out the heavens and laid the foundations of the earth?" (Isaiah 51:12,13). Those who fear men will find themselves in one compromising situation after another. Their fear becomes their snare (verse 25); they are caught in it.

The solution is clear. Don't be afraid of men. Trust in the Lord.

Verse 26 expands on verse 25. Many look for security and justice from the earthly powers-that-be. The real power resides in God's hands. As Jesus told the Roman governor Pontius Pilate, "You would have no power over me if it were not given to you from above" (John 19:11). Solomon, who himself was a great king, tells us where to take our prayers and in whom to put our trust—the Lord.

Verse 27 is a fitting close to the Second Collection of Solomon's Proverbs. The righteous and the wicked are lined up against each other in poetic parallelism. Throughout this collection we've seen that we are either on God's side or on the side of the unbelieving world and Satan. The two cannot be reconciled. Jesus says, "He who is not with me is against me" (Luke 11:23) and "If the world hates you, keep in mind that it hated me first" (John 15:18).

Were it not for Christ, we would still be enemies of God and friends of this world. But we have been reconciled to God. Now, with the Lord's help, we walk in the way of wisdom. We pray and we witness, that by God's grace others might be won to Jesus' side.

PART SIX

Appendixes to the Second Collection
(30:1–31:31)

This last section of Proverbs divides into three parts: the Sayings of Agur (30:1-33), the Sayings of King Lemuel (31:1-9), and the famous passage on The Wife of Noble Character (31:10-31).

Sayings of Agur

30 The sayings of Agur son of Jakeh—an oracle:

This man declared to Ithiel,
to Ithiel and to Ucal:

This verse has been called the most difficult in the entire book of Proverbs. Who is "Agur son of Jakeh"? And as for Ithiel and Ucal, these Hebrew terms can be translated in another way instead of as proper names: "I am weary, O God; I am weary, O God, and I am worn out."

Some have contended that Agur is another name for Solomon. But that seems unlikely, since nothing in the Bible leads to that conclusion. It seems that Agur was a wise man who is not mentioned elsewhere in Scripture. The fact that we are told nothing about Agur is not unusual, in that the names of several inspired writers occur only in passing in the Bible. For example, we know next to nothing about such Old Testament prophets as Habakkuk, Haggai, and Obadiah.

In regard to the names Ithiel (occurring twice) and Ucal, it seems best to understand them not as proper names but as exclamations. We would then translate, "This man declared, 'I am weary, O God; I am weary, O God, and I

295

Proverbs 30:2-4

am worn out.'" This seems to fit well with the context that follows. Incidentally, the Hebrew term *El* (as in Ithiel) is the word for God; at times it occurs in the names of people or places, such as Bethel, which means "House of God."

At any rate, we now turn to the inspired wisdom of Agur:

God is a mystery!

> ² **"I am the most ignorant of men;**
> **I do not have a man's understanding.**
> ³ **I have not learned wisdom,**
> **nor have I knowledge of the Holy One.**
> ⁴ **Who has gone up to heaven and come down?**
> **Who has gathered up the wind in the hollow of**
> **his hands?**
> **Who has wrapped up the waters in his cloak?**
> **Who has established all the ends of the earth?**
> **What is his name, and the name of his son?**
> **Tell me if you know!**

These verses are reminiscent of the book of Job. There God challenges Job with a series of questions designed to show the greatness of God compared with man's limited mind and abilities: "Where were you when I laid the earth's foundation? Tell me, if you understand . . ." (38:4–39:30). Here too the writer humbly stands in awe before God's great creation.

Each of the five questions in verse 4 implies the answer: God. In regard to the first question, Genesis 11:7 speaks of God going down to the tower of Babel. Referring to himself, Jesus also used words reminiscent of this verse: "No one has ever gone into heaven except the one who came down from heaven—the Son of Man" (John 3:13).

The Son of Man of course is also the Son of God. Psalm 2 is another Old Testament reference to God's Son: "[The LORD] said to me, 'You are my Son; today I have become

Proverbs 30:5,6

your Father'" (verse 7). How blessed New Testament believers are that we have the fuller revelation by which we know the name of God's Son. His name is Jesus Christ, our Savior!

In our humanistic age, people are sometimes overly impressed with human intellect and accomplishments. It is good, along with Agur, to recognize our smallness—both in knowledge and in power—compared with our Creator's omniscience and omnipotence. This helps put a proper perspective on life and shows us how completely dependent we are on God.

The strength of God's Word

> ⁵ **"Every word of God is flawless;**
> **he is a shield to those who take refuge in him.**
> ⁶ **Do not add to his words,**
> **or he will rebuke you and prove you a liar.**

Since verse 5 is almost a direct quote of Psalm 18:30, a psalm of David, it seems Agur was familiar with the psalm. The psalm says God's "way is perfect." The proverb says his word is "flawless." Both of course are true. And both are of great comfort. In God's Word, the Bible, we have a flawless guide through life and death.

Many people today, even in Christian churches, deny the inerrancy of Scripture. Yet Scripture asserts it in many places. Because it is flawless, we can always count on God's Word—all of its promises and warnings, its commands and assurances. This is the place to go with all of our needs and problems.

Because God's every word is perfect, it is not for us to add our own ideas or man-made rules to it. Verse 6 reiterates Moses' inspired warning in Deuteronomy 4:2: "Do not add to what I command you and do not subtract from it, but keep the commands of the LORD your God that I give you."

297

Proverbs 30:7-9

Although many verses in Proverbs bring to mind other portions of Scripture, these two are the only clear references to other Old Testament passages.

A prayer

> [7] **"Two things I ask of you, O Lord;**
> **do not refuse me before I die:**
> [8] **Keep falsehood and lies far from me;**
> **give me neither poverty nor riches,**
> **but give me only my daily bread.**
> [9] **Otherwise, I may have too much and disown you**
> **and say, 'Who is the Lord?'**
> **Or I may become poor and steal,**
> **and so dishonor the name of my God.**

This is the first of Agur's numerical proverbs, in which he enumerates and thus emphasizes his subject. (For comments on this type of proverb, please refer to 6:16.)

The two requests of this brief prayer have one focus: Make me a godly person. As in verse 2, Agur expresses his humility before God. Here he recognizes his sinful weakness, and he asks that God (1) keep him honest and (2) deliver him from temptation.

Both poverty and riches can be temptations—the one a temptation to steal, the other to become proud. Agur's request for neither poverty nor riches is not far from what Jesus teaches in the Lord's Prayer: "Give us today our daily bread" (Matthew 6:11). As is Agur's prayer, this is a request for the necessities of life, not the luxuries—Jesus teaches us to ask for bread, not cake.

Instead of trusting in money for financial security, we trust in God's daily providence. That's not to say it's wrong to invest money in the bank or elsewhere. Our confidence, however, is in the Lord and not in how much earthly wealth

Proverbs 30:11-14

we've accumulated. Agur's prayer is also similar to the Bible's many other passages that urge contentment (for example, 1 Timothy 6:6-8).

If we pray as Agur did, and yet God answers by giving us either poverty or riches, we will accept his answer to our prayers. Then we will pray that he help us deal wisely with whatever our circumstances.

Notice that the sage prays for these blessings "before I die." We struggle with some of our sinful tendencies for years. No doubt, at times we've become frustrated when we fall into the same sinful habit over and over again, each time promising ourselves and God that we'll do better. Still, we keep working at it, relying on God's grace and renewed in his strength.

Against slander

> [10] **"Do not slander a servant to his master,**
> **or he will curse you, and you will pay for it.**

Here we are told not to take advantage of a person's lowly position. It might be tempting to think we can say whatever we want about somebody, simply because that individual is not in a position of influence. Such slander, like other sins, will only come back on us. Unlike the curse mentioned in 26:2, this one would be deserved. In one way or another we'll pay for bearing false witness against another, no matter who that person is.

Four kinds of people

> [11] **"There are those who curse their fathers**
> **and do not bless their mothers;**
> [12] **those who are pure in their own eyes**
> **and yet are not cleansed of their filth;**
> [13] **those whose eyes are ever so haughty,**
> **whose glances are so disdainful;**

Proverbs 30:11-14

¹⁴ those whose teeth are swords
and whose jaws are set with knives
to devour the poor from the earth,
the needy from among mankind.

"There are those" is, literally, "There is a generation." Or we might say, "There is a class of people." In verse 10 we saw the evil of slandering anyone, even a person of lowly station; now we see four more classes of wicked people. (Of course, the wicked often aren't limited to merely one class of evil.)

The first consists of people who curse their parents. Usually when we think of cursing it has to do with using certain bad words. But to curse really means to belittle, to treat as insignificant. To disobey, to dishonor, to show disrespect, to put down—these are all forms of cursing one's parents. God wants us to honor our father and mother. In the words of Martin Luther's explanation to the Fourth Commandment: "We should fear and love God that we do not dishonor or anger our parents and others in authority, but honor, serve, and obey them, and give them love and respect."

Verse 12 describes the second class of people—the self-righteous. Although they are sinners, they don't see their own sin.

Verse 13 continues with a similar class of people—the self-righteous who look at others with contempt. In the Sermon on the Mount, which often reflects Proverbs, Jesus warns against this sin:

> Why do you look at the speck of sawdust in your brother's eye and pay no attention to the plank in your own eye? How can you say to your brother, "Let me take the speck out of your eye," when all the time there is a plank in your own eye? You

Proverbs 30:15

hypocrite, first take the plank out of your own eye, and then you will see clearly to remove the speck from your brother's eye. (Matthew 7:3-5)

Finally, the wicked are described as *devouring* others (verse 14)! There has been a progression in these four verses. First came the people who mistreat their own parents, then those who think too highly of themselves and look down on others. Now we have people who run roughshod over others. Perhaps they are all the same people, showing a progression of evil that begins at home at a young age and gradually extends outward and becomes more blatant.

In Psalm 14:4, David used the same imagery of the evil devouring others: "Will evildoers never learn—those who devour my people as men eat bread and who do not call on the Lord?" But not only are those who openly ignore the Lord capable of "devouring" the poor, sometimes it's those who put on the appearance of being religious. Jesus spoke of those who like to have "the most important seats in the synagogues": "They devour widows' houses and for a show make lengthy prayers" (Mark 12:38-40). To devour, then, is to take advantage of the vulnerable in business or other dealings.

At times we may have been among these four classes of people. We need God's forgiveness and power to overcome these sins. Lord, help us replace self-righteousness with humility and the urge to devour others with the desire to help and befriend them!

Human bloodsuckers

> [15] **"The leech has two daughters.**
> **'Give! Give!' they cry.**

This verse is really saying: "The leech has two daughters—'Give!' and 'Give!'" (The words "they cry" are added

301

Proverbs 30:15,16

by the translators.) In others words, greed is incapable of giving birth to anything but more greed. Those who devour the possessions of others will never be satisfied. They'll keep wanting more. Like a leech that sucks blood from whomever it's attached to, greed just keeps taking and taking from others.

Four things that are never satisfied

> **"There are three things that are never satisfied,**
> **four that never say, 'Enough!':**
> [16] **the grave, the barren womb,**
> **land, which is never satisfied with water,**
> **and fire, which never says, 'Enough!'**

The sage gives four examples of unquenched longing for satisfaction. Two of them—the grave and the barren womb—deal with human beings. The painful, unfulfilled longing of a barren woman was expressed by Jacob's wife Rachel when she exclaimed, "Give me children, or I'll die!" (Genesis 30:1). At the other end of life, the grave keeps taking in people and never says, "I've had enough."

The other two examples of unfulfilled longing—land and fire—deal with the physical world. Land keeps soaking in water, and fire keeps burning as long as there's something left to burn. Agur is showing that all of nature is caught up in the cycle of dissatisfaction.

In the opening verses of Ecclesiastes, Solomon sounds a similar theme: "Generations come and generations go. . . . All streams flow into the sea, yet the sea is never full. . . . The eye never has enough of seeing, nor the ear its fill of hearing" (1:4,7,8). We have here the picture of a world fallen into sin. Instead of peace and satisfaction, unrest and dissatisfaction prevail everywhere. This is true among human beings and in nature itself.

Proverbs 30:18,19

Our only solution is to find nourishment that can satisfy. Jesus said, "Whoever drinks the water I give him will never thirst" (John 4:14). As long as we look to the things of this world, we won't find satisfaction no matter how much we acquire. True contentment and fulfillment are to be found only in Christ.

Incidentally, this is the first of five times in chapter 30 in which Agur uses the technique of citing four examples to illustrate an idea.

Disrespectful children: their punishment

¹⁷ **"The eye that mocks a father,**
   that scorns obedience to a mother,
will be pecked out by the ravens of the valley,
   will be eaten by the vultures.

Since the eye is the window to a person's inner feelings, the mocking and scorning eye symbolizes the person's attitude.

Under Old Testament law, parents could have a "stubborn and rebellious" child put to death by stoning (Leviticus 20:9; Deuteronomy 21:18-21). The implication of verse 17 is that a disrespectful child will be put to death, lie out in the open, and have his eyes plucked out by birds of prey.

We no longer have capital punishment for this kind of sin; nor does the Bible anywhere endorse physical abuse of children. Yet the fact that children could be punished in this manner for disobedience indicates how serious a matter it is to God.

Four things of intrigue

¹⁸ **"There are three things that are too amazing for me,**
   four that I do not understand:
¹⁹ **the way of an eagle in the sky,**
   the way of a snake on a rock,

Proverbs 30:20

the way of a ship on the high seas,
and the way of a man with a maiden.

Commentators have offered several suggestions as to what these four things have in common that makes them "amazing." Some say that what is amazing is the mystery of how they accomplish their effect—the wonder of an eagle soaring through the air or a snake slithering along without any feet. Others see the wonder in that none of the four leave behind a trace. Still another suggestion is that each of the four travels where there is no path; they chart "virgin" territory.

A reason for this possibility is that the word translated "maiden" can also be translated "virgin." It is the same Hebrew word as in the famous passage: "The virgin will be with child and will give birth to a son" (Isaiah 7:14). There, as the New Testament asserts, we have a reference to the birth of the Savior (Matthew 1:22,23). In the Proverbs passage, the reference may well be to the wonder of a young man courting, winning, and consummating his love with a young woman.

Through these four amazing activities, Agur demonstrates that even this fallen world is full of wonder, mystery, and beauty.

Immediately following "the way of a man with a maiden," we encounter the way of another type of woman—the adulteress:

About the adulteress

²⁰ "This is the way of an adulteress:
She eats and wipes her mouth
and says, 'I've done nothing wrong.'

What's amazing about this woman is that apparently adultery to her is merely an innocent physical satisfaction, like eating food. This verse really hits home in that it so concisely

Proverbs 30:21-23

describes the attitude of many modern, "liberated" people. Adultery and other sexual sins are considered natural and morally neutral. If there are feelings of guilt, they are viewed as hang-ups from an overly strict childhood training. If it feels good, do it! That's the motto today.

Some view the reference to eating and wiping the mouth as an indirect reference to the actual act of intercourse. At any rate, the adulteress has hardened her conscience, a very frightening course for anyone to take!

Four things that are intolerable

**²¹ "Under three things the earth trembles,
      under four it cannot bear up:
²² a servant who becomes king,
      a fool who is full of food,
²³ an unloved woman who is married,
      and a maidservant who displaces her mistress.**

Concerning this section, one commentator remarks, "The sages were the enemies of social and political revolution, considering it a prime cause of oppression, violence, and disorder. These four illustrations all serve to underline their view."[16] A closer look indicates that the problem is not social or political change but wrongful change.

Agur is speaking about going against God's order. It is not for us to usurp authority that is not ours. First Kings 16:8-20 relates the short (seven-day) and bloody reign of Zimri, an official who killed the king of Israel and seized power for himself. Earlier in Proverbs chapter 30, we saw what can happen when a fool comes into wealth (and consequently is full of food); he becomes proud and forgets about God (verses 7-9). Genesis 29:31,32 relates the sadness of an unloved wife; Jacob loved one of his wives, Rachel, more than the other, Leah. And the story of the problems between Abram's wife,

Proverbs 30:24-28

Sarai, and her maidservant Hagar illustrates the last of the four things under which the earth trembles (Genesis 16:1-6).

In each case, the problem is sin—(1) wrongful seizing of power, (2) love of material possessions, (3) polygamy or a marriage not following God's ideal, (4) contempt toward someone in authority. These sins disrupt relationships and cause heartaches and all sorts of troubles. Under them, even the earth trembles.

Four things small—yet smart and strong

> [24] **"Four things on earth are small,**
> **yet they are extremely wise:**
> [25] **Ants are creatures of little strength,**
> **yet they store up their food in the summer;**
> [26] **coneys are creatures of little power,**
> **yet they make their home in the crags;**
> [27] **locusts have no king,**
> **yet they advance together in ranks;**
> [28] **a lizard can be caught with the hand,**
> **yet it is found in kings' palaces.**

Bigness is not the same as greatness. Nor is it synonymous with wisdom and virtue. In contrast to the four sins of verses 21 to 23, here we learn four virtues. Interestingly, Agur used people for negative examples (verses 21-23), but now he turns to the animal kingdom to teach the positive.

From ants we can learn to provide. While we trust the Lord, we also plan ahead and are careful not to squander his blessings so that we have nothing left in time of need.

The coneys—also translated as "rock badgers" or "marmots"—are little mammals, about the size of rabbits. At the first hint of danger, they scurry into their rock shelters (see Psalm 104:18). They teach us a God-pleasing caution. As Jesus answered when Satan tempted him to throw himself

Proverbs 30:29-31

down from the temple, "It is also written: 'Do not put the Lord your God to the test'" (Matthew 4:7). While we will not tempt God with foolish risk taking, at the same time we have the assurance that he is our rock. The hymn writer put it this way: "Rock of Ages, cleft for me, let me hide myself in thee!" (CW 389:1).

Locusts teach order and cooperation. Individually, they are tiny and weak. Collectively, they form a "mighty army" (see Joel 2:3-9).

From lizards we can learn boldness, as these little creatures appear even in the palaces of kings. There is a time for caution but also a time for boldness. Through Christ, we can be bold enough to bring our prayers and needs before the throne of the King of all.

Behind nature and the animal kingdom, of course, is the great Creator. If we but open our eyes, we can see his wisdom in the wisdom of his creation. And from it we can learn.

Four things that move like a king

> ²⁹ **"There are three things that are stately in their stride,**
> **four that move with stately bearing:**
> ³⁰ **a lion, mighty among beasts,**
> **who retreats before nothing;**
> ³¹ **a strutting rooster, a he-goat,**
> **and a king with his army around him.**

Again turning to the animal kingdom, the sage points out examples of royal bearing. Since ancient times, the lion has been considered the king of the beasts. The rooster is still known for its strutting. Although not so familiar to Westerners, in the Middle East the he-goat with its haughty stare remains a symbol of dignity.

As for the king with his army, that too is no longer a common figure for most people. But with our imaginations

Proverbs 30:32,33

we can see the royal entourage—trumpets announcing the king's approach; chariots, horsemen, and infantry, armed with swords and spears, preparing the way; bright banners waving in the wind; the royal carriage covered with gold and silver and upholstered with purple; and the king himself with his royal crown. (See Song of Songs 3:6-11 for a description of a such a procession.)

The most stately appearance of all will take place when the King of kings returns in glory at the end of the world (Revelation 19:11-16).

In his description of four stately things, Agur neither censors nor endorses this kind of bearing. Certainly as children of God, we can hold our heads high, boasting not in ourselves but in our Savior (1 Corinthians 1:31). There is, however, another kind of proud behavior that is wrong. The next verses speak of it.

Keep calm and quiet

> [32] **"If you have played the fool and exalted yourself,**
> **or if you have planned evil,**
> **clap your hand over your mouth!**
> [33] **For as churning the milk produces butter,**
> **and as twisting the nose produces blood,**
> **so stirring up anger produces strife."**

The chapter began with a call to humility; it also ends that way. Commentator Derek Kidner rightly notes how humility appears in Proverbs 30—as reverence (verses 1-9), restraint (verses 10-17), wonder (verses 18-31), and finally peaceable behavior (verses 32,33).[17]

The fool forgets his smallness before the Almighty and exalts himself. Putting oneself, instead of God, at the center of life can lead to nothing but evil. The me-first philosophy leads to evil plans and to conflict with others: If I want to get

308

Proverbs 31:1

ahead in this world, I'm going to have to step on some feet. Right?

Wrong! says Agur. If you've been plotting like that, put a stop to it now. Clap your hand over your mouth before another self-serving word comes out. Churning up milk makes butter; twisting the nose brings blood. Likewise, stirring up the anger of others by your self-centered ambition brings strife.

Instead of pushing ourselves forward, the Bible urges us to humble ourselves before God. James 4:10 is but one of many passages that address this important truth: "Humble yourselves before the Lord, and he will lift you up." Humility before our Creator and Savior—that's the chief lesson from Agur, son of Jakeh.

Sayings of King Lemuel

Introduction

31 The sayings of King Lemuel—an oracle his mother taught him:

As was the case with Agur in the last chapter, we are not sure who King Lemuel is. Ancient rabbis took this to be a pen name for Solomon. The name Lemuel means "He who is for God." But there is nothing to indicate that this was another name for Solomon. On the other hand, we know nothing about another king by the name of Lemuel.

An old Jewish story relates that Solomon married Pharaoh's daughter on the day the temple was dedicated. He overslept, with the keys to the temple gates under his pillow. This delayed the morning sacrifice and led to the following words of advice from his mother.

While interesting, such stories are mere speculation. We take Lemuel to be another ruler-wiseman, unknown except for this reference in Proverbs.

Proverbs 31:2,3

Clearly, Lemuel's mother played a key role in his training. In the ancient Near East, mothers were strong influences. We think of women like Sarah and Rebekah or of Solomon's mother, Bathsheba.

Don't make yourself vulnerable!

> ² "O my son, O son of my womb,
>   O son of my vows,
> ³ do not spend your strength on women,
>   your vigor on those who ruin kings.

Lemuel's mother reminds him how much he means to her. He is her son, whom she went through the pain of bearing. He is the son of her vows—perhaps a reference to his name, that she had vowed to devote him to God. This reminds us of Samuel's mother, Hannah, who prayed for a son: "O LORD Almighty, if you will only look upon your servant's misery and remember me, and not forget your servant but give her a son, then I will give him to the LORD for all the days of his life" (1 Samuel 1:11).

Having reminded Lemuel of her care for him, the mother warns him against two dangers for leaders. The first is women.

Women proved the downfall for one as wise and great as Solomon. He had seven hundred wives and three hundred concubines. Years later Nehemiah recalled how Solomon's foreign wives had led him into idolatry: "Among the many nations there was no king like [Solomon]. He was loved by his God, and God made him king over all Israel, but even he was led into sin by foreign women" (Nehemiah 13:26).

For a king or any man in a position of leadership to spend his energy in the delights of the harem instead of concentrating on his duties could bring ruin. Many a modern politician has also been brought to ruin by getting caught up with

Proverbs 31:4-7

women, in particular in illicit affairs. Lemuel's mother does not tell her son not to have a wife; she does warn against dissipating his strength on women.

The use of liquor

> [4] "It is not for kings, O Lemuel—
>   not for kings to drink wine,
>   not for rulers to crave beer,
> [5] lest they drink and forget what the law decrees,
>   and deprive all the oppressed of their rights.
> [6] Give beer to those who are perishing,
>   wine to those who are in anguish;
> [7] let them drink and forget their poverty
>   and remember their misery no more.

Wine poses a second great danger for leaders. As with women (verse 3), it seems here that Lemuel's mother is not advocating complete abstinence. Rather, she teaches him to avoid craving beer and drinking to the point of forgetfulness.

One hears stories of political leaders today voting on legislation while under the influence of alcohol. We pray that God will keep our land and its leaders from this. It can only result in unjust laws, which almost always hurt those already oppressed. The New Testament points out that leaders in the church are also to avoid drunkenness (Titus 1:7).

Beer and wine can be the ruin of leaders. At the same time, if used properly, they can be a blessing to dull the pain of those who are suffering. When Jesus hung on the cross, he was offered wine. Even in his suffering, our King refused (Mark 15:23). He chose to bear the full pain as he suffered in our stead.

A good king is not concerned about indulging himself; he is too interested in the welfare of his people:

Proverbs 31:8,9

Defending the poor and the needy

> **8 "Speak up for those who cannot speak for themselves,**
> **for the rights of all who are destitute.**
> **9 Speak up and judge fairly;**
> **defend the rights of the poor and needy."**

These powerful verses lend themselves to many applications, such as defending a person who is an object of gossip. They are frequently applied to the many babies who are killed through legalized abortion in our day. Who is less able to speak for himself or herself than an unborn baby, who is being deprived of the very right to life? We support those lawmakers who are trying to help the infants, as well as others in need.

The words of Lemuel are aimed at leaders. Yet they apply to every Christian. As we help those in need, we show our love for Jesus himself. He tells us, "Whatever you did for one of the least of these brothers of mine, you did for me" (Matthew 25:40).

Epilogue: the wife of noble character

The final verses of Proverbs are the well-known poem about the wife of noble character. The poem is an acrostic: each verse begins with a successive letter of the Hebrew alphabet. Since there are 22 letters in that alphabet, there are 22 verses. Some of the psalms have the acrostic structure (see especially Psalm 119), as do the first four chapters of Lamentations. This literary form served as an aid in memorizing passages. It also gives a sense of completeness—the wife of noble character from A to Z.

Before we look at specifics, some general comments are in order. Back in 18:22 God declared, "He who finds a wife finds what is good and receives favor from the LORD." Now he elaborates on that theme. In describing this wife of

Proverbs 31:10-31

noble character, Proverbs describes a capable woman who enjoys many responsibilities.

This noble woman stands in sharp contrast to the nagging and unfaithful women mentioned elsewhere in Proverbs. It has been said, "Nothing in ancient literature equals this remarkable attestation to the individuality of woman." While much of Proverbs is addressed to "my son" and deals with male-oriented themes, the beautiful closing section focuses on ideal womanhood.

We see in the following verses a woman of means. Many wives are not in a position to carry out all the transactions of this woman. But every Christian wife is in a position to meet her responsibilities as one "who fears the LORD" (verse 30).

Whether this closing portion is still part of the words of Lemuel (31:1) is unclear. Because of its different structure, it would seem to be a separate addition. Moreover, in the Septuagint, the earliest translation of the Old Testament, Proverbs 30:1–31:9 are placed five chapters earlier, with Further Sayings of the Wise (24:23-34).

An alphabetic poem

10 A wife of noble character who can find?
She is worth far more than rubies.
11 Her husband has full confidence in her
and lacks nothing of value.
12 She brings him good, not harm,
all the days of her life.
13 She selects wool and flax
and works with eager hands.
14 She is like the merchant ships,
bringing her food from afar.
15 She gets up while it is still dark;
she provides food for her family
and portions for her servant girls.

313

Proverbs 31:10-31

¹⁶ She considers a field and buys it;
　　out of her earnings she plants a vineyard.
¹⁷ She sets about her work vigorously;
　　her arms are strong for her tasks.
¹⁸ She sees that her trading is profitable,
　　and her lamp does not go out at night.
¹⁹ In her hand she holds the distaff
　　and grasps the spindle with her fingers.
²⁰ She opens her arms to the poor
　　and extends her hands to the needy.
²¹ When it snows, she has no fear for her household;
　　for all of them are clothed in scarlet.
²² She makes coverings for her bed;
　　she is clothed in fine linen and purple.
²³ Her husband is respected at the city gate,
　　where he takes his seat among the elders of the land.
²⁴ She makes linen garments and sells them,
　　and supplies the merchants with sashes.
²⁵ She is clothed with strength and dignity;
　　she can laugh at the days to come.
²⁶ She speaks with wisdom,
　　and faithful instruction is on her tongue.
²⁷ She watches over the affairs of her household
　　and does not eat the bread of idleness.
²⁸ Her children arise and call her blessed;
　　her husband also, and he praises her:
²⁹ "Many women do noble things,
　　but you surpass them all."
³⁰ Charm is deceptive, and beauty is fleeting;
　　but a woman who fears the Lord is to be praised.
³¹ Give her the reward she has earned,
　　and let her works bring her praise at the city gate.

Although many of these verses are self-explanatory, a number of comments are in order.

The first verse sets the noble wife in a proper perspective; she is a priceless find. When young people look for a life-

Proverbs 31:10-31

long partner, what do they look for? Physical attraction is usually high on the list. So is having fun together. Somewhere down the list comes the person's character. The Bible puts it at the top. Godly character is rare, and to find it in one's spouse is a very, very special gift from above. As rare jewels are the most valuable, so the rarest of traits are also the most valuable.

The noble wife is trustworthy (verse 11). We might liken marital faithfulness to the foundation upon which marriage rests. Without confidence in one another, a marriage can never be ideal. When there is complete confidence in the other person, everything else of value falls into place.

Verse 12 speaks of the woman's dedication to her husband. She continually—all the days of her life!—seeks to be supportive and encouraging. She doesn't bring him down.

Verses 13 to 27 show the woman's industry, concern, and care for her household, and also for others in need (verse 20). The listing of her activities in these verses pictures an energetic, happy, and optimistic person. It's interesting that a number of these activities involve business. God's Word doesn't advocate that a woman stay at home and not venture into the world beyond. At the same time, her concerns clearly center around her home and family.

When verse 13 states she "works with eager hands," it literally says, "She makes according to the pleasure of her hands." It's as if her very hands enjoy the work. In other words, she likes what she does. And she does it with vigor (verse 17).

The allusion to merchant ships of verse 14 brings to mind the ships of Solomon: "The king had a fleet of trading ships. . . . Once every three years it returned, carrying gold, silver and ivory, and apes and baboons" (1 Kings 10:22). From the Red Sea port of Ezion Geber, his ships sailed to Arabia and

315

Proverbs 31:10-31

possibly on to faraway India. The noble wife goes out of her way to obtain the best for her family.

The mention of servants in verse 15 gives the impression of a wealthy family. The context also indicates that the wealth came honestly and that her love extends to her servants as well as to her own family. While many Christian wives may not have the kind of wealth described here, all can have her kind of character.

The planting of a vineyard (verse 16) need not mean that she personally did it. Similarly, when Solomon speaks of "the temple I have built" (1 Kings 8:44), that doesn't mean he personally did the building. She, like Solomon, may have overseen the work.

Mention of her lamp not going out at night (verse 18) could refer to her working into the night. It could also mean that the household is prosperous enough to keep a lamp burning all night. Having one's lamp go out was symbolic of God's disfavor (Job 18:5).

Her concern for the poor (verse 20) reflects an earlier proverb: "A generous man will prosper; he who refreshes others will himself be refreshed" (11:25). A number of verses in 31:10-31 refer to the woman's hands and arms. In a concrete way, they represent the activity of her entire person.

Winters in Palestine are cold and rainy, and sometimes it even snows. Yet her family remains warm (verse 21). Not only does she see to it that they are kept warm, but she also provides the finest clothing possible. Purple (verse 22) is the color of royalty (see Song of Songs 3:10). She is the consummate seamstress, doing everything from spinning thread (verse 19) to selling linen and sashes (verse 24).

When verse 23 tells of her husband being respected at the city gate, it refers to him meeting with city leaders. The city

Proverbs 31:10-31

gate was the place at which business and important discussions were held in Middle Eastern towns. A good part of that respect comes from the kind of wife he has. She brings him admiration.

Much is said of how she clothes her family. The real beauty of her appearance comes not from the materials she wears but from her inner qualities—strength, dignity, confidence, wisdom, faithfulness, concern, and industriousness (verses 25-27). So many couples today futilely try to find love and satisfaction in outward appearances and possessions. The Bible constantly directs us to the attitudes of the heart.

No wonder her family praises her (verses 28,29)! It is a thing of beauty to see children raised by a believing mother; as they grow older they return her love more and more. Her husband, who owes so much to her, also showers her with heartfelt praise.

What she does for her family isn't done to glorify herself. But as a by-product of her fearing the Lord, they—and others—praise her. She's praised not only in the privacy of the home but in the city gate as well (verse 31).

Verse 30 summarizes the poem. Beauty is fleeting. Literally, it is "a breath"; it evaporates like a fleeting breath on a cold day. (This is the same Hebrew word translated "meaningless" in Ecclesiastes 1:2,3.) The Prologue to the Book of Proverbs stated, "The fear of the LORD is the beginning of knowledge" (1:7). This is the motivating drive in the noble woman's life. What comes from fearing God is anything but fleeting. It lasts a lifetime and beyond.

It's fitting that Proverbs should end as it began, with the fear of the Lord. This theme has run throughout the book. To fear God is to stand in reverent awe before him and to love and trust in him. This is the beginning, the middle, and the end of godly wisdom.

317

Endnotes

On this encouraging note we conclude our study. But it's not really the end. As Luther put it, "Anyone who intends to become righteous might well take this [Proverbs] as a handbook or prayerbook for his daily use, read it often, and ponder his own life in it."[18] May our study of Proverbs continue as a lifelong adventure. And may all of us grow wiser—through Jesus Christ, who is the very wisdom of God!

ENDNOTES

[1] Martin Luther, *Luther's Works*, edited by Jaroslav Pelikan and Helmut T. Lehmann, American Edition, Vol. 35 (St. Louis: Concordia Publishing House; Philadelphia: Fortress Press, 1955–1986), p. 258.

[2] Robert L. Alden, *Proverbs—A Commentary on an Ancient Book of Timeless Advice* (Grand Rapids: Baker, 1983), p. 9.

[3] Ibid., p. 10.

[4] A. Cohen, *Proverbs* (London: Soncino Press, 1985), p. 1.

[5] Derek Kidner, *Proverbs: An Introduction and Commentary* (Downers Grove, IL: InterVarsity Press, 1964), p. 61.

[6] Martin Luther, as quoted in *Meditations* daily devotions (Milwaukee: Northwestern Publishing House, 1968), p. 63.

[7] Kidner, *Proverbs,* p. 83.

[8] Franz Delitzsch, *Proverbs,* translated by James Martin, *Commentary on the Old Testament in Ten Volumes*, Vol. 6 (Grand Rapids: Eerdmans, 1975), p. 15.

[9] Martin Luther, *What Luther Says,* edited by Ewald M. Plass, Vol. 3 (St. Louis: Concordia, 1959), p. 1495.

[10] Alden, *Proverbs,* pp. 114,115.

[11] Ibid., p. 155.

[12] As quoted in Alden, *Proverbs,* p. 168.

[13] Luther, *What Luther Says,* Vol. 3, p. 1156.

[14] Delitzsch, *Proverbs,* p. 142.

[15] C. Hassell Bullock, *An Introduction to the Old Testament Books* (Chicago: Moody, 1988), p. 158.

[16] J. Coert Rylaarsdam, *Proverbs, Ecclesiastes, Song of Solomon* (Atlanta: John Knox Press, 1964), p. 92.

[17] Kidner, *Proverbs,* p. 182.

[18] Luther, *Luther's Works,* Vol. 35, p. 258.

The author gratefully acknowledges the use of the helpful section headings as found in *Proverbs,* the New Evangelical Translation (Cleveland, NET Publishing, 1991).

TOPICAL INDEX

This index is not exhaustive but should prove helpful in topical studies of Proverbs. Since many of the proverbs are antithetical, to find the subject you are looking for, you might try its opposite (for example, work—laziness). Except for references to material in the Introduction, all references are to chapters and verses.

Accusations, 3:30
Acrostic, 31:10-31
Adultery, 2:16-19; 5:1-23; 6:20-35; 7:1-27; 22:14; 30:20
Advice, 25:20
    parental, 23:22-25
Agur, 30:1
Agur, Sayings of, 30:1-33
Amenemope, Introduction p. 3; 22:17-21; 23:4,5
Anger, see Temper
Animals
    regal, 30:29-31
    small, 30:24-28
Anxiety, 12:25
Associations, 13:19,20; 18:22-24
Attitudes, 18:12-16

Benefits of wisdom, 2:1-22; 3:1-35
Blessings, 10:22,23
Boasting, 27:1,2
Boundary stones, 15:25; 22:28; 23:10
Bribe, 17:8,23; 18:16; 19:6; 21:14; 28:21

Caring (for others), 24:10-12; 27:18; 29:7
Character, 12:1-4
Charity, see Generosity

Children, 1:8; 5:20; 9:16; 13:22,24; 15:32; 17:6,21; 19:18; 20:7,11; 22:15; 23:13-16,25; 28:9,24; 29:3,15,17; 30:17; 31:28
Christ, as wisdom, 8:22-31
Companions, see Associations
Confession (of sins), 28:13
Contentment, 15:16,17; 17:1; 30:7-9
Correction, 27:17,19; 29:15
Courage, 28:1
Creation, 3:19,20,33; 24:24; 30:11
Curse, 3:33; 24:24; 26:2; 27:14; 30:10,11

Death, 1:19,32; 2:18,19; 5:11,23; 8:36; 10:16; 11:7,19; 12:28; 14:11,12,32; 21:16; 23:13,14,17,18; 24:14,19,20; 27:20
Deceit, 12:17-20,22; 14:25; 17:20; 19:5-9; 21:8; 26:23-28; 27:6; 28:17
Discipline, 10:13; 13:24; 15:32,33; 19:18; 20:30; 22:15; 23:12-14; 29:15,17
    (of) children, 13:24; 19:28; 22:15; 23:13,14; 29:15,17
    from God, 3:11,12
Disputes, see Quarrels
Drinking, see Wine

319

Index

Elderly, 16:31; 17:6; 20:29
Enemies, 16:7; 24:29; 25:21,22
Enticement, 1:8-19
Envy, 3:31; 13:21; 14:20; 23:17;
   24:1,19,20

Fairness, 24:23-26; 28:21; 29:14
Father, 1:8; 3:12; 4:1-6; 6:20; 10:1;
   11:29; 13:1,24; 15:5,20; 17:21,25;
   19:13,26; 20:20; 23:22-25; 28:7,24;
   29:3; 30:11,17
Fear of the Lord, 1:7,29; 2:5; 3:7;
   8:13; 9:10; 14:2,26,27; 15:16,33;
   16:6; 19:23; 22:4; 23:17; 24:21,22;
   31:30
First collection of Solomon's
   proverbs, 10:1–22:16
Flattery, 22:11; 25:3; 27:21; 29:5,12
Folly, 12:23; 22:15
     consequences of, 15:10-12,
       24-27; 17:7-10
     personified, 9:13-18
     warnings against, 6:1-5
Fools, 14:7-9; 24:7; 26:1,3-12;
   27:3,22; 28:26; 29:9
Fountain of life, 10:11; 13:14; 14:27;
   16:22
Friend, 12:26; 14:20,21; 17:17; 18:24;
   19:7; 20:6; 22:11; 23:6-8; 25:19;
   27:6,9,10
Friendship, 12:26; 27:9,10

Generosity, 3:27,28; 11:24-26; 19:17;
   22:9
Gifts, 7:14; 10:22,24; 14:27; 16:16;
   17:8,23; 18:16; 21:14
Gossip, 10:18,31,32; 11:13; 16:28;
   17:4; 18:8; 20:19; 25:9,10,23;
   26:20-22; 31:8,9
Government, see Kings
Greed, 15:27; 23:4,5; 28:20,22,25;
   29:4; 30:15

Hatred, 29:27
Health, 3:8
Heart, 11:20-23
Hezekiah, 25:1
Honesty, see Integrity
Hope, 23:17,18
Humility, 22:4
     see also Pride

Immortality, 12:28
Inheritance, 28:10
Instruction, 1:3,4,8; 2:1; 4:1-6,10;
   8:10,33; 9:9; 10:1,17; 13:1,13;
   16:20; 19:16,20,27; 20:7; 22:6,17-
   21; 23:12; 27:12; 29:15; 31:26
Integrity, 11:1-3; 12:22; 16:8,9;
   20:10,23
     hated by wicked, 29:10
Interest, 28:9
Intolerable things, 30:21-23

Jealousy, 27:4
Joking, 26:18,19
Joy, 14:10-13; 15:13-15,23,30; 25:25;
   27:11; 29:6
Judgment, human, 20:20-27
Justice, 8:20; 11:21; 12:5; 16:10;
   17:23,26; 18:5; 19:28; 21:15;
   22:22,23; 24:23; 28:4-6; 29:7,26

Kings, 14:28,35; 16:10-15; 19:12;
   20:2,8,26,28; 21:1; 25:2-7; 28:2,3
     just, 16:12; 25:5; 29:4,14

Lawsuits, 25:8-10; 29:9
Laziness, 6:6-11; 12:24,27; 18:9;
   19:15,16,24; 20:4,13; 21:25,26;
   22:13; 24:30-34; 26:13-16; 28:19
Lemuel, 31:1
Lemuel, Sayings of, 31:1-9
Life, 3:1,2; 4:10; 9:11; 10:16,27;
   11:19; 12:28; 14:32; 16:31; 28:16

320

Index

see also Fountain of life,
Tree of life
Light, 4:18; 6:23; 13:9; 21:4
Loans, 6:1-5; 22:26,27; 27:13
Love, 27:5
Lying, see Deceit

Mercy, 21:13
Mockers, 1:22; 9:7,8,12; 13:1; 14:6,9;
15:12; 18:6-8; 19:25,28,29;
21:11,24; 22:10; 24:9; 30:17
Money, 3:13-16; 10:2,3,16; 12:12;
13:11; 16:8; 17:16; 19:4,6,7; 20:4;
22:1,2,7,9,26,27; 23:4-8;
28:8,11,22; 29:8
Mother, 1:8; 6:20; 10:1; 15:20; 17:25;
19:26; 20:20; 23:22,25; 28:24;
29:15; 30:11,17; 31:10-31
Motives, 16:2; 20:5,9,11,12,27; 21:2
Mystery
of creation, 30:18,19
of God, 30:2-4

Neighbors, 14:20,21
Numerical proverbs, 6:16-19; 30:7-
9,15-19,21-23,24-28,29-31

Outcomes, 12:8-14

Parents, 1:8,9; 17:6; 19:13,14;
23:22-25
Patience, 16:32; 19:11
Peace, 16:7
Personality patterns, 14:14-19;
15:18,19; 16:25-30; 30:11-14
Plans, 10:22; 12:5,20; 15:22;
16:3,4,33; 19:21; 20:18; 21:30,31;
24:5,6,27
Plot, 3:29; 12:20; 14:22; 24:2
Plotting harm, 14:22; 24:8,9
Poetry, Introduction pp. 5,6

Poor
destitute, 13:8,23; 17:5; 18:23;
19:1-4,7,22; 22:2,7; 27:7;
28:3,6,27; 29:13; 31:20
lazy, 6:11; 11:24; 21:5,17;
22:16; 24:34; 28:2
oppressed, 3:34; 13:23; 15:15;
22:22,23; 29:13; 30:14;
31:5,8,9
Prayer, 15:8; 28:9
Pride, 8:13; 11:2; 13:10; 16:5,18,19;
21:22-24; 25:27; 28:11; 29:23
Prologue to Proverbs, 1:1-7
Promises of God, 2:20-22; 3:9,10
Property, 22:28; 23:10,11
Prostitution, 23:26-28; 29:3
Proverb, definition of, Introduction
p. 1; 1:1-6
Proverbs, Book of
divisions, 1:1,8; 8:1; 10:1;
22:17; 24:23; 25:1; 30:1;
31:1,10
outline, Introduction pp. 7,8
place in the Bible,
Introduction p. 7
purpose, Introduction pp. 4,5
title, Introduction pp. 1,2

Quarrels, 17:14,19; 18:17-19; 20:3;
26:17

Rebuke, 1:23,30; 3:11; 9:7,8; 13:1,2;
15:5,31; 17:10; 19:25; 25:12; 27:5;
28:23; 30:6
Rejecting wisdom, 1:20-33
Reputation, 22:1
Revenge, 20:22; 24:28,29
Righteousness, 10:2,3,6,7,24-32;
11:10-19; 12:5-7; 13:5,6;
15:9,28,29; 28:18
(in) government, 14:34,35
loss of, 25:26; 27:8

321

Index

rewards of, 11:27-31; 12:21; 13:21,22,25; 20:7
triumph of, 28:12
value of, 11:4-9; 24:15,16
Rural life, 27:23-27

Safety, 18:10,11
Satisfaction, 30:15,16
Sayings of the wise, 22:17–24:22,23-34
Second collection of Solomon's proverbs, 25:1–29:27
Self-control, 17:26,27; 25:28; 29:11
Selfishness, 18:1,2; 23:6-8
Sluggard, see Laziness
Socializing, 23:1-3,6-8; 25:16,17
Speech, 10:8-14,18-21,31,32; 12:17-20; 13:2,3; 14:3; 15:1-7; 16:1,20-24,27; 17:28; 18:6-8,20,21; 20:14-17; 22:11,12; 23:9; 25:15; 29:19,20
(of) messengers, 25:11-14
Strength of character, 14:4-6
Stubbornness, 12:15,16; 29:1

Temper, 16:32; 19:19; 22:24,25; 29:22; 30:32,33
Testimony, 12:17; 24:28,29; 25:18
Testing, 27:21
from God, 17:3
Tree of life, 3:18; 11:30; 13:12; 15:4
Trust in God, 3:5,6; 29:25

Unfaithfulness, 25:19

Warnings
against folly, 6:1-5
against rejecting wisdom, 1:22-27
Wealth, 3:9; 10:15-17; 11:4; 13:7,8,11; 14:24; 18:11; 19:10; 21:20,21; 22:2,7; 28:8

Wickedness, 21:27-29; 24:1,2
aspects of, 18:3-5
consequences of, 17:11-15; 21:7,12; 22:5,8
(in) power, 28:15,16,28; 29:2,12,16
Wife, 2:16-19; 5:18-20; 6:23-29; 7:4,5; 12:4; 18:22-24; 19:13; 21:9,19; 23:26-28; 25:24; 27:15; 31:10-31
of noble character, 12:4; 31:10-31
quarrelsome wife, 19:13; 21:9,19; 25:24; 27:15
Wine, 20:1; 21:17; 23:19-21,29-35; 31:4-7
Wisdom
(in) behavior, 13:15-18
benefits of, 2:1-8; 3:1-4,16-18; 24:13,14
discourses of, 8:1–9:18
effect of, 9:7-12
eternal existence, 8:22-31
general, 1:1-7; 14:33
invitation, 8:1-11; 9:1-6
personified, 1:20,21
protector, 2:9-15; 3:23-26
self-description, 8:12-21
spurned, 1:28-33
value of, 3:13-15,21,22; 16:16,17; 24:3,4
warning of, 8:32-36
Wisdom literature, Introduction pp. 2-4
Women, 14:1; 31:2,3
Word of God, 30:5,6
Work, 10:4,5; 13:4; 14:23; 22:29
see also Laziness

Youth, ten discourses to, 1:8–7:27